"Oliver O'Donovan's *Finding and Seeking* is characteristically learned and well written, but it is more than this. It is a fresh reading of the gospel for our current situation. O'Donovan has penetrating insight, like Kierkegaard, into the temptations that are endemic to our culture, and he has the skill of giving acute and vivid examples, in which we recognize ourselves unexpectedly. Only when we see the disease can we start to see the remedy."

— JOHN HARE
Yale Divinity School

"Rich and challenging. . . . Far from being a summary of the author's already known ideas, this is a provocative wake-up call for ethics in general and Christian ethics specifically. We can only ignore this book at great loss to ourselves and the urgent discussions of our times."

— G. C. DEN HERTOG
University of Apeldoorn

SELF, WORLD, AND TIME

Ethics as Theology 1

AN INDUCTION

FINDING AND SEEKING

Ethics as Theology 2

Forthcoming:

ENTERING INTO REST

Ethics as Theology 3

Finding and Seeking

• •

Ethics as Theology 2

Oliver O'Donovan

WILLIAM B. EERDMANS PUBLISHING COMPANY
GRAND RAPIDS, MICHIGAN / CAMBRIDGE, U.K.

Published 2014 by
Wm. B. Eerdmans Publishing Co.
2140 Oak Industrial Drive N.E., Grand Rapids, Michigan 49505 /
P.O. Box 163, Cambridge CB3 9PU U.K.

Printed in the United States of America

19 18 17 16 15 14   7 6 5 4 3 2 1

Library of Congress Cataloging-in-Publication Data

O'Donovan, Oliver.
Finding and seeking / Oliver O'Donovan.
pages   cm.   — (Ethics as theology; 2)
ISBN 978-0-8028-7187-9 (pbk.: alk. paper)
1. Christian ethics.   2. Self-knowledge, Theory of.
3. God.   I. Title.

BJ1251.O3634   2014
241 — dc23
                              2014025022

www.eerdmans.com

Contents

CONTENTS

Contents

Preface

In *Self, World, and Time,* the first part of *Ethics as Theology,* we described Christian Ethics, alias Moral Theology, as an intellectual discipline: distinct from moral thinking on the one hand and from moral teaching on the other, it offers to each of them an ordered reflection on their assumptions and procedures in the light of the Christian gospel. We came finally to focus on a conceptual trajectory which would encompass the logic of moral thought within the three virtues of faith, love, and hope (the sequence in which the three most usually occur in the New Testament). This now gives rise to two further tasks. One lies before us in this second part: to follow moral thought from self-awareness to decision through the sequence of virtues from faith to hope. The second, guided by the claim made for the sovereignty of love, is to explore ends-of-action, penultimate and ultimate, the objects, natural and supernatural, that we may anticipate and pursue.

"Today, if you shall hear his voice, harden not your hearts . . ." (Ps. 95:7). "Today" is the day *of some agent,* some "I" or "we" who find ourselves addressed in that "you"; more precisely, *this* "I" or "we" — ourselves, as we take up the question of what to do as our own question. Another agent's day is not "today," but "then." We do not deliberate about it. We deliberate about the today on which it is given to you, or me, or us, to live and act. But there can be no framing this "today" — it remains no more than a pleasing philosophical abstraction — unless the "you," "I," or "we" in question have come to know ourselves as agents summoned by God to answer him in action, and in that knowledge have addressed the question of what we are to do as the supremely important question. And there can be no framing this "today" except as a moment within world-time. The subjective "here and now" of action has to be correlated to the objective "there and then" that can be seen and spoken of all around us. The "today" we face presupposes our agency and presupposes the world with its time. Ethics, in helping us face it, must point us to the knowledge of self and world that is actually given us, a knowledge through which the Spirit of God leads us to the action and life that are offered to us.

To the expressions of gratitude in the Preface of *Self, World, and Time,* most of which are relevant also to this volume, I must add thanks to the editors of *The American Journal of Jurisprudence,* in which parts of chapter 9 appeared, and of *The Journal of Law, Philosophy and Culture,* which hosted parts of chapter 8. A section of chapter 6 first appeared on http://www.fulcrum-anglican.org.uk, and, translated into German, in *Wie kommt die Bibel in die Ethik?* ed. Marco Hofheinz, Frank Mathwig, Matthias Zeindler (Theologischer Verlag Zürich, 2011), 229-42.

Those who find themselves perusing a volume called *The Authority of the Gospel: Explorations in Moral and Political Theology in Honor of Oliver O'Donovan,* edited by Robert Song and Brent Waters, shortly to be published by Eerdmans, will find an unusual degree of overlap, I fear, between my essay there and some pages in this book. It was not quite what was intended, but that is how it turned out. *Ignoscat lector!* It is not for anything *I* have contributed, after all, that that book will make its appeal to the reader, but for the interpretative insight of a remarkable constellation of contributors. May the reader gain no less profit from it than I do, and make better use of it! Finally, in that context, I mention the staff of Eerdmans, of whom the conventional word of thanks says too little. In an age when publishers despair, they continue to encourage us all.

CHAPTER 1

Spirit and Self

Ethics in the Spirit

"The Spirit comes to our aid in our weakness" (Rom. 8:26). Weak in confidence, weak in understanding, weak in endurance, our sickened agency is restored, our ill-conceived undertakings are given good effect. What do we mean by weakness? Paul has described it, borrowing a telling image from the Isaianic Apocalypse, as a world that groans and labors in the pangs of childbirth (8:19-22). Striving to produce something but unable to tell what it would produce, it is wholly bent upon painful effort, a world with a historical destiny but no vision of fulfillment. The future is laid upon it as a goal to strive for, but it is opaque and beyond any clear imagination. Within this world there are some who "possess the firstfruits of the Spirit" (8:23), who share in the cosmic groaning of history with a certain self-awareness, knowing that their own accomplishment is bound up with a point of arrival for the material universe, the "resurrection of the body."[1] But neither the unconscious groaning of the world nor the conscious groaning of the spiritually aware achieves anything. They are formless aspirations towards an object that is neither envisaged nor realized. The salvation they look for is hidden behind the curtain of the future; it has no presence, and they can only wait.

This shortfall in agency cannot be made good from the side of its object. From an abstract future there is no clarity or energy to be drawn, no meaning sufficient to direct or command. The shortfall must be supplied from the side

---

1. οὐ μόνον δέ, ἀλλὰ καὶ αὐτοί . . . (Rom. 8:23): the spiritual not only *know* of the world's groaning, but groan *with* it.

of the subject. And here Paul speaks, remarkably, of a third groaning, one that arises in the being of God himself. God's Spirit groans for the fulfillment of God's purpose, and if the Spirit's groans are "inexpressible," that does not mean that they are doomed, like ours, to be contentless and ill-focused. The divine purpose may be incommunicable, but the secret understanding of the future which the Father and the Spirit hold between them comes to our assistance. "We do not know how we are to pray aright"; yet prayer can be effective if it springs from the praying of the Spirit. Our formless aspirations, taken up and woven into God's purposes, aim at more than we can know.

The Spirit comes to our aid, and active life with its active purposes comes within our reach. Rescuing us from a futile passive-reactive immanence, the Spirit of God strives and works with and through our practical thinking. But as active life becomes thinkable, so does *reflection upon* active life. The Spirit comes to our aid in the practice of Ethics, too — not only, that is, in how we think about what we are to do, not only in our mutual communication and instruction as to what we are to do, but in the reflective analysis we bring to bear on them. For Ethics is not itself practical reasoning or moral instruction, but a reflection upon both. Especially the Spirit teaches us to reflect upon the moral instruction of Jesus, illuminating it for each successive attempt to understand, obey, and communicate. It was with well-justified astonishment, then, that Johannes Fischer complained twenty years ago that the Spirit "plays almost no part in contemporary theological ethics."[2] The essential note of an evangelical ethics will be missing if the freedom of the Gospel is not understood as life in the Spirit. Failure on this point must mean the failure of Theological Ethics as a whole.

There is, to be sure, some reason for hesitation. It might appear that the only effect of reflection on active life is to subvert the logic of action. Reflection and action, it may be thought, are mutually exclusive postures. Action is exertion seeking satisfaction in a point of rest. It seeks that it may find. It has an end-of-action set before it to attain. In the foreshortened view of active intelligence the end-of-action melts into the end-of-history. The whole of future time is divided into time before and time after, the time of exertion and the time of rest: "If I can only get this rose bush to bloom on this plot, the garden will be really pleasant!" Ethics knows how foreshortened

2. Johannes Fischer, *Leben aus dem Geist* (Zurich: Theologischer Verlag Zürich, 1994), p. 11. "In contrast to dogmatics," Fischer added, though he might justly have given the credit for recognizing the importance of the Spirit for Pauline ethics to New Testament exegetes following Herman Gunkel. The point has been emphasized again in relation to justification by N. T. Wright, *Paul and the Righteousness of God* (London: SPCK, 2013), pp. 912-1037.

that perspective is. It reflects on the place that the goal occupies within the world's happenings, and foresees many more months and years of further aspiration in the garden after the blooming of the rose bush. Life does not stop and enter a new register of restfulness with each practical achievement. "Find, and you shall seek!" says the reflective ethicist back to the moral thinker. That is not good news for practical reason. It carries the warning of an illusory character in its ends and a futility in its exertions. As soon as we set practical thinking in a framework of reflection, we view the world of action as Qoheleth viewed it, bewildered at the vanity of each and every undertaking.

Yet that view cannot be escaped. Everyone who steps into practical thinking must at some point step out of it, and look back uneasily over the shoulder, wondering whether the project has been an illusion.

If an Ethics consists solely of reflective observations on the practice of moral thinking and teaching, it will lead into the stagnant marshes of nihilism. A "moral science" that begins and ends in an observer's account will be a salt that has lost its savor, reducing practical thinking to a process. As P. T. Forsyth remarked, "a process has nothing moral in it."[3] There is room enough in Ethics, to be sure, for disciplined observations, generic (as in sociology, economics, or anthropology) or particular (as in history), which can contribute to the forming of a moral imaginary. Taken on their own terms, they are modest and useful scouts, reporting on the terrain. The trouble lies with a moral science that offers observations on the terrain in place of a strategy. An observational science can do nothing to help us evaluate our ends; it can only say that they are similar or dissimilar to the common run of human ends. It can only deflate us with the sad wisdom that action has no real end at all, but returns after every finding to seek some more, at best allowing the illusion of an end. For Kierkegaard the ethicist was trapped on the ground of "resignation," cultivating self and life assiduously in the absence of ultimately satisfying grounds for doing so.

There is a certain practical coherence about conforming to the common run of humankind and the exigencies of natural existence. We begin most unreflective moral experience with little more than these to go on, and may tolerate an Ethics that speaks of them familiarly, even if it never takes us a step forward. Yet the question "why?" takes us beyond any such Natural

3. *The Work of Christ* (London: Independent Press, 1938), p. 67: "An act, on the other hand, can only be done by a moral personality. . . . Science knows nothing about acts, it only knows about processes."

Ethics. It is not an unreasonable or sophistic "why?" but a "why?" that asserts itself logically as soon as we achieve a sense of responsibility, as soon, that is, as we acknowledge that there is a reality to which we owe the questioning of social norms and natural exigencies. Since it is not a "why?" of theory but of practical reason, the only answer to which it is open is an end of history. Of itself Ethics knows nothing of an end of history, but it can point to a moral teaching that does. "Seek, and you shall find!" (Matt. 7:7). Like other teachings of the Sermon on the Mount, this word has two aspects, as acknowledged practical wisdom, on the one hand, as eschatological promise on the other. The proclamation of the Kingdom has, it seemed, stepped in to vindicate the cheerful logic of practice against the sad disillusion of ethical observation.

And with that vindication new possibilities arise for reflection. It becomes thinkable that "Find, and you shall seek!" need not deflate "Seek, and you shall find!" The perpetual return to seeking becomes a preliminary mapping of the way to the promise of an ultimate finding. Of itself Ethics has no resources to make such a promise, but it can hear it, and it can proceed on the basis that it has been heard. Such is Ethics undertaken in the Spirit. The Spirit is "warranty" of the promise (2 Cor. 1:22; 5:5; Eph. 1:14), and under its leading Ethics can think about the perpetual seeking-and-finding of moral thinking, about its native ends-of action and its formal accomplishments, in the light of what is promised over and beyond every intermediate finding and seeking.

Let it be said, first of all, that such an Ethics will speak of God's action. It will speak of the groanings of creation and of the firstfruits in whom these groanings reach articulacy, but it will speak of them as moments in the purpose and work of God. Its discipline will be theological — not disregarding the contributions of philosophical analysis and phenomenological interpretation, but stepping beyond them to reach decisions which philosophy quite properly holds back from, decisions authorized and required by the Spirit who searches the deep things of God. In the second place we must add that it will speak of our human life and action as it is to be undertaken "today," in the time that is given us to live. Here there is a delicate but important division of labor between a theological Ethics and a doctrinal theology. Doctrine rests in truth. It has to struggle hard for it, and can never perfect its articulation of it once and for all, but the truth of the matter and nothing else is its term, and to that extent it sets the activities of time in the light of eternity. It speaks *of* temporal moments in their unique unrepeatability, but since its concern is with what God accomplishes in them, it does not speak *to* those moments. In telling of God and his work done once for all in history, it tells truths that are good yesterday, today, forever. Christ was crucified under Pontius Pilate in the reign of Tiberius (not Herod the Great or Nero), but the truth of his death in the reign of Tiberius was no less true in the reigns of Herod and Nero. If we say that he was "crucified before the foundation of the world," we mean that his crucifixion by Pilate was always God's purpose for mankind; if we say that he was "crucified again" in the martyrs, we mean that the power of his death under Pilate lived on in his suffering church. All times and places equally are governed by the truth that he suffered under Pontius Pilate. The perennial validity of this proposition belongs to no proposition framing a practical purpose or pursuing a moral deliberation. Deliberation is always a matter of "today, if you will hear his voice." Ethics must speak, though reflectively, *to* each today, as each today is a fresh today, not a repetition of yesterday.

This means that Ethics has neither the first nor the last word in Theology. Those words belong to a doctrine that speaks of God's purposes, acts, and ultimate ends. But because God's purposes are alive and active, there is place for a word in between first and last words, a word that speaks reflectively on the Spirit's aid to our present weakness, which discerns the present converse of the Spirit in guiding the human spirit to the service of God's further ends. We are summoned to be alert and understanding, not passively reactive, and that means thinking what it is we are to do while it is ours to do it.

The point may be expressed crudely by saying that Ethics, though reflective, is still a *practical* discipline, not a *theoretical* or *speculative* one. It is not a branch of dogmatics, distinct in its special themes as the doctrine of the church is distinct from the doctrine of creation. Yet the polarity of "practical" and "speculative" should not seduce us into thinking that truths of dogmatic theology are without interest for practical life. An impatient would-be-up-and-doing theology may have a hate-list of doctrines it stigmatizes as "purely speculative" — the Trinitarian doctrines, for example, or the doctrine of God's electing decree before the foundation of the world. Yet these truths, too, can enrich and enlarge the moral imaginary. No theologian should accept that a truth about God is a function of its utility, and yet truths *are* useful to creatures such as we, who need truth in order to live by it. The despised *Quicunque vult,* with its "almost mischievous" exchanges of "metaphysical confidences," may elicit a moral conversion, as a memorable passage in one of Charles Williams's novels suggests.[4] The simple truth that

4. *The Greater Trumps* (London: Faber & Faber, 2011), p. 110.

God is good in his being, and in his working good *for us* — "Good art thou, and doest good!" (Ps. 119:68) — focuses the "excess" of praise, where belief utters things beyond practical application while never ceasing to speak of moral reality. That is why Ethics must wait on Doctrine, content to say the second word, never succumbing to its worst temptation, which is to conceive itself as a kind of alternative doctrine, speculatively valid on its own terms, a mistake of some nineteenth-century advocates of the Ritschlian "primacy of ethics." This yields an impoverished substitute doctrine, shorn of the "excess" of praise and reduced to those divine workings we find most immediately to our purpose, and, if carried through to the end, will fail to yield ethics at all, since its false pretension to speak eternally loses sight of the distinct time of practical action.

Ethics can claim no primacy in theology, then, but neither should it be willing to grant one, however much it may accept that it can speak only after Doctrine has spoken. The two branches of theology are mutually complementary: Doctrine completes Ethics by speaking of an end of God's works; Ethics completes Doctrine by offering it an understanding of itself as a practice of praise. Yet the two still proceed in a certain independence. If the truths they attend to are the same, the rational order in which they place them is different. Ethics, watching reflectively over practical reason, orders theology towards deliberation; Doctrine, with its task of expressing the truth of the divine, orders it narratively, following the work and self-disclosure of God. That is one sense in which not only the "first" but also the "last" word is given to doctrinal theology. When it reaches its last word and speaks of the end of God's works, it may entertain the thought that, since God shall be all in all, the actions of men can be no more than a pale and insignificant reflection of what God has done, a proper idea to entertain and perhaps God's own last word on all human endeavor. Yet Ethics cannot allow itself to be brought to rest there before the time has come. It must call us back from the apocalyptic viewpoint to the moment that confronts us now: "Today, if you will hear his voice, harden not your hearts." And that is something most definitely to be heard and received with an impressionable and active heart.

The Giver of Life

The Spirit is "the lifegiver" (John 6:63). There are other titles that highlight other aspects of the Spirit's work; if we give priority to this one, it is not that the others are of lesser weight. The giving of life comes first not in the logic of divine being but in the order of divine works. The Spirit will preside over our loves and our hopes, our knowing, our enduring, and our final glorification, but it is from the giving of our life that all subsequent life must flow. We are creatures of time, whose beginnings precede their continuations and their endings. Our first thought of life in the Spirit, therefore, must be directed to the gift received.

The word "life" has various levels of meaning, even confining its reference to humans and ignoring the life of plants and non-human animals. It is true of us as humans that we are sentient and capable of feeling; it is true of us as humans that we are existentially self-aware: both these powers are elements in what "living" means for us. But it is not to these that the title "lifegiver" points, but to something more lively, to the power of purposing and acting, of what we call "living our lives," which human nature to all appearances possesses, yet is constantly in peril of losing. We note in the first place the connection of the verb "to give life" *(zōopoiein)* with the divine act of raising from the dead.[5] Death has no quarrel with biological life; it is indispensable to recycling it. Death has no quarrel with consciousness, which can view the prospective limit of its own continuance with reasonable equanimity. But death is the enemy of all our purposes, and the Spirit's power in raising the dead is of a piece with our *moral* recovery, the restoration of imperiled or decayed agency. Ezekiel's famous vision of the dry bones of a battlefield reconstituted by the Spirit into a mighty army is meant precisely as a description of moral renewal (Ezek. 37:11-14).

To speak of moral recovery is to speak of a word in our mouths that is true and effective. "The flesh is of no avail; the Spirit is the lifegiver; the words I have spoken to you are spirit and life" (John 6:63). Or, again, contrasting the two covenants of law and spirit, "the letter kills, the spirit gives life" (2 Cor. 3:6). "Give me life according to thy word!" was the repeated prayer of the poet of the Long Psalm, who meant not merely to claim a promise but to appropriate a word of God that was itself the life for which he longed. God-given speech commands and orders the elements, and makes the life of the Hebrew poet, marshalling the letters and lexemes of his language, one with the very speech of God. When Jesus addressed the crowds on the last day of the Feast of Tabernacles, inviting "anyone who thirsts" to come to drink, he added, "Whoever believes in me, as the Scripture has said, 'Out of his heart will flow rivers of living water'" (John 7:37-39) The believer was to receive, and become, a source of words of life, one in whom the understanding and

5. Cf. John 5:21; Rom. 4:17; 8:11; 1 Cor. 15:22; 1 Pet. 3:18.

command of the Son of Man would be immanent. This was meant, John explains, of the Spirit, to be given when Jesus was glorified.

Intelligence, articulateness, authority, understanding self-command and self-disposal, the framing and execution of purposes that overcome death and decay, these are all elements of life in the Spirit. Taken together, they allow us to speak clearly and comprehensively about freedom, over which there can always be a temptation to equivocate. Freedom implies an emancipation from powers that oppress our agency and reduce us to a passive-reactive existence. It is an event, and as such it can and must be experienced, once and more than once if need be. But the one event, taken on its own, is not enough to imprint the character of freedom upon a whole course of life. Some who have been emancipated busy themselves thereafter oppressing others as they were once oppressed, as though freedom were no more than an exchange of roles. Some attempt to recover and re-live the pathos of emancipation over and over again, as though a step beyond it would be a step back into the old oppression. Emancipation is only the negative moment of freedom; it should open the way to fulfillment in self-government. Freedom is a way of living that builds on the event of emancipation, preserving its gains and realizing its promise. "*For* freedom Christ has set us free," as Paul declared (Gal. 5:1). That is why life liberated from the oppression of law, which is how Paul understood evangelical liberty, is anything but a lawless life. To fly from law-bound arbitrariness to spontaneous arbitrariness is simply to oscillate between passivity and reactivity, always threshing about within the toils of legal consciousness. It is the mark of true freedom that it can see the moral law from a new vantage-point as a witness to God's purpose to order and bless the life of the human race. What previously looked like disconnected arbitrary norms come together to form a coherent "law of Christ," the love of neighbor as self. As with the claims of moral law, so, too, with the claims of community. Liberty may strike out to gain a certain initial distance on community, but it cannot take a permanent form as solitary independence, for freedom is grounded in communication. It is discursively engaged, not only with other agents, but in dialogical intimacy with God himself, who speaks with those who possess the Spirit as he did with Moses, face to face. "Led by" the Spirit and "walking in" the Spirit, they find their human purposes shaped responsively to his purposes.

We may say that life in the Spirit is nothing less than a condition of moral *maturity*, in which the elements of moral experience — norms, good, demands of other people — are integrated into a competent discernment of God's will, founded in an understanding of the order and destiny of the world. Yet "nothing less" does not mean nothing more. For the idea of maturity, prominent in Paul's exposition of spiritual freedom in the Epistle to the Galatians, is not solely a matter of individual maturation, gaining confidence, exercising better judgment, seeing more clearly the purpose of different requirements and their application to different cases, and so on. It is not even a matter of power to will or courage to venture beyond what seems possible. The maturity of the believer is set against the background of a world-historical narrative of new creation through the Son of God, a story of a once-for-all recovery of humankind that reaches its crisis in Christ's death and resurrection. The world itself had to groan in labor-pains. Morality had to come to its fulfillment in history. Until the disclosure of the "Last Man," the lordly servant of God (1 Cor. 15:45), no authority could make sense of the moral law, no prophetic vision could tell of the life of the Kingdom of God. Life in the Spirit is the life of a post-resurrection mankind, taken into the friendship of God, admitted to divine direction and guidance. "I live, yet not I, but Christ in me" (Gal. 2:20). And as the first gift conferred on two disciples on the first Easter evening was the gift of interpreting history, so an Ethics of the Spirit is an Ethics learned in Christ's school of interpretation: the moral law fulfilled in himself, the Kingdom of God coming in himself, the authority to live in the world conferred by himself.

The concept of Spirit in Ethics, then, is an evangelical one, referring us to the narratives of resurrection and Pentecost, not, as Johannes Fischer expounds it, a formal one, framed to overcome the philosophical antinomy of deontology and teleology. First resolving that Spirit refers to a "unity of life and action" which "determines us to and in communication," Fischer is led to posit behind every question of discursive practical reasoning a deeper question about "the spirit that determines us to and in our communication, behind our back, as it were."[6] A great variety of spirits, each specific to its own "context of communication," leaves to Christian Ethics the "essentially critical" task of distinguishing among the multitude of spirits "in quest of the Spirit that ensures 'real' life" and "led by the question of 'true' life."[7] That Christian Ethics is guided in this task by the Pauline ethics of the Spirit, which fills the general concept "paradigmatically" with Christological and ecclesiological content, may seem to be no more than a particular variant on the general theme.[8] Why should a critical Christian Ethics expect to

6. Fischer, *Leben aus dem Geist*, p. 51.
7. Fischer, *Leben aus dem Geist*, p. 132.
8. Fischer, *Leben aus dem Geist*, p. 190.

identify just one such spirit, especially if the spirits are differentiated by a variety of cooperative tasks — banking, washing up the dishes, teaching in universities — in any of which we may frequently engage? Fischer's two-level method represents at its starkest the paradox of contemporary communitarianism: loudly protesting the sovereign rights of the particular, it keeps its own distance from it within a general theory of particulars. The ambivalence in which this leaves Fischer is suggested by the quotation marks that stand guard over every use of the words "real" and "true": what is *real* from the point of view of the particular inner circle is only *"real"* from the point of view of the general outer circle, and in principle exchangeable with a thousand alternative "realities." The gift of Pentecost, the reality of renewed mankind in Christ, these evangelical elements are kept strictly within the inner circle, while Fischer's own "Ethics of the Spirit" roams free of commitments in the outer circle, ready to greet any new communal practice, and any new ethic derived from it, with the same kindly offer of a niche within the structure of the "spirit-directed life." We should not hesitate, of course, to speak of the Spirit of God as source and guide of every creaturely aspiration of human practical reason. But if we are to make that affirmation, we must be bold enough to remove the quotation marks that ghettoize the reality-claim, and state, "what you worship in ignorance, I declare to you!" (Acts 17:23).

On one point at least, however, we must attend to Fischer carefully. Life in the Spirit, as he understands it, is a life of "communicative reason," taking up the watchword of those who have used it to free the legacy of Kant from its relentless individualism. It participates in a moral awareness and responsibility that takes shape in dialogue between an "I" and a "Thou." Practical reason cannot be solitary; it can only be an invitation and response. Behind every report of practical reasoning there is an invitation it has heard, an address to which it makes answer with a responsible and considered self-disposal. In all the masterful discernment for which the Spirit equips us there must be an attentive response to the searching, questioning, and summoning of God.

Naming God

In a curious story from Genesis (32:22-32), primitive in detail and subtle in structure, the patriarch Jacob struggles with an unknown assailant in the night. The drama of the story lies in its unexpected outcome: Jacob's life-and-death struggle becomes an encounter with a God who could, and would, bless him, a conclusion which turns upside down all the expectations built up in the course of the narrative. The slippery patriarch did not wrestle with God knowingly; he wrestled with a nameless threat, as he had often had to do before, and, as before, succeeded. The night visitor, one of those malign spirits that prowl in desert places, perhaps, and have power in the hours of darkness, struggles to get free as dawn approaches. But at this point the story assumes a new aspect: by a simple touch on the thigh the adversary asserts his power over Jacob in hurting him without killing him. Jacob, still refusing to relax his hold, demands a blessing from his victorious adversary. Told to state his name, the patriarch is given a new one, with a new moral import (Jacob means "trickster," Israel "striver"), and in this form the blessing is given. When in turn he demands the name of the one who has blessed him, he meets refusal, but the very refusal contains a clue of self-identification: "Why is it that you ask my name?" Why else, but because in all his struggles Jacob has been in search precisely of one who is not to be named as other beings are, the nameless one? And so he can announce with confidence that he has seen God, and lived.

Nameless, because he is not one among others, God grants mankind a way of calling on him, a "name." In the Mosaic narratives God names himself in a reduplicated expression as "I am that I am" (Exod. 3:14). As Being itself God needs no name, for God's being is all the identity he can require. But in making himself known he gives himself to mankind a second time with a name to be called on. The reduplicated being is not *other* than God's being, but neither is it *simply* God's being. The self-naming of God is not a non-event, a mere emanation of its unnamable eminence. Divine being is offered in self-repetition, for our sakes. Self-naming is the excess of the fullness of divine being, the moment at which it affirms itself in giving itself. The gift attains its end as we, in response, learn to name him. As he calls himself "I am that I am," so we call him "He is" (YHWH), or, as one of the Psalms insists, we call him by that name by which he is known and worshiped everywhere, "God," *Elohîm* (Ps. 48:10).

It is a moment that constantly enchants the poets of Israel, the agent-self emerging from anonymity to invoke God in answer to his self-naming. "Thou hast said, 'Seek ye my face,'" a poet declares, and in response to that invitation (in the plural), he steps forward in a sudden self-awareness to announce himself in the first person singular, "My heart says to thee, 'Thy face, YHWH, do I seek!'" (Ps. 27:7-9). Another Psalmist in a similar self-awakening cries, "Bless YHWH, my soul!" (Ps. 103:1), discerning in one and the same moment the object of blessing, "HE IS," and "my soul." With the cry that recognizes God the self leaps to self-recognition. There could have been no discourse with "my soul," no talk of "what is within me," before that exclamation, "Bless YHWH!" Impressions, sensations, feelings, impulses, whatever flits across the surface of consciousness like shadows across a stone, come together to constitute a *me,* when they are concentrated upon the blessing of "HE IS." There is more: the world, too, makes its appearance in the very act of the self's praise of God. As the subject-agent is given continuously from one moment of blessing to the next, he finds himself delivered over to a world of objective content that gives dimensions to his memory: "and forget not all his benefits!" The self-donations of the world's Original comprise a story of goods unfolding upon earth, to be recalled and narrated by a self that has historical identity in poetic recounting.[9]

"Call unto me and I will answer," the prophet is commanded (Jer. 33:3). Ethics begins with calling on God, the first human act. But that call is not the first event; God's call to us to call on him precedes it, and only at his summons does our agency come to consciousness. "You have opened my ears," another Psalmist cried, "and so I said, 'Here I come!'" (Ps. 40:6f.). It is not that there can be no self-knowledge of any kind apart from the opening of our ears. We may know ourselves at the level of the sensory consciousness through feelings of comfort or pain; we may know ourselves at the level of existential awareness through anxiety and care. But we cannot know ourselves as *agents,* of whom it is written in the scroll of God's purposes that we may do his will.

Jesus addresses God neither as "God" nor "YHWH," but as "Father," teaching his disciples to do so, too. This does not repudiate the truth that God is "I am who I am," but builds on it: "Our Father" is the source of our being. We may take or leave the suggestion that the use of the intimate form "Abba" in prayer was an innovation on Jesus' part.[10] It scarcely matters, since the underlying Christological point is clear:[11] his address to God as Father corresponded to his understanding of himself, and in summoning disciples to call God "Father," he invited them to enter the position before God which he claimed for himself. As we call God "Abba! Father!" our agent-identity is united with that of the Son. The Spirit who enables us to pray in such words is the Spirit of adoption, the one who makes us a member of God's family

9. Ps. 57:7ff. invites a similar line of commentary, while the subtle interweaving of life and art in the Long Psalm (Ps. 119), where "meditations" on divine law blend seamlessly into "songs" about the language of God's speech, take the thought much further.

10. Joachim Jeremias, *The Central Message of the New Testament* (London: SCM, 1965), pp. 9-30.

11. Cf. Origen, *On Prayer* 22.

(Rom. 8:23; Gal. 4:5-6). And so the first petition of the form of prayer that Jesus gave his disciples, "Our Father, hallowed be thy name!" calls on the name of God to ask for its "hallowing" precisely by our calling upon it. Luther's famous interpretation of the clause, that God's name, "always holy in its essence," may be holy also "in our use of it," is well-judged and, of course, traditional.[12] In one sense, then, the petition is granted at the moment of its utterance; precisely by calling on God as Father we hallow his name as we pray that it may be hallowed. Yet that does not make it redundant. If in calling on the name we assert our agency as grounded on the gift of the name, in praying for it to be hallowed we pray for effective encounter with the Holy in all our living and acting. It is a prayer for the grace to live life as God has given us to live it, as a member of his family.

Agency is the exercise of freedom, and freedom is the responsibility for self-disposal. We must be called to it. To know ourselves as agents is to know that we have been called to make decisions about ourselves. It is to know, too, that the decisions we must make do not rest with us to think up or invent, but are thrust upon us in the form of certain definite possibilities, challenges, and opportunities as we find ourselves delivered over into a world that is as it is, not as we might have wished it to be. To know ourselves as responsible is to know that a response to *these* possibilities, challenges, and opportunities is required of us. And on how we shall make a response to these, rather than others, the fate of our freedom depends, and with it our final welfare. Success or failure lies before us, not only piecemeal in relation to particular endeavors, but as a whole. To know ourselves as agents is to know that we may win our souls or lose them; our lives shall at the last have been well lived or wasted.

The command to exercise responsibility, then, arises from outside us. We are responsible to our context, to the world we find ourselves in. But it arises, too, within our consciousness: it is as immediate as it is objective, neither open to our evasion nor subject to our control. When responsibilities are imposed on us from outside, we can interrogate their authority, call them in question, and finally refuse them. We have a certain transcendence over them, and can teach ourselves to treat them with scorn, a lesson illustrated in antiquity by the famous hypothesis of the philosopher cheerfully roasting to death in the brazen bull of Phalaris. Even if we are resolute enough to say, with Levinas, that responsibility to the Other makes subjectivity "initially

---

12. Luther, *Great Catechism* (*WA* 30.I.198). Sources may be found in Gregory of Nyssa, *De oratione dominica* 3; Augustine, *Sermo* 56.5.

and as such a hostage," we reserve the privilege of all hostages, to attempt escape.[13] But the demand which lays claim on us by virtue of what, as agents, we *are,* cannot be eluded in this way. The demand to exercise our freedom well is categorical. It is the demand the Spirit lays on us, and in acknowledging that, we acknowledge it as the demand both of our own existence and of God.

The Flesh

One aspect of Paul's treatment of Spirit is too important to pass by. He does not oppose divine spirit to human or demonic, or good spirit to evil, but persistently opposes life in the Spirit to "life by the flesh."[14] Any proposal to speak of life in the Spirit stands or falls by its success in addressing this point. For flesh and spirit are not two concepts, but one concept of an opposition of poles. In speaking of one, we must speak of both, and if we overlook the contrast of the two, the "spirit" of which we speak will not be the Spirit of Pentecost.

At first glance the opposition points to a simple psychological tension: there are higher and lower impulses within the complex motivating drives of human nature, intellectual on the one hand, sensuous on the other. But placed within the narrative of new creation, it becomes an opposition of two moral eras, before and after Christ. It is not enough to say with the later Augustine that life *secundum carnem* means life *secundum hominem,* for though this points in the right direction, it ignores the elevation of humanity into the sphere of spiritual life with the ascension of Christ.[15] Humanity may turn in either of two directions: it may remain self-enclosed within its own immanence, or it may be lifted up to share the life of God. Life "according to the flesh," for Paul, is life that has not entered the triumph of Christ's *new* humanity. It is lived in subjection to prevailing anthropological dynamics, not only sensuous impulses but intellectual and emotional needs, too, and psychological or social pressures. Spontaneous impulses and imaginations, unreflective trains of reasoning and *idées reçues,* overburdening social demands and expectations, all cut the nerve of responsibility and numb our

---

13. Emmanuel Lévinas, *Éthique et Infini: dialogues avec Philippe Nemo* (Paris: Fayard, 1982), p. 96.

14. The key texts are Gal. 3:3; 4:29; 5:16-26; Phil. 3:3; 1 Cor. 3:1-3; Rom. 8:4-17.

15. *City of God* 14.2ff. *De continentia* 4.10.

understanding and self-control, generating strife in communities, both selfish strife over immediate advantages and high-minded strife over principles
we cannot agree on. Apart from the Spirit's rule there is no hermeneutic
authority, no overarching framework of mutual service commanding the
play of moral and practical imagination on every side. As John Chrysostom
read Paul, "flesh" stands for "a kind of reasoning that is earthly, superficial,
and inconsiderate."[16]

We may speak of life by the flesh in a more general or a more specific
sense. Generally, first of all, it is coextensive with the category of sin. Sin is
a form of evil, and evil, according to the theological tradition, has no being,
but only failure of being. As there is no alternative God and no alternative
creation, so there is no alternative reality. "Evil never was, never is, and never
will be a subsistent with a nature of its own," wrote Maximus Confessor. "It
has nothing by way of substance, nature, subsistence, potency or operation
among things that really are; it is not a quality, quantity, relation, place, time,
purpose, effect, motion, disposition, or experience observable within the
nature of things that have being; nor in the totality of things does it subsist
in its natural identity as beginning, middle, or end, but, to offer a summary
definition, evil is a *failure of operation* in any of nature's immanent powers
to attain its ends; apart from that it is nothing at all."[17] And as there is no
alternative God and no alternative reality, so there is no alternative action,
only failed action, by which is meant, of course, not only failure to attain
subjective ends, as when I try to kill my enemy but my hand slips, but *objective* failure, as when I hate my enemy because I fail to recognize his real
status as a lost child of God.

Critics object to this negative account of sin as a palliation, a refusal
to take the radicality of sin seriously. The truth is exactly the opposite: it is
the only way of taking sin seriously *as offense to God.* One may be "serious"
about sin in various ways; Milton's Satan illustrates one of them. Satan is the
original Manichaean, believing in the possibility of an alternative reality, an
alternative scale of values and an alternative god, who will, of course, be himself. His sin is the occasion for heroic self-esteem. According to the logic of
that alternative reality God cannot be offended that Satan should do his own
thing in his own way. Once it is granted, our own routine failures become
quite different from real sin, so much inferior to it that they are hardly worth

16. *In Epistolam ad Galatas Commentarius* (PG 61:671-72). Here and elsewhere throughout this volume, unless otherwise indicated, translations of ancient texts are my own.

17. Maximus Confessor, *Quaestiones ad Thalassium,* introduction (PG 90:253).

noticing. Offense to God is thus evaded on two sides: real sin is too dignified for it, mere failure too undignified. The rebel angel rises above God's wrath, the erring human does not rise to his notice.

Even while avoiding this Manichaean extreme, one may derive from it the seductive thought that the only offense to God is one offered by a reflection of his own absoluteness, the offense of an heroic will. A hard and sharp line is drawn between voluntary and involuntary, so that nothing of real importance is held to occur apart from an unencumbered and unclouded free choice. Here we are at the center of gravity of "voluntarism." It is a term widely applied across the Western tradition and therefore difficult to use with precision; if our stipulative paradigm leaves some views that may bear the name to one side, so much the better, for we shall not lack other instances to talk about. From a work such as Slater's *Manual* one might form the idea that sin is very difficult to commit — real, honest-to-badness sin, that is, as distinct from mere "imperfection." A sin requires that one "always apprehends that he is doing a wrong action, an action which his conscience condemns," and with "actual advertence to the malice of the action done," to which demanding psychological conditions one must add a yet more demanding one, "free consent of the will." The thief who has never learned to distinguish *meum* from *tuum*, the kleptomaniac who is "powerless to refrain," are mere inadequates, not clear-sighted, steely-nerved sinners.[18] Few of our failings qualify, in fact, since so much wrongdoing has to do with failure to understand, see, or appreciate. If I have told the company a funny story that puts a colleague in a foolish and ridiculous light, I need feel no compunction, it seems, so long as I have been heedless of the painful implications for my victim. Only if I were quite clear that the story was unkind, would it give me something to repent of. If *that* degree of self-awareness, self-control, and moral apprehension is required for the exercise of free will, those Reformers who denied the freedom of the will outright may have had a point! But this is all the fruit of an exaggerated voluntarism devised in order to qualify Moral Theology as an art of *judgment* — judgment on other people's sins, that is, in relation to which it is naturally right to give the benefit of the doubt, to set high conditions for the proof of guilt and to pronounce acquittal when uncertainty remains.

18. Thomas Slater, *A Manual of Moral Theology* (London: Burns, Oates & Washbourne, 1925), vol. 1, pp. 83-84. The point of criticizing a text from the old and discredited "manualist" tradition is simply that it illustrates certain default assumptions which persist in vigor to this day.

When moral thinking, serving pastoral uses, cares for others' faults more than our own, it must be open to excuses: "tout comprendre rend très indulgent." Yet that does not take us as far as it may seem to. As close as possible to an imperfection that was not a sin might be the case of an elderly person who puts water on to boil, forgets about it and starts a fire, endangering other people's homes and lives. A teenager who did the same while distracted by the social media would feel the full force of our anger. A fully competent adult would be expected at least to make a very clear apology, reparation for damage, credible promises of future precautions, and so on. But with an elderly person we suspect an early symptom of decline, and we do not want to scold where scolding cannot mend. Responsibility may be limited. Yet we still treat the offender as responsible, and set about helping him or her find ways of taking responsibility — by replacing an old saucepan with an automatic-switch kettle, for example, or accepting that he or she cannot continue to live alone. What we do not do is decree that since the culprit is not wholly responsible, nothing of moral interest or importance has transpired. Limited responsibility is still responsibility, and the more responsible as it takes responsibility for its limits: the kleptomaniac never goes shopping without a companion, the alcoholic lets someone else keep charge of his cash and cards, the older person gives up driving, and so on.

There is a place for an art of judgment; it is called, generically, "politics," and Moral Theology does not belong under its paradigm, but lives and works this side of the frontier-notice, "Judge not, that you be not judged!" And as soon as we turn from caring for other people's sins to caring for our own, the whole excusatory line of thought becomes irrelevant. The plea, "I couldn't help it!" gets me nowhere. My whole problem is, I *didn't* help it! My awareness of sin comes down to this, that when I meant to do good, I did mischief, and my best purposes miscarried. Either I lacked strength to do the good I intended or the circumstances were too much for me; I misjudged myself, or I misjudged the world. In the face of these misjudgments nothing else matters.

We have noticed already two complementary ways of talking about sin in theology: the dogmatic theologian's thesis of its *necessity,* and the moral theologian's thesis of its *possibility.*[19] The dogmatician's sin is "original," i.e., located in the origins of our agency, and since sin is where human beings *necessarily* start from, it is also "radical," i.e., bound up with our membership of the human race — not, to be sure, in its creation and its destiny, but in its historical actuality. Circumstantial and temperamental differences in human

19. See *Self, World, and Time,* pp. 82-84.

sin are not of much interest to dogmatic theology, and especially uninterest-ing is any attempt to rank sins according to their gravity.[20] The dogmatician has no interest in exploratory descriptions. Sin lies behind us, and can safely remain a "mystery," a senseless contradiction of the right of God, of which no rational account could ever be given, or should be attempted. Moral Theology, always speaking in second place and after the dogmatic theologian has finished, views sin not as a presupposition but as an open possibility. Sin lies ahead of us as well as behind us, not as a necessity but as a danger. It "crouches at the door," as God said to Cain (Gen. 4:7), warning him of the sin that lies *ahead,* which he may either succumb to or escape from. This "*possible* sin," to use a phrase more suitable than the tradition's "actual sin," needs to be recognized and described in its various presentations. We must, of course, be careful here. To describe the varieties of sin is not to grade them by severity, but to understand the differing grounds on which sin offers itself as possible: we may sin by being unfeeling, we may sin by being stupid, we may sin by being hasty, we may sin by being insecure, and so on.

It follows that there is a variety of legitimate ways of surveying the scope of possible sin, depending on the route the moral inquiry is taking.[21] In pro-posing to speak of sin against faith, sin against love, and sin against hope, we simply follow the order implied in the trajectory of moral reason as attending to self, world, and time. Let us give each of the three a provisional name: we shall speak of the sins of *doubt,* of *folly,* and of *anxiety.* To which must be added a fourth kind of sin, the failure to give love its proper finality as the point of rest, the sin of *pride.* Sin is always "against," since it is constituted as refusal of some aspect of good reality, and all sins are against God, the creator, sustainer, and redeemer of all good reality. But as a relation to the creator and redeemer is mediated through nature and time, so it is with our failures to relate to him. We cannot accept Abelard's voluntarist dictum that the only true sin is immediate contempt of God. Our sins do indeed evince contempt of God, but we are not capable of shaking our fist at God and defying him outright. We are capable only of forgetting him, and of forgetting what he has made and what he has done. And as the direction of moral thought proceeds from self to world and time, so our contempt for God takes form as the refusal

20. Cf. Martin Luther, *On Good Works* (*WA* 6.206): "All works become equal, and one work is like the other; all distinctions fall away, whether they be great, small, short, long, many, or few." The source of the thought lies in James 2:10.

21. Augustine often uses the threefold sin of 1 John 2:16, "the lust of the flesh, the lust of the eyes, and the pride of life," because it fits the anthropological schema of body, soul, and mind, but he by no means confines himself to it.

first of our own agency, then of the created goods we are set in the midst of, of the historical moments in which we are given to act, and ultimately of the destiny to which we and the world are summoned. These classifications are, of course, no more than heuristic. To classify sin is to classify failure, which can be done only by locating it at points where it typically occurs. To classify sins according to self, world, time, and rest is not to classify the failures as though they were *something,* but to mark their position as one might warn of a hole in the road by drawing a white circle round it.

From these focal points there opens a vista of further possible specifications, stretching to the imagination's horizon. But a theoretical Ethics must know its limits; it should be suspicious of too elaborate a taxonomy of sin. Wrongdoing is a wearisomely repetitive business, and though it may be necessary in a juridical context to narrate it in great detail, the yield for understanding is slight. Discernment of temptation, on the other hand, is an exploratory matter, to be done on the ground and not reflectively. The pilgrim may see a temptation beside the road, and may warn us of it; the moral teacher, guiding others to find the road, may tell of some characteristic temptations. In either case they speak to a cultural context in which their discernments belong; unfamiliarity with the context may make what they tell us puzzling. When we read, for example, of conscientious anxieties in the fourth century about singing hymns, or about reading novels in the nineteenth, we find ourselves embarrassed. Yet by listening to these testimonies with respect, acknowledging the limits not only of their understanding but of our own, we can attune our sensibilities to temptations we must face in our time. No treatise by Aquinas or Calvin can tell us what challenges confront us, no grand theory of all conceivable temptations can be formed. Yet that does not leave nothing for Moral Theology to do. The underlying structure of sin corresponds to the underlying structure of action, and its recurrent and necessary forms can be, at least, illustrated, the possibilities which open up from them pointed out. It can provide a framework within which our own and others' temptations may be intelligently discerned.

Sin against the Self

In the second place, then, we speak of life by the flesh in a more restricted sense, as the paradigm of sin *against the self.* Of the three immediate contexts of sin the first stands apart from the other two. All sin is against the self, since we cannot refuse God's world in loveless folly, or God's time in impatient anxiety, without self-harm, but there is a sin that harms the self not consequentially but primarily, when we deny what God is calling us to be. As we have said that life in the Spirit embraces all moral life, the spheres of love and hope as well as of faith, yet speak first of the Spirit as lifegiver and of faith as the root of love and hope, so in speaking of "life in the flesh," though it includes the failures of love and failures of hope, we must give priority to the failure of faith which forms the horizon of our moral life *a limine.* There is a failure which consists essentially in refusing responsible agency, a failure to think morally, a passive-reactive immanence that is deaf to the call of God to act and live for him.

Sins against world and time can be described as we describe their objects, speaking of anxiety as we speak of the future, speaking of folly as we speak of worldly reality. In each of these cases the reality is before our eyes, but we mistake it. But the self is not before our eyes; it is not so much mistaken, as never grasped. We act and think as though we were not agents, but disposed of by outside forces like stones scattered on a hillside. We decline, as it were, to exist. And yet it is not possible to decline our agency effectively, actually to become non-agents. Passive self-imagination is a deception. We conceal from ourselves what we cannot help being and doing. Scope for bad faith is at its widest when we toy with the idea of non-existence. "Ere nescience shall be reaffirmed how long, how long?" Thomas Hardy made so bold as to inquire.[22] To which we can only reply: if nescience was what he craved, why ask, why ask?

The possibility of self-loss invests with danger all temptations that arise in the spheres of world and time. Is there an innocent mistake of love or a harmless wavering of hope? Certainly, there are failures of love and hope which *turn out* innocent and harmless, but that is only when faith has been active in repentance. Viewed in prospect, every such failure, however minimal, may have the loss of self crouching at the door beside it. And as those possible concrete sins are not only dangerous but tempting, so they may lend the loss of self a false attractiveness. We can be attracted by the thought of simply giving up trying, and we can be attracted by the thought of making a better agent-self than what God offers us. For it is a Protean sin, taking on the forms and colors of its setting, difficult to describe with precision. It can be seen equally in the glum disheartenment of the unemployed and the polished self-possession of the epicure, in the timid insecurity of the girl and the pushy bullying of the boy. Its common thread lies in an element

22. Thomas Hardy, "Before Life and After," *Collected Poems* (London: Macmillan, 1919).

of refusal and withholding, a *ressentiment* which closes down on the gift given and diverts energy away from it. Generically we describe this sin as "doubting," which is not a good name for it in modern English, having too strong a suggestion of propositional uncertainty or emotional timidity. The focus of the sin is neither cognitive nor emotional, but existential. "Let him ask in faith!" is the first word of the most practical of apostles, Saint James, who continues, "He who doubts is like a wave of the sea that is driven and tossed by the wind" (1:6).

What is it, then, that we "doubt," when we fail to ask in faith? That God exists, or that he rewards those who seek him (cf. Heb. 11:6)? Quite possibly, yet more fundamentally we doubt the selves God holds out to us and the God who offers us ourselves. As such, doubt is the radical sin, the sin that undermines agency at its root. It may present itself, on the one hand, as refusal of responsibility, burying the talent in a napkin for fear of the mistakes we may make if we venture on the exchange of life and action. Seen in this light it is the "shrinking back" which the Apostle says gives God no delight in us (Heb. 10:39). "Something we were withholding made us weak," as Robert Frost observed in his idealizing reflection on the conquest of North America.[23] The condition God has set upon the agency he gives is that it should be exercised; one who fears to exercise it is called "base servant!" (Luke 19:22). We are mistaken if we limit this to a simple lack of confidence; it may very well be lazy over-confidence, which sees no need to put itself out by exertion. Nor should it be confused with self-denial. When we consciously forgo some finite good in regard for the claims of the neighbor or God, we do not shrink from agency but affirm ourselves as agents who can and will decide.

On the other hand, it can consist in setting up a rival self to that which God would give us. Here is the bad form of self-love, "to the contempt of God" as Augustine described it, which is at the same time "self-hatred."[24] "Complacency" — or, to speak more properly, *self*-complacency *(complacentia de se)* — grounds the affirmation of self on an ideal and fantasized imagination, refusing the self that is real. True self-love responds to a summons addressed to self; bad self-love clings to a self that is self-conceived. Luther's well-known description of the *incurvatus in se,* "self-enclosure," captures perfectly the vicious circularity.[25] Self-complacency reduces world

---

23. "The Gift Outright," *Collected Poems* (London: Cape, 1943).

24. Augustine, *City of God* 14.28. For the paradox of sin against the self, and especially of Psalm 11:5 (10:6), cf. my *The Problem of Self-love in St. Augustine* (Eugene: Wipf & Stock, 2006²), p. 44.

25. Among many examples, this from his exposition of *Paul's Letter to the Romans* (*WA*

and time to materials for its own self-imagination, the world to a setting for self-display, time to an occasion for striking a pose. Self-assertive in manner but diffident in motive, it thirsts to be the object of admiration. Not the miser hiding his wealth from the eyes of his fellows, whose sin is anxiety, but the spender, the party-thrower, the householder with the elegant mansion, the garrulous talker who hogs the conversation, the driver of fast cars and private aeroplanes (or what substitutes a modest income may allow), all try to knead together out of friable materials a self that God would cast in the metal of spirit. Worldly ambition has all to do with the conspicuous, with wealth, power, or simple publicity, with whatever excites the emulating gaze, for the gaze is what the doubter lives on. Doubt is a predatory relation to the world; its inner resources are over-leveraged and its power over-extended when it comes to any course of action involving obscurity or public rejection.

The sin against the self, the passive-reactive immanence that shrinks from concrete action, requires a certain reflectiveness even to notice it. We come to recognize it in a moment of painful self-discovery, a token of common grace in our fallen human nature which offers us the chance to emerge from immanence and come to self-knowledge. We speak at this point of *shame*. Shame is commonly distinguished, correctly enough, from fully reflective moral self-awareness; it is a feeling, not a cognition, and is largely instinctive. It can be inflamed by trivial occasions and unresponsive to great ones. Its reactions in any instance must be questioned, and may often be dismissed when we are told by someone we can trust, "That's nothing to be ashamed of!" Shame is a bewildered attention to the self, astonished by the inner contradiction of failed agency. Where, it asks, is this boasted agency of mine? But its concern is with the appearance; it cannot submit a failure to a reflective appraisal. We can feel shame even when others are to blame. Earlier generations described this as "dishonor," and Augustine had a long struggle against the prejudice of his contemporaries which held that the most terrible dishonor one could suffer was to be the victim of rape.[26] Offenses against our person are, indeed, a cause of shame, for they defeat our self-possession and self-disposal. More broadly, we can be humiliated by any disappointment of expectations we have had of others. The position we assumed in the world, the plan of life we laid claim to, the very way we understood what we "meant"

56:356): *"Et hoc consonat Scripturae, quae hominem describit incurvatum in se adeo, ut non tantum corporalia sed et spiritualia bona sibi inflectet et se in omnibus quaerat."*

26. Notably in *De mendacio* and *City of God* 1.

to them, are shown up as ineffectual. The agony of shame lies in the collapse of a self-ideal.

Shame is not a recovery of agency, merely a symptom of its loss, and can even stand in the way of recovery if its painfulness so dominates the practical horizon that any further view is blocked. If renewal is to be given us, we must look for it beyond shame. That was the highly personal discovery of Martin Luther, which so unsettled the medieval synthesis of penitence and restoration. A step that goes beyond shame will not flow from self-contempt, but only from the intervention of God to remake our lives, and that intervention is not proportioned to shame in recognition of some would-be "congruent merit" of compunction, but is independent of it. This has given shame a bad reputation with some Christian moralists: "Shame, depart, thou art an enemy to my salvation!"[27]

And yet, like a fever produced by infection, at once a pathology and a defense, shame can point in either direction. There is an infinite difference between shame and repentance, that "change of mind" *(metanoia)* which leaves us facing in the opposite direction. Shame prepares the way for repentance by setting us to the task of accounting for how and why we failed, but it cannot guide us in that task, cannot sift details, weigh considerations, frame a narrative, but only establish our existential position. It chases us down the paths of self-questioning, but does not lead us through and out of their labyrinthine windings; it brings us round in a circle to where it first took up with us. Yet if the Spirit is calling, shame may be the first moment of repentance, not merely an antecedent but already an act of faith in itself, from which repentance cannot be separated: "Repent and believe the Gospel!" (Mark 1:15). The agony of the self protesting against its failure thus prevents the knowledge of agency from escaping down the channels of indifference, excuse, and despair, impressing on us that it is we who have failed, no less and no more, and that once we are responsible for wrongdoing we are responsible eternally. Only in believing can we seriously say of ourselves, "We have left undone those things which we ought to have done. And we have done those things that we ought not to have done. And there is no health in us."[28] Not a report of events, but a self-acknowledgment, a valid form, we might say, of the notorious *Cogito ergo sum*. In that acknowledgment, drawn from us by the living presence of the God against whom we have sinned, there is a new discovery of the self.

27. John Bunyan, *The Pilgrim's Progress* (Oxford: Oxford University Press, 1900), p. 69.
28. *The Book of Common Prayer.*

CHAPTER 2

Faith and Purpose

The Root of Action

Faith, as Christians have spoken of it, is a response to the summons of God, at once action and reaction, response and initiative, cognition and intention. It is, as we have put it, the root of action.[1] To unpack that phrase, two observations suggest themselves: first, faith is already an act, the first act, and not merely the presupposition of an act; second, faith confers meaning on subsequent acts which spring from it, and they in turn give concrete expression to faith.

(a) Thomas Aquinas defines faith as an "imperfect" cognition — imperfect, in that it needs to be carried through in hope and love if it is to come to rest in its object. Apart from hope and love the act of cognition is not effected. In any complete act of a rational being the two powers of knowledge and will must be coordinated. We need make no difficulty over the two rational powers, one power of being impressed by reality, the other of making an impression on reality; they can sensibly be distinguished, though they cannot sensibly be separated. Yet if faith is assimilated to the function of knowledge and hope and love to the function of will, faith cannot be an act, only an aspect of an act. To speak of a first *act,* an act from which other acts flow, we must speak of one in which faith is conjoined with an act of will (whether we call it "hope" or "love"), which accompanies faith from the very foundations up. But this foundationalizing of the will is, at the same time, a partial defoundationalizing of faith. Faith continues to be foundational,

---

1. *Self, World, and Time,* pp. 105-12.

but only as "implicit," not as active faith, a knowledge waiting to be supplemented with a volition, lacking the energy in itself to initiate anything. It was from this position that the Reformation's reassertion of the active character of faith sought to recover.[2]

Augustine had been less ready to tie faith down to the cognitive function of the mind. For him faith, too, and not only hope and love, was a prayer, and his rendering of the relation of the three was as a dynamic unfolding of the *working* of faith. The cognitive aspect of faith had as its object God's *goodness*, which is recognized as the cause of all that is. In this recognition faith is already intentional as well as cognitive, while love and hope, correspondingly, are cognitive as well as intentional. The distinctions among them are not to be made in terms of the different powers of reason, but have to do with the successive phases in moral thinking.[3]

(b) Unreflectively we may be tempted to think of our acts as separate and sequential, ranged one after the other, first this and then that, like beads on the string of time. If this were all there was to be said, understanding what someone had done would simply be to observe the act, classify it, and situate it in the sequence. Acts do follow and precede other acts, but they also spring from them, necessitate them, comprise them, and contribute to them. There may be logical implications which require that we do this after having done that; there may be actions that precipitate further actions, not to mention mental dispositions and commitments that demand to be enacted physically. The logic of action is built up in layers: acts and dispositions evoking and interpreting sequences of acts, sequences of acts expressing more fundamental acts and dispositions. To understand and interpret any one act, we must expose the practical logic that it reveals. Interpretative questions direct us to motives and purposes, which in turn direct us to questions about the history and situation of the agent. The question, "What is he *really* doing?" is always apt. If sometimes the answer is, "no more than he appeared to be doing," that simply means that not all we do is done as part of a larger purpose. But a great number of things we do are.

Someone stoops to pick up a fragment of paper. She may be tidying up, she may be concealing evidence from the police, she may be searching for a missing note, trying to find out what has been going on in the room, improving the environment of a public place, or an infinite number of other

---

2. *Compendium* 2.1.

3. *Enchiridion* 1.5; 2.7; 3.9. I here stress the contrast between Thomas and Augustine more than I did in *Self, World, and Time*.

things. Stooping to pick up paper has not much determinate meaning in itself; it derives its meaning from its active context. It is, we sometimes say, an "operation" rather than an "action." But consider an action which does have meaning in itself: tidying up. It can be its own justification, needing no further explanation. Yet in any particular instance it may very well have a further explanation. It may fulfill the terms of a contract of employment, steady the nerves for an important encounter, express a compulsive obsession, ritually mark the end of the day at bedtime. Action-types are intelligible in themselves, and yet every concrete instance of them is open to further interpretation. We see someone comforting a weeping child and we grasp the elementary meaning of the situation at once, but what relation is the child to the comforter, what are the tears about? Someone donates a sum of money to a charity, and we approve — but how was the money come by, what is the charity going to do with it? Apparent meanings may be deceptive. "Hypocrisy" is the name we give to exploitation of surface meanings of acts to conceal their deeper and larger direction. A fuller narrative may throw strange light on an apparently straightforward action, and turn our first impressions of it upside down. Knowing more may often mean knowing less.

The Reformers who declared that only such acts pleased God as sprang from lively faith, were looking to discern the fuller narrative that could integrate good acts into good agency. They sought to understand what makes a string of actions cohere as life, and asked what makes a life as a whole worth living, acceptable to God as a totality. The separate acts that go to make it up cannot bear the burden of conferring meaning on the whole. Their meaning must be given by the life, not vice versa. Faith is the moral center of the life, around which other acts cohere and find their larger justification. None of which denies the inherent worth of various action-types (comforting a weeping child, giving gifts to charity, etc.); it simply understands that every act is performed by someone; its concrete meaning is not merely a function of its type, but also of the agency behind it. Imagine someone performing an act of bountiful generosity and following it immediately with an act of savage cruelty. We cannot simply declare that a generous act is a generous act, and ignore the context of what follows it. Tyrants specialize in such interlacing of generosity with cruelty, and it gives their generosity the suspect character of an assertion of arbitrary power. There are those who think they should never accept even unencumbered gifts from donors with blood, or other doubtful substances, on their hands, and, whether or not we agree, we must be clear at least that the moral personality of the giver is relevant to the moral meaning of a gift.

If we speak of a "first act" that determines all subsequent acts, we cannot be speaking of something self-contained. Some representations of a "fundamental option" seem to present the matter as though a uniquely privileged moment of moral determination settles everything there and then, making subsequent decisions indifferent, subject solely to the judgment of an amoral practical rationality. But faith not only initiates, enables, and shapes a life; it accompanies it, acquiring concreteness through the actions which it animates. There may be paradoxical tensions between the inner and the outer aspects of an active life, between (let us say) the humility of a scholar and the proud boasts he makes for the truths he has discovered, or between the affectionate disposition of a ruler and the harshness of the judgments he makes. Yet such paradoxes must, in the end, be resolved in a coherent narrative. We cannot simply stipulate, with the romantics, that it is the inner person that counts, and that outward actions neither add to nor detract from the innocence within. What the outer act can do is reveal and express the inner person. Without a coherent narrative of acts the act of faith is, as James put it, "dead" — which is to say, it is *not* an act of faith, but an empty and ineffectual gesture that imitates it, rather as one might imitate the acts of a conductor by beating time to recorded music. Faith is the *categorical* act, the source of a life's activity, and precisely as such may be known from the acts that spring from it.

Faith, then, is a beginning, and beginnings point beyond themselves; they anticipate subsequent developments. Faith thus anticipates the conditions of worldliness and temporality that affect all action; it is an openness to world and time, a competence to appreciate meaning and to form purposes. We shall explore this thought in its two aspects, treating first of faith's competence for purpose, under the three designations of obedience, self-offering, and self-consistency.

Command and Obedience

Faith's initiative springs from a prior initiative. The phrase "obedience of faith" (Rom. 1:5; 16:26) is not correctly rendered as "obedience to the faith" (KJV), nor as "obedience that comes from faith" (NIV), nor even as "faith and obedience" (NEB, REB). It is precisely the act of faith itself, which is already obedience to the voice of God. There is something at stake in this grammatical nicety: the summons of God, to live and act before him, is not *first* a universal message of good news and *then* a particular command for each individual to obey. It is from the start a command as well as a message, a particular address as well as a universal address; to believe it is to obey it, and to obey it is to believe. It confronts the agent now, as this agent and not another. To be sure, it is a universal message and a universal command. It summons all men everywhere to repent, it offers eternal life to all who believe. Yet its universality can mean nothing to us until we have received it as a particular message and command, addressed to us as the agents we are to become, a matter for our obedience or disobedience. Without this there is nothing we can call "belief." Cognitive and intentional aspects of our response belong together. They are distinct, for James suggests that the devils believe and tremble. But we are not devils, and if we disobey, we disbelieve.

Here we observe the strength of an approach to Ethics which some philosophers of our time have advanced under the heading of "divine command." Its advocates defend the claim that morality is rooted in obedience, and, perhaps without always being conscious of it, renew two typical claims of the Reformation: (i) that true morality (pleasing to God) is conceivable only as response to God's initiative; (ii) the "good unbeliever," the ideal person in whom the moral life is supposed to flourish independently of faith in God, either is an illusion or is suffering from one. They do not generally propose that morality is *definitionally* equivalent to God's command, but that since among things we rightly judge to be good some goodness lays claim on our action in a way that not all goodness does, God's command accounts for this morally transcendent claim. If the language of obligation and value is rooted in our social expectations and practices, there remains, nevertheless, a possibility of *criticizing* those expectations and practices. The transcendent point of view from which we can undertake such criticism is the command of God. The thesis thus accounts for a phenomenon of thought and experience that is otherwise mysterious and impenetrable.

There are difficulties in making the term "command" do all the work, as is well understood by those who have pursued this line of thought most persistently.[4] The important point is simply the communication between God and the human agent, the sign that gives a particular possibility its special significance. When Luther wrote that "there is no good work apart from that which God has commanded, and likewise no sin apart from what God has forbidden," he apparently meant to *limit* the ways in which we might

---

4. See John E. Hare, *God's Call: Moral Realism, God's Commands, and Human Autonomy* (Grand Rapids: Eerdmans, 2001).

appeal to divine action as a criterion for our own well-doing and evil-doing to an explicit communication of God's will.[5] "Command" as the privileged communication intervenes into our moral thought rather than simply giving rise to it, and so imposes a definite claim.

But on whom does it impose it? And for what? Upon one agent only, or upon all agents? For one action only, or for all actions? There is apparently more than one question to which divine command may be thought to be the answer. There is the question of how an obligation of any kind may come to bear upon *me* — the "why bother being good?" question. There is the question of why certain *kinds* of practice (e.g., family loyalty, honesty) are good practices, other kinds (telling lies, spitting in public places, forging coins or works of art) are bad kinds, while others again (e.g., sleeping, sailing) are generically neither good nor bad. And a third group of questions concerns how these virtues, prohibitions, and things indifferent bear upon me *at this particular moment:* why am I required to spend this coming Christmas with my wife's mother, rather than with my great-uncle? A full answer to any one of these three kinds of question may involve a reference to God; yet, as the questions do not arise together or with the same force, neither does the reference to God arise at the same point in answering them, nor with the same effect.

R. M. Adams has argued that the proper role of divine command in moral thinking is to propose an answer to questions of *obligation* rather than to questions of *good.*[6] This distinction defends the theory against a longstanding objection to it, often made with reference to the formulation of the dilemma in Plato's *Euthyphro:* "Is what is holy holy because the gods approve it, or do they approve it because it is holy?"[7] What this formulation draws to our attention is the foundation of holiness, or any kind of goodness, in a world of ordered being. Nothing is good, and therefore, perhaps, nothing obligatory, which is not coherent with the ordered reality of a world in which good has its foundations. The idea that a command could ever be foundational of good is put in doubt. A divine commander who merely decreed from moment to moment that this or that was to be done would be incapable of generating moral authority. This does not imply that God is *subject* to some ideal good prior to and independent of his being and doing; it means

---

5. Luther, *On Good Works* (WA 6.204).

6. *Finite and Infinite Goods* (Oxford: Oxford University Press, 1999), pp. 249-52.

7. *Euthyphro* 10a2. Trans. Lane Cooper, *Collected Dialogues,* ed. Edith Hamilton and Huntington Cairns (Princeton: Princeton University Press, 1941).

simply that the idea of an absolute discretion to command things contrary to the order of goods, e.g., that we should hate good and love evil, is beyond our powers of conception. God's "absolute" power is a truth of speculation only, for in meeting God we meet him as Creator and Preserver, faithful to the good that he has made. Adams has accepted all this: an account of obligation is formed against the background of a knowledge of the good. "Divine command" does not explain why anything is good (though divine creation may), but simply why this or that good rests upon us *as an obligation*.

We should certainly follow Adams up to this point. But there are ambiguities, in my view, arising from the binary opposition he proposes between the good and the obligatory. This obscures an important distinction in the idea of obligation, between the concrete duty that confronts me now, and the categorical, or existential, truth that how I am to live and act is laid upon me, not simply chosen or embraced. An attempt to explain each and every concrete obligation in terms of a divine command seems bound to fail. Those commands would themselves have to be concrete, taking the form, "Now do this!" or "Now go there!" like special commands given to the prophets of old, and though we may credibly claim to receive such commands from time to time, by far the greatest number of our concrete obligations are discerned by understanding how a generic demand applies to the circumstances. To invoke a distinct and concrete command of God to explain why I should offer such and such a sum in exchange for a bottle of milk I have removed from the shop's refrigerator is metaphysical overkill. Circumstances, including implied contracts, come together at this moment to point to such an act. I rightly attribute to God's government the general norms governing contracts of sale and purchase; I rightly attribute to his providence that I am in a position to purchase a bottle of milk. Beyond these I have no need for an additional sign to establish a concrete obligation. I infer from the general norms of sale and purchase what God commands me to do at this point; I do not infer the norm from the command. The divine command is hypothetical, reached from a moral judgment on the circumstances.

It is quite different when I ask why in principle I should not cheat the shop. Why should the norm matter to me? Practical reasons may be insufficient: the check-out attendant is distracted, the milk can be concealed under my coat. There are intermediate answers I may give to the question, but they are liable to be inconclusive, and it is here that a divine command, addressed immediately to the agent, proves illuminating, accounting for a sense of responsibility which most of us have but cannot give reasons for. Awaking to responsibility, I am aware of a calling which lays claim on me regardless of its particular content. I know I must do right, whatever right may be. I discover that aspect of moral consciousness known to an earlier generation of theorists as "unconditionality," and to more recent philosophy as "overridingness." Its force has nothing to do with *what* is required; when we say that the protection of a human life or the salvation of a soul is always of overriding importance, we are making a judgment about the moral field, and the word "overriding" means simply "of much greater importance than most other things." In relation to the agent, however, we have to do with a demand that is prior to all content, the demand of responsibility itself which bears upon us, binds us and forces us to ask about relative claims presented in the moral field whether they interest us or not, extracting our acknowledgment that some things have unnegotiable seriousness and reducing our convenience and utility to the status of trivialities. We find, gladly or reluctantly, that we *are* responsible, which brings the question "Why bother being good?" to a stand, not by *giving* the reason why, but by *being* the reason why.

To refer to this unconditional prior demand as a "command" is an impoverished use of language, for that term suggests a definite rather than an indefinite objectivity, a mediated rather than an immediate authority. One may always make enquiries about the authority and scope of a command, but this authority can only be encountered, its scope allowed to be indefinite. Responsibility points to one who holds us answerable. How could we ever think of ourselves as responsible without knowing, or suspecting, a reality to which our response is due? Responsibility is not a power; it is the knowledge of oneself as summoned to act in ways one did not prescribe for oneself, and so it must ask about its own vis-à-vis. And that question cannot find its answer in the wills of other people, which are mere facts-in-the-world, nor in the self, which is a mere tautology. The answer lies in a prior agency that calls our responsibility out to active engagement. Seeing myself as so placed is to be open to a demand I have not laid on myself, the scope of which I cannot determine.

The reference to God in this train of thought is not inescapable. God enters moral reasoning by inductive inference. It is always possible that the experience and language of moral transcendence is an illusion to which nothing in reality corresponds. Yet the induction is persuasive, for all that. A defiant positivism that asserts the feeling of responsibility as a projection of the conscious self — I just *am* responsible, no matter to whom, for what, or why! — lacks resources to sustain itself, and once tempted to think itself an illusion, will become one. Only a culture which *first* learned to think of itself as responsible to God and *then* found difficulties of other kinds in thinking about God could ever suppose that responsibility could float in mid-air. "Ah, love, let us be true to one another!" cried Matthew Arnold before the retreating sea of faith on Dover Beach. It is a typical philosopher's "delay," a pious gesture to cover the retreat into moral skepticism. As though we *could* be true to one another with no truth that could lay claim on us! To be true is precisely to be set before a horizon of responsibility stretching before and behind every consciousness we have of one another.

Together with a self-contained, this-worldly sense of moral obligation we meet the "good unbeliever," that unstable object of so many theoretical discussions, usually supported by inverted commas. There is, of course, a real phenomenon to describe; the good unbeliever is not a fantastic object like a unicorn or a griffin. Since the inference from concrete obligation to God's summons is not transparent, the agent who achieves perception of the one and not the other has to be taken seriously, not only as a performer of good deeds but as a subject with an interiority, one who *thinks* about what is right to do and why, but cannot pursue the "why" back to its foundations. But in this state of incomplete interrogation the good unbeliever is not an exception to the world in general. Everywhere there arises the same paradox: God attested in the goodness of his works, yet unrecognized and unacknowledged. This paradox is intelligible, but only as a *moment* in the exercise of freedom and discernment. Either the works must decay and lose their goodness for us, or the immortal goodness from which they spring must come to be acknowledged. The good unbeliever, we may say, exists, but does not subsist. A sense of obligation and unbelief in God may occur together in one mind, but it is not a stable condition; it will evolve one way or the other, since the decision about the reality of good must finally be encountered and made.

There is, of course, more than a slight impropriety in theorizing about the good unbeliever in the third person, since third-person discourse can be no more than an exercise of thought to lead us back to a first-person question. To take the word "good" on our lips without playing cheap games means asking about its challenge to ourselves. "Why do you ask me about the good?" Jesus demanded of the rich young man (Matt. 19:17), not because he should *not* have asked about it, but because he needed to understand that in asking about the good he asked about himself. Nothing can be said about the good unbeliever that fails to take the words "good" and "belief" as meant for us, too. The goodness of practical reason and the courage of belief are what we ourselves are called to demonstrate. Is it to *pursue* the good that we ask about good people? Is it to *exercise* belief that we ask about unbelief? There is no measurable quantity of good in the good unbeliever, no measure of the failure of belief, nothing to be talked about in quantitative terms. We speak about a moment in the course of inquiry and reflection, and we do not bring our reflective inquiry to a conclusion unless we see goodness and unbelief as a practical alternative before us, a matter for decision. To ask about the good unbeliever is to learn that some combinations of commitments which we find attractive and plausible will prove unavailable to us.

Self-offering

"Here I am!" cries the agent-self in obedience to the God that has called it forth. Agent-identity is given as we know ourselves addressed by a command to responsibility.

Responsibility for what? "In the scroll of the book it is written for me. I desire to do thy will" (Ps. 40:7-8). There is a "scroll," an account of world and history in which the agent-self finds itself inscribed, and there is a desire to be doing. As the Bible often expresses it, those who name God receive a name, a determination of their agent-identity (cf. Rev. 2:17). If identity speaks, in the first place, of being differentiated from others and individuated within the world, with the qualifier "agent-" it speaks of being the intentional subject of one's own actions, self-continuous in time.

Patristic theologians described the agent-name as an "individual quality" *(idia poiotês)*.[8] It is a paradoxical expression, apparently a contradiction in terms: a "quality" is a likeness, a feature by which one thing is comparable with another, but individualities are not more or less alike, but simply other. John's striking resemblance to Jean does not make him any less *other* to her than either to James, who is unlike both of them. What constitutes individuality is not some feature that no one else possesses, but being the subject of a unique history. That is enough to make us easy in our minds about such problems as the individuality of identical twins. But a unique history is not something we can grasp simply in its unicity; like a mathematical point, it

8. Origen, *On Prayer* 24: "A name is a summary designation which captures the individual quality of one named, as, for example, the individual quality of the Apostle Paul: the quality of soul by which it is as it is, the quality of mind by which it understands what it does, the personal quality of body which makes it appear as it does. The individuality of his qualities makes him unmistakable for any other person; clearly, another Paul precisely similar to this one does not exist. But when men's individual qualities undergo a kind of change for the better, we find in Scripture that their names are changed, too."

has to be given dimensions in order to be imagined. Reading the phrase "individual quality" sympathetically, then, we can see it as an invitation to approach individuality by way of a distinctive constellation of likenesses and unlikenesses which expresses and reveals it. Pontius Pilate was an irreplaceable subject with a part in unique events; yet his unrepeatable history is that of a weak judge yielding to expediency, typical of all such judges in every age and place. Our unique histories take form in likenesses and unlikenesses, external and internal. "How like him!" we exclaim, when someone behaves as we have learned to expect.

When we say that the person is the subject of a history, more is meant than that a narrative sequence of verbs has one and the same grammatical subject: "That woman lost her money in the bank crash, and now she has been hurt in a road accident." When we speak of the subject *of a history*, we speak of a capacity to create a coherent narrative around oneself by directing and taking responsibility for one's active powers so as to own one's doing and living, planning what one does, acknowledging what one has done, sustaining a policy of doing one thing from one circumstance to the next, and so on. The subject stands behind the history, neither disinvolved from the sequence of events nor dissolved into it. The history discloses the subject through the qualitative continuities. No longer hidden, the agent emerges (still unique and irreplaceable) through events that in themselves are comparable to other events. Being self-continuous is not a necessary posit, but a moral self-accomplishment: agent-identity is revealed by living and acting *as* the continuous self one is given to be, in likeness to oneself. It is a matter of reflective intention. The concept of "person" points in two directions: on the one hand, to the individual *hypostasis* that is presupposed in the very condition of human existence; on the other, to its expression in the sphere of responsibility and action, the realm of "personality." Being a person, the subject of a history, is to "make" beginnings and continuations, not only to "have" them. But to make a beginning is to intend a continuation of one's act, and to intend a continuation is to intend a likeness of what follows to what was begun. Here is the essential sense in which human agents are "in the image of God," who begins, continues, and perfects all things.

A short narrative of Saint Luke (2:41-52) tells of a visit by Jesus on the threshold of adult responsibility to the temple in Jerusalem. It looks at first like a *Wunderkind* story, but the amazement Jesus excites is not the point of greatest importance; the weight falls on the anxiety and pain he causes. William Blake had it partly right:

34

Was Jesus gentle, or did he
Give any marks of gentility?
When twelve years old he ran away,
And left his parents in dismay.[9]

But neither is the story a prophecy of Jesus' destiny, for of his suffering, as distinct from that of his parents, nothing is said. No sapling grows meaningfully in the near background to provide wood for the cross, as in Renaissance artistic representations of the scene. It is a story of mutual incomprehension, focusing on the growing independence of youth from age. We are shown the moment of awakening, when a young and unformed boy, knowing himself called like Samuel, responds directly, throwing every expectation of a devout family into confusion and disarray. Their devotion had brought Jesus to Jerusalem, but it was his own devotion that kept him there. He discovered himself an agent summoned by his Father.[10]

The story presents the boy "listening and asking questions," avid for learning, absorbing the tradition from the teachers. But the enthusiasm was not speculative. "Did you not know I must be at my Father's business?" he asks his parents, in the traditional, and probably correct, translation of the words.[11] There is a "must," framed within, but not constituted by, the hallowed practices of the community. "Must" has become "I must," and indeed, "I must *be.*" The imperative takes possession, quickening the boy's sense of himself, though form and content are unclear and there is yet no concrete task, no mission of healing and teaching. All he can do is listen and inquire, and yet that is not a preparation for some future decision, but a decision already. If the crowd was amazed at his "understanding" and "answers," it was because his forwardness among learners and inquirers *already* bore traces of an understanding and an answer, an understanding that his Father called him and a readiness to respond. "I must be" — the imperative of being himself — became "I must be at my Father's business" — the imperative of active response. The moment captured here is self-offering in the simplest sense, a surrender to the service of God without condition and without foreknowledge.

9. *Songs of Innocence and Experience.*

10. The placing of the story among the infancy narratives owes nothing to the evangelist. It could better be conceived as an introduction to Jesus' ministry, placing his vocation before the Baptist's appearance and so stressing his priority to John, a typical theme of Luke's Gospel (e.g., 1:43-44).

11. The now more favored translation of ἐν τοῖς τοῦ Πατρός μου, "in my Father's house," emphasizes the reception of tradition rather than the vocation to service.

Not, of course, without a contextual frame, for the temple and the teaching comprise a world of God's good purposes which enables the call to be heard and understood. Yet the indeterminacy of the call, its open-endedness towards the future, is of importance. If the nature of the service were clear, even in outline, Jesus would commit himself only to a certain ambition, a certain role in line with the plan disclosed to him. It would not be left to God to make of his service what he would. The sacrifice God required transcended concrete obligations, yet was still an offering *of service*, in full awareness of his powers of agency. Correspondingly, the tradition of God's deeds and purposes, the temple and the teaching, though not a comprehensive "worldview" but full of openings for questioning, was no less than a vision of a world in which God reigned, a vision of the world *from*, and a vision of the world *as* God's temple, the place where God made himself known.

What is meant by speaking of faith's active beginnings as self-offering? Offering can be a symbolic act, which conveys more than its material content. Materially no more than a day or two spent in the temple, when good time might have been made on the road, this limited content conveyed unlimited implications: a life of single-minded service. A teacher may give a student thirty minutes of time and attention, two lovers may give each other a night of passion, and in either case that may be the end of it. But with self-offering no end is in sight. It is given as a token of more to follow, a recognition of unlimited claim.

Not even unlimited self-offering, of course, can match what God will give. Yet among all the things he gives for no return, there is one that he gives with the purpose of receiving it back again, "ourselves, our souls and bodies."[12] What he has in view is that we should be at his disposal. The end of our action is to offer God our "works," the accomplished performance of our lives, and we are told that that is what we shall be judged on at the end. But at the beginning and in the middle we must offer him our possibilities, our mental and physical capacities as yet uncommitted, even undeveloped and unrecognized, for him to make what he will of. Ancient Israel offered living beasts, which represented not what the worshipers had done or made, but the essential resource on which their existence depended. And so in Christian liturgy we bring our offering in the form of money, the point of which is that it is nothing concrete at all. Our money is the unexploited potential for whatever we *may* become capable of, the pure symbol, the un-

12. *Book of Common Prayer.*

actualized resource, which represents the material conditions of our being and doing. To those who wish to employ the liturgy to "express" their works and accomplishments, "fruit of the earth and work of human hands," this is scandalous. But to offer God only what we have made is not to offer him ourselves. That demands an agency unresolved, open to whatever service it may be directed to.

The indeterminate offering is made with the intent that God shall determine it. The offering God accepts may be repeated, but not *de novo,* since he has taken in hand the active life of the one who offers it. God asks ourselves of us precisely in order to bestow an identity upon us, making of us a definite somebody. Whatever follows, however passive in itself, will unfold that first offering and make a history of it. It has concrete material content, "the trivial round, the common task" or "new treasures still of countless price," which are its "road to bring us daily nearer God," but its traffic is with the unknown, the course of life unlived, the experience untasted, the challenges yet not confronted.[13] The offering of opportunity becomes a way for the individual life, through its variety of passions and actions, its experiences and risks, to be bent and molded into a consistent pattern directed to a consistent goal. This traffic is still at its disposal when material circumstances are restricted to the very minimum. In states of utter weakness when exertion is out of the question, when we lie helpless on our last bed needing assistance with the most ordinary bodily movements, sacrifice can make a path that continues the way set out on long before.

This is why the act of faith may take form as conversion. This concept, which in Catholic moral theology has tended to be absorbed into the idea of penitence, emerges distinctly in modern Protestant theology as a biographical event of unrepeatable significance, a conscious moral analogue to the sacrament of baptism. The turning to God which takes place in conversion is an awakening such as can only happen once. There are, of course, dangers in the suggestion of regeneration focused in a single moment of moral experience, swallowed, as it were, in one gulp of decision. It may lead to the mistaken thought, flirted with and shrunk from by "experimental religion" since the eighteenth century, that after this one moment there is no call for further surrender, only "assurance," grounded on recollection of a past event. But in avoiding this mistake we should not lose sight of the truth it misunderstands: moral life in Christ does allow of a self-conscious beginning, a decision that conveys representatively, in one sacrificial surrender, what is

13. John Keble, "Morning," *The Christian Year* (Oxford: Benediction Classics, 2009), p. 12.

to be rendered in steady service over years to follow. Conversion is the first act of freedom. Misunderstanding of conversion arises when it is forgotten that a beginning must envisage a continuation, the logic of the initial act worked out and elaborated.

Self-consistency

Turning from the first to the last stage of Jesus' ministry, we find in the prayer in Gethsemane (as reported in Matthew and Mark) a similar confession of reality and the most famous of all expressions of self-giving. "Abba, Father, all things are possible to you!" the prayer begins in Saint Mark (14:36). The act of self-giving is founded on the confession of a world governed by God's good purpose, a world in which nothing is purely tragic, but all serves the good that the Father ordains.[14] In Saint Matthew, who alone reports the prayer in two forms, God's sovereign power of disposal is expressed as an alternative: "If it be possible . . ." on the first occasion, "If it be not possible . . ." on the second (Matt. 26:39, 42). This highly reflective formulation develops the claim that "all things are possible." The meaning of God's sovereignty is not that he "can" do whatever we may suggest to him. His purpose, which he will carry through, is consistent with some imaginable developments and inconsistent with others. Jesus, viewing the moment before him from an acute angle, cannot discern which is which. That need hardly strike the sympathetic reader as surprising, or inconsistent with his earlier predictions of the death and resurrection of the Son of Man. Whatever he might have seen and taught in the course of his ministry, here in the deadly sorrow of his soul his sight is restricted to this "if." It is enough. The Father's purpose is sovereign, and his own "cup" will be administered or withheld as befits that purpose.

From this point he can repeat his concession of the right of God to command his whole active life: "Not my will, but thine!" (Mark 14:36). It is not that Jesus should will *nothing*, but that his willing should flexibly follow the contours of his Father's will. The "will" denied in that prayer is not Jesus' agency as such, not his capacity to decide and perform, but the concrete object of desire, life itself, which would be present to the imagination of any human being who wanted to live. From that natural human object of desire,

---

14. St. Luke's version of the prayer (22:42) absorbs the expression of faith in God's sovereignty into the focus on the two wills of the Father and the Son.

which could prompt him to qualify the obedience he offered, he turns away in search of the Father's purpose. "The spirit is ready, but the flesh is weak" (v. 38), describes not only the disciples' failure but the experience Jesus has himself been through. The assertiveness of self-protective instincts against the readiness to do God's will is the very meaning of temptation as inner division.

The word "faith" *(pistis),* which belongs equally to beginnings and continuations, develops dialectically in a way that allows English, like some other modern languages, to produce a secondary variant, "faithfulness." "Faithfulness," which we sometimes speak of as "keeping faith," is a consistent adherence to an acknowledgment once made. When *pistis* is ascribed to God, it is always in this sense. There is, of course, no other reality in which God has believed. The reality to which he responds is himself, and his response is from eternity. God's "faithfulness" is how we experience his "self-sameness" within the economy of time. We ourselves are not "self-same." We are continuous with ourselves physically, and may become consistent with ourselves morally, too, but that can only be as we respond to the reality God has made present to us.[15] We reflect his self-sameness not by persisting in our own likeness but by formation into his, that "likening to" God of which the fathers often spoke.[16]

Yet it is a consistency *with ourselves.* If we break with the unity of life that has been given us — "reinventing ourselves" as we call it scornfully — we destroy ourselves. But self-consistency is not an easy thing to envisage clearly. Anyone can be stubborn. Anyone can view his own past contradictions with narcissistic self-admiration. But self-consistency is a matter of being true to the truth given us, and involves our constant self-attention as to what that truth has been and how we may be true to it. Self-consistency is not stiffness, but persistent memory and acknowledgment of something received. "I have not forgotten thy commands!" the poet of the Long Psalm repeatedly affirms, meaning the summons that was given to him, the poetic vocation to hear and shape words of truth and praise. In that summons lay his identity; to recall it was to recall himself.

15. "Get into the way of being one!" — *"Assuesce unus esse!"* — is quoted by Ambrose (*Ep.* 63.30) as an "old saying," probably of Stoic origin, since it was a thought also dear to Seneca. But it was left to Ambrose to see that this aspiration to be *"unus et idem"* could be reality only in conformity to the God who was self-same (cf. *Ep.* 7:21).

16. For two examples of ὁμοίωσις Θεῷ among many, Clement of Alexandria, *Stromateis* 2.22; Methodius of Olympus, *Banquet* 1.4. The simultaneous recollection in this phrase of Gen. 1:26 and Plato, *Laws* 4.716 goes back to Philo of Alexandria.

Consistent agency is by no means confined to the singular agent, the individual subject alone in self-reflection. It is constantly predicated of communities. Losing the vision is a risk every established enterprise runs: banks need to rediscover their "core business," associations to pursue some goal set for the purpose of re-envisaging it. The church runs it, too, of course, though it has this strength in facing up to it: it knows that its engagement with the truth is a personal and ongoing one, and it calls by name on the one who has named it in the name of his Son. *Ecclesia semper reformanda,* said the Reformers, and there is only apparent inconsistency between that saying and the assertion that it is built upon the rock so that the powers of hell shall not prevail against it (Matt. 18:18). The church's "indefectibility" is a promise that God wills to reform it perpetually, to keep it faithful, to bring it back to its calling.

New Testament ways of speaking about faithfulness are built primarily on metaphors of position and location. "Standing" is opposed to "falling" (1 Cor. 10:12; Rom. 14:4); "in faith" one stands, "in unbelief" one may be "cut off" (Rom. 11:20). Such metaphors are as easily applied to the community as to the individual: in Colossians 4:12 "standing" speaks of the church's retention of its character and obedience, while in Ephesians 6:11-18 it is woven into an elaborate simile of military engagement.[17] The more common metaphor of "securing" and "being secured" has in view a community that must not "fall out" of its established order (2 Pet. 3:17) but must "secure" elements of its life which are otherwise liable to "die away" (Rev. 3:2). It is concerned with consistency of speech and action (2 Thess. 2:17) and with community of resolve (1 Thess. 3:13; James 5:8). Securing the community is supremely God's work (Rom. 16:25; 2 Thess. 3:3; 1 Pet. 5:10), though the pastorate has its part to play in it (Luke 22:32; Acts 18:23; Rom. 1:11; 1 Thess. 3:2), and it is the fruit of communion between one church and another (1 Thess. 3:12-13). In the Johannine literature the equivalent thought is supplied by its distinctive verb, "remaining." Here agency is stabilized by being drawn into the mutual indwelling of the divine and the human, through sacramental and moral participation in the life of God, Christ, and the Holy Spirit, as in 1 John 2:24; 4:13 (of the community) and 4:16 (of the individual), so that its use is reciprocal, "he/you in me and I in him/you" (John 6:56; 15:4) — a matter not only

17. The Colossians' "assurance" is a settled common purpose in respect of what God wills for them. See Walter Bauer, William F. Arndt, and F. Wilbur Gingrich, *Greek-English Lexicon of the New Testament and Other Early Christian Literature* (Chicago: University of Chicago Press, 1957), on πληροφορέω, and cf. the uses of the same verb at Rom. 4:21; 14:25.

of remaining but of being remained *in,* by God's word, by the baptismal anointing, by eternal life itself. The parable of the vine in John's Gospel (15:4-9) is the paradigm: participation in Christ's life is like the attachment of branches to their trunk; his indwelling "words" or "commands" afford the constant reality of "remaining in my love," i.e., the life of the godhead. The application at this point is collective, though in the Epistles, with their interest in who does and does not belong, a similar point is made with an individual thrust (1 John 3:24), while at 1 John 2:6 and 3:6 "remaining" is a matter of the individual believer's imitation of Christ and love of the brother (1 John 2:10).

If these ways of describing faithfulness in terms of objective situation seem to avoid the subjective point of self-consistency, the balance is redressed by language about the *formation* of the agent, taking on the pattern of the humanity God wills in Christ. The life of Christian individuals and communities (here, too, both kinds of agency are in question) is a continual emergence of the "form" *(morphē)* of Christ in their midst (Gal. 4:19). It is a "con-forming" *(summorphizesthai),* in which Christ's "image" is in view (Rom. 8:29), and especially the image of his death (Phil. 3:10), and a "trans-forming" *(metamorphousthai),* incremental but qualitatively transcendent (Rom. 12:2; 2 Cor. 3:18). It is described, too, as "renewing" *(ananeousthai),* for the human life which is given in Christ is *given back* to those created for it who were lost to it. Repeatedly this new formation of human life is associated with a renewal of mind and knowledge (Rom. 12:2; Col. 3:10).

In this context we can understand language about a *human spirit* made actual by the working of the Holy Spirit in and through human agency. In ancient authors "spirit" was widely and loosely used to refer to biological motion and psychological excitement. On the one hand it was breath, which accounts for the dead being called "spirits," since the body surrenders its breath in dying. On the other, it was disturbance of feeling and emotion; in the New Testament restlessness and comfort are located in the spirit (1 Pet. 3:4; 1 Cor. 4:21; 2 Cor. 2:13; 1 Cor. 16:18). Some ancient philosophers made a distinction between "soul" and "spirit" that was equivalent to that of "soul" and "mind," but this was not commonplace, and in general the two were not distinguished.[18] But when Christians spoke of the Holy Spirit in their midst, they found it natural to speak of a human spirit moving in responsive sym-

---

18. When the author to the Hebrews speaks (4:2) of the word of God cutting to the point of division between the two, it is an elegant turn of speech for making the finest imaginable discrimination.

pathy with the Spirit of God.[19] Man indwelt by God experienced the relation dialectically, spirit to spirit (Rom. 8:16). The depths of human self-experience were deepened and its scope widened; it became a "spiritual" partner to the Spirit who searched the deep things of God. So in Philippians 1:27, encouraging that fractious church to work together, Paul urges its members to exert themselves not only "with one soul" but "in one spirit," which is the spirit of the community emerging in response to the action within it of God's Spirit. And when he prays for the Thessalonians to be sanctified "entire and whole, spirit, soul and body" (1 Thess. 5:23), we can only understand that list of aspects in the light of the warning, "Quench not the Spirit!" (v. 19).[20] Temptation to over-precision, lexicographical or anthropological, must be resisted. It is the genius of the word "spirit" to move seamlessly between human phenomena and divine. The human spirit is not a distinct hypostasis, different from soul or mind on the one hand, and from the person on the other; it is a miraculous product of the working of God upon human moral and practical endeavor. Those who are "renewed by the spirit of the mind" (Eph. 4:23) are *themselves* renewed; their *mind* has been opened up to encompass spirit.[21] So Origen, using more material imagery, understands the spirit as "that which clings to the souls of the righteous," the "part of the soul which is made in the image and likeness of God," which can, nevertheless, be torn away from the soul in the final judgment.[22] The spiritual is a realm that extends wherever God is at work.[23]

Alongside this correlation of human and divine spirit we may place another human-divine correlation, that of "holiness." In classical Trinitarian language the terms "holy" and "spirit" are both attributed to the third per-

---

19. Possibly James 4:5 is relevant to this point, following the interpretation of the English RV margin, the RSV, and Bauer, Arndt, and Gingrich: "God yearns to the point of jealousy over the spirit he has made to dwell in us." Other translators (REB, NIV) treat *pneuma* as emotional disturbance: "the spirit that dwells in us lusts to the point of envy."

20. Paul's prayer for his churches that "the grace of the Lord Jesus Christ be with your spirit" (Gal. 6:18; Phil. 4:23) is to be read in the same way. Nor, if we are not blinkered by a conception that Pauline and Johannine Christianity are mutually sealed against each other, shall we overlook the parallelism between Rom. 1:9 and John 4:24.

21. In one notable instance Paul had urged that the working of God on an offender, excluded from the church and left to the dominion of Satan, could enable the saving of "his spirit" from the destruction of the flesh "on the day of the Lord Jesus" (1 Cor. 5:5).

22. *De principiis* 2.10.7; *Comm. in Ep ad Rom.* 2.10.

23. In the law, Rom. 7:14; in the special gifts of church members, 1 Cor. 12. The term "the spiritual" is used at Gal. 6:1 and 1 Cor. 2:14-15 of those who live in the medium of the Spirit, resembling the risen humanity of the Second Adam (cf. 1 Cor. 15:47).

son of the Trinity as a proper designation (though God as such is said to be both holy and spirit), since the indwelling of the third person imparts both holiness and spirit as human characteristics. "Holiness" has a human moral content. When Paul declared, "This is God's will, your sanctification" he was concerned with how the Thessalonian Christians managed their sexual energies. Yet, equally clearly, this language points to the transcendent root of the moral life in a participation in the indwelling of God. As the holy nation was of old conceived as the nation in which God set his presence and his throne, so it still was. The capacity to *be* holy, as the capacity to *be* spirit, is something to which human existence is opened up by Holy Spirit, not immanent, yet at the same time not alien, but at one with the purposes for which God called forth mankind from the created world, "that I may dwell among them." It requires "daring," as Jean-Yves Lacoste has said, to take up the term by which Hegel designated the human race, "finite spirit." We can justify it only if we conceive that infinity may offer us a peaceable self-possession. "Spirit is not an entity. It is the way of being that goes further than existence and carries with it the ultimate stakes of life. . . . 'Spirit' names what we cannot name in any other way, goes beyond what we say of ourselves as subjectivities, goes beyond what we say when we call ourselves 'existents' or 'mortals.' It is included in a description of life to bring clarity to what living means."[24]

Doubt of Purpose

We have made some general observations on the sin against the self in the last chapter, and may now take some provisional soundings into the forms that doubt may take, and here, first, see it as a failure to intend, shrinking from the opening of faith to time. We speak of *indecision* as a simple incapacity to begin things, rebounding from one projected action to another, always looking over the shoulder and hedging against each decision almost before it is made. *Half-heartedness* will then serve as a name for the incapacity to continue what is begun.

They are two aspects of one and the same failure, the refusal of commitment to action. Someone who never continues, but makes new beginnings all the time, does not actually begin. Yet the two aspects are worth distinguishing, since the temptation to doubt can arise from either pole of an oscillation of mood, from enthusiasm or from exhaustion. One who announces

24. *Être en Danger* (Paris: Cerf, 2011), pp. 310-11.

excitedly that now for the first time after years of marriage true love has come his way, is not in a very different case from one who sinks mournfully under the strains of his marriage and crawls off to find such comfort as he can. As failures in marriage they are in the same position; they simply feel different, sitting at opposite peaks of the mood-cycle.

"He who doubts is like a wave of the sea that is driven and tossed by the wind" (James 1:6). The ups and downs of feeling are natural enough, but the way of practical thought is to find a passage through them, not to be tossed from one feeling to the next. To be at the mercy of the bipolar oscillation of mood-swings, pitching and tossing between self-depreciation and self-vaunting, between *Fatum* and *Fortuna,* is to be deprived of practical purchase on ourselves. Doubting is failure to engage, and when the moment for action elicits no definite engagement from us, it may fill us at any moment either with despair or elation. "From being anxious or secure, dead clods of sadnesse, or light squibs of mirth . . . good Lord, deliver us!"[25] The oscillating moods are, as it were, the roar of an engine accelerated out of gear, with no thrust on the road beneath the wheels.

It lies beyond the sphere of Ethics to pursue the questions of causation that arise here. We know that mood instability can be a function of biochemical irregularities or unstable blood pressure, that it can be caused by genetic inheritance or external stimulation, and that it can be medically offset. Something similar can be said of great achievements, too. Intelligence is genetically conditioned, and the flow of adrenalin is helped by a supportive crowd. Bipolar pathologies present no greater mystery to practical reason than the familiar mystery, that we are objects at the same time as we are subjects, products of causal sequences at the same time as we initiate them. This may generate obscurity about other people's actions — can they help themselves? is it a result of medication? — but it cannot generate obscurity about our own *projected* actions, for as soon as we ask ourselves, "Can I help it?" we are already helping it. We have adopted a reflective distance on it, and though we do not know how much we may be able to control from that distance, we know that there is *something* we can do: we can pray, we can apologize, we can recognize the onset of an episode and can make provisions against it. Odysseus tied to the mast is Odysseus in control of his loss of control. In such ways we ordinarily take responsibility for our moods, even where there is no question of actual pathology. When we are bored,

25. Donne, "A Litanie," *Divine Poems,* ed. Helen Gardner (Oxford: Clarendon, 2001²), p. 21.

we settle down to amuse ourselves; when we are lonely, we seek company; when excitement makes us giddy, we calm one another down, and so on.

There are less emotional ways of pitching and tossing, which may even strike us as proof of cunning or boldness. We may become so used to cutting loose from old decisions and making new ones that what passes for our decisiveness is simply indecisiveness, the rebound to the opposite pole whenever we doubt our capacity to stand by a decision. Institutions have their own well-known patterns of decisive indecision: policies carefully made and quickly lost sight of, long-term aims swallowed up in short-term tactics, disciplines of consultation overridden by managerial fiat, important record-keeping lost in a mountain of ephemeral documentation, guidelines issued and reissued so frequently that not even the software can keep pace with them. No one truly makes a decision who cannot stand by one; the decision is "made," finally, only when it is carried through.

Indecision should not be confused with hesitation, which may also sometimes take the form of a mind wavering between alternatives. Hesitation in itself is simply caution, a claim upon the time decision needs, reflecting the truth that a moment for resolving must be waited on. It may indicate a self ready and poised to move as soon as the pieces fall into place and the signal given. The hesitant agent decides slowly, but may decide definitely. Judicious hesitation may, however, serve as a mask for indecision. If the reasons that would allow us to decide are not to hand, we must wait before deciding. It may be, however, that we hunt for reasons to defer decision.

Half-heartedness, too, may be masked, as adaptability. All long-term commitments require adaptability, since conditions change and our powers increase or decrease. Beginnings are beginnings, subject to the law of the relation between sowing and reaping. We need from time to time to reconsider how we may proceed further in the direction on which we set out. Refusal to accept adjustments is usually a refusal to accept some aspect of our mutability, which we need to come to terms with if we are to learn how to be true to ourselves. But the difference between adaptability and half-heartedness begins to emerge precisely at this point. Half-heartedness can be close to a false perfectionism that cannot endure the tension of creativity, self-criticism, and adaptation. In any complex undertaking it is easy to lose interest in some functions and processes. Seated at a meeting we manipulate the telephone beneath the table, quietly signaling, perhaps, that we do not care for these wearisome deliberations but have more important things to get on with. Dividing attention is a typical expression of disdain. At the same time half-heartedness can appear as enthusiastic engagement with business that is beside the point, a readiness to be diverted into proceedings that promise more gratification in themselves than in their service to the undertaking as a whole. To recover a true engagement and adaptability what we need is to re-envision the connection between the undertaking as a whole and the proceedings which serve it. We may be justified, of course, in thinking some proceedings unfit for their purpose. But if we know what that purpose is, we can take an interest in how the proceedings that serve it may be conducted better. The man who would build a tower and the king who would go to war both need to think about how a task may be effectively carried through (Luke 14:28-32). Such thinking is itself an aspect of single-mindedness. To throw ourselves at something without thinking about how it is to proceed may earn an accolade for motivation or leadership, but it is just another way of withholding the investment of ourselves. But if we think clearly about how an undertaking can *best* proceed, we must also think clearly about how it may proceed *well enough*. The tower needs *enough* bricks, the king *enough* trained soldiers, which may not be as many could be wished. Thinking clearly about means to ends involves weighing compromises, distinguishing the necessary and tolerable from the self-defeating. There is an old proverb, "If a thing is worth doing, it is worth doing well," which warns of a half-heartedness that fails to take care of the performance. The wit who turned it on his head, "If a thing is worth doing, it is worth doing badly," identified a different but no less potent form of half-heartedness.[26]

Adjustments, interruptions, changes of strategy or method, lie within the sphere of concrete operations and projects, which are the gift of temporal circumstances. How, then, may we be wholly consistent? What is the categorical undertaking that does not change when it encounters change? It is the commitment of the self to the service of God. To stand by that commitment, putting ourselves at its service and growing with it and into it as it unfolds before us, is what brings us into unity with ourselves.

26. *The Oxford Dictionary of Quotations* (Oxford: Oxford University Press, 1979³), p. 148, tells us not improbably that the wit in question was G. K. Chesterton.

CHAPTER 3

Faith and Meaning

Know Thyself!

Faith has no discursive content of its own. Its native understanding is immediate. We call on God as "He is," and identify ourselves as "Here I am!" But the "I am" of faith is summoned further, not only to forming definite purposes in time but also to comprehending meaning in the world. "Call to me and I will answer you, and will tell you of great and hidden things that you have not known" (Jer. 33:3). Faith seeks understanding — so runs Anselm's famous principle. Belief opens outward towards the space of the world. What we have found in faith commits us to seeking. What we have found is an agent-self; what we seek is an occasion for agency, to be unfolded to us in terms of world and time. Beyond that first call to awaken in faith, in which the self finds itself set before God, there is a second call, mediated through the good world God has made and the time God has foreordained, calling the wakened agent-self to practical engagement. Without the second call agency would be empty and inchoate, a false pregnancy that produced only wind, a responsibility with no determination. Balthasar, commenting on Abraham's call, marks a sequence, as "the moral subject . . . constituted by the call of God and obedience" and "isolated for encounter," is subsequently "enframed by the covenant, grounded in call and faithful response, on every side: not only in risk of faith, but also the flesh and its possibilities."[1] The same sequence may be seen in the famous response of Mary to the angelic

---

1. Hans Urs von Balthasar, "Neun Sätze zur christlichen Ethik," in Joseph Ratzinger et al., *Prinzipien Christlicher Moral* (Einsiedeln: Johannes Verlag, 1975), pp. 80-81.

message, confessing the vis-à-vis of self to God and then reaching forward to embrace the vocation: "Behold the handmaid of the Lord; let it be to me according to your word!" (Luke 1:38).

With this "enframing" we pass from the unmediated to the mediated summons. "Does not wisdom call?" (Prov. 8:1). Created, as the ancient poem declared, at the beginning of the creator's work, wisdom stood by him like a master-workman in charge of his works (Prov. 8:22, 30). What wisdom demands is a response to the goodness of God's world, which is to say, to know it and to love it, to realize ourselves in engagement with it. But not every knowledge and love of the world is wisdom. Our human nature displays immense capacity for knowing and loving things, but these are also capacities for ignorance and deception. Real knowledge depends on demands and opportunities that are offered, and so Gray could suppose that in the rural graveyard there lay sages and savants *manqués*:

> But Knowledge to their eyes her ample page
> Rich with the spoils of time, did ne'er unroll.[2]

Even the successful acquisition of knowledge can trap us in ignorance and deception. Discovery can dazzle, blinding us to other things we should have known. To realize ourselves as knowing and loving agents, then, it is not enough to acquire items of knowledge or objects of appreciation. It requires the organization and critique of our knowledge and love. Wisdom as "master-workman" demands of us a reflective and critical relation to knowledge, exercised in judging what this or that item of knowledge is worth, how it is contextualized among other items, what it licenses us to conclude and what it does not.

It is in this context that early Christian thinkers took up the celebrated counsel of the ancient Greeks, "Know thyself!" When they came to it, they found an inherent tension in it. Those who first placed that advice over the temple at Delphi meant it as a warning against a dangerous sense of world-transcendence. To be an agent one must give up the affectation of infinity, and focus intention upon the realities and possibilities of the world: "Nothing in excess! Give guarantees, and ruin will follow! Know thyself!" Prompted by Socrates and Plato, philosophy turned this mundane warning on its head: to know oneself was to know one's transcendence as a contemplative being, to discover an affinity between the soul and the divine.

2. Thomas Gray, "Elegy Written in a Country Churchyard."

Christian theologians, bringing to the phrase a fuller account of the self, reconciled these opposite leanings. Worldly effectiveness was precisely what the transcendent self was meant for.

It might seem that we could *be* ourselves, *affirm* ourselves, even *offer* ourselves, but that we could hardly *know* ourselves. My self is what I cannot get a purchase on. "We do not possess ourselves. We are not ourselves in totality . . . the self always escapes us in part."[3] How does the outer space of the world come to include the self? Or, the same question turned around, how does the self acquire inner space enough to enclose the world? It was the question Augustine faced when at the end of his great autobiographical narrative he wished to proceed from "what I have been" to "what I now am." "I am a great question to myself," he had observed earlier, and in the extraordinary tenth book of the *Confessions* he pursued that question into inner space, beginning from the a priori certainty of his love of God.[4]

By identifying the initial vis-à-vis with God as love rather than faith, Augustine saw it as a motivation driving a path through all his subsequent dealings with the world. It contained the power to draw him out of himself into his search. There are, as we have said, dangers in letting love move over into the role of faith, presenting it from the beginning with God as its object.[5] It can encourage an aspiration to worldless transcendence, of which some critics have thought Augustine guilty. Yet against the temptation of world-lessness he had a strong defense in the conviction that love was inseparable from knowledge. This was why his journey led him through psychological "caverns" of memory which unfolded the world to him in all its irreducible variety. The need to distinguish God from not-God (and consequentially self from not self) forced the complex realities of world and time before his

---

3. Jean-Yves Lacoste, *Être en Danger* (Paris: Cerf, 2011), pp. 295-96.

4. *Confessions* 10.3.4; 4.4.9. The phrase "inner space" was coined by Philip Cary, *Augustine's Invention of the Inner Self: The Legacy of a Christian Platonist* (Oxford: Oxford University Press, 2000). Did Augustine "invent" this idea of the self, as Cary claims? The answer must be, No. There was always a complex and dialectical character about "the heart" in Hebrew Scriptures, "elusive above all things," as Jeremiah observes, "and fainting, so that who can comprehend it?" (17:9). Jesus' own teaching constantly reverted to the heart as the source of action, and to the importance of solitude in prayer. And if it is true that the counsel to turn inward and explore the soul owed much to Plotinus, that inspiration had already led Ambrose to find in the Psalms an encouragement "to wander around in our heart as in an expansive house, and converse with it as with a good companion" (*De officiis* 3.1.1). Yet Augustine pursued the thought of inner space with a complexity and philosophical inquisitiveness that forms a landmark in Western philosophy.

5. *Self, World, and Time*, p. 105.

gaze, ranged in their logical order. Much care is given to that order: earth and its contents (including the physical self), the "force" that ties the soul to the body, the "force" that commands the senses in common with the beasts, the memory, involving both "images" and the contents of an "inner memory" — categories of reason, laws of mathematics, and the awareness of temporal distance — and finally the self itself, for though transcending its experiences, self is still the object of its own remembering, and therefore not immutable, not to be confused with God. The capacity to hold oneself before one's eyes is the central core of memory, the point furthest removed from the empirical images it has acquired. The ascent through memory displays the power of self-objectification, and its climax is the discovery of the self as "under" God, suspended on divine transcendence. How, then, can God be seen, or known, or loved? Only as the memory's categorical presupposition, the undefined "happiness" that makes sense of active life. Divine transcendence is reflected through memory as the object of striving — always within it, yet beyond it, never right in the focus of its eye.

Whereupon Augustine turns from the speculative to the practical, taking another route of ascent, that of moral discipline, or "continence," mounting the anthropological ladder of body, soul, and mind. At its climax he discovers the idea of justice, and with it the neighbor, whose entry is the more powerful because long delayed. It would have been possible, Augustine thought, to try to get to neighbor-love too quickly, taking too much for granted, assuming we knew what the neighbor was, and therefore what he needed. In a sermon contemporary with the *Confessions,* he asked why it was not enough to say, "You shall love your neighbor," and replied that if we did not know how to love ourselves, we should go wrong in loving our neighbor. "So the Lord resolved to give you a form for your love of yourself in the love of God, and only then entrusted you with your neighbor, to love him as yourself."[6] Without a self-love shaped to the love of God we are not equipped to care for a neighbor's welfare. The discovery of self in God is the precondition for ranging self alongside neighbor in a just equality. But the neighbor, when he arrives, is also accompanied by God. Indeed, the neighbor *par excellence* is God himself in Christ. So the God who lay behind Augustine's memory can now be seen to have walked with him throughout his search: "You have always walked beside me, truth

6. Augustine, *Sermo* Mainz 40.12. Cf. *Sermo* 128.3.5: "First see whether you have learned to love yourself; then I will trust you with your neighbor to love as yourself. If you have not learned how to love yourself, I am afraid you will cheat your neighbor as yourself!"

that instructs me!"[7] The exertion of the soul to realize its own inwardness has left it as God's hostage, subject to his ordering of all things in justice.

Christian moral theory has been intrigued by Augustine's paradox about the foundational love of self and its diametric opposite, also called "self-love," a self-complacency which entrenches us at the center of our own universe. The first self-love paves the way for engagement with not-self, the second precludes any relation to not-self other than "concupiscence," which is the attempt to absorb the not-self into the self. The relation to the self is unrepeatable; no other can be a self to me. Unique, coming first in the order of moral responsibility, "every man is nearest to himself." Yet we are human beings like others; our unique center of perception confers no privileged moral status. When we speak of self-love in a subjective sense, we do not make the self an object of love preferred above other objects, but identify the self, called by God and responsible to God, as the presupposition of love. Self-love can assert no claim on material and spiritual goods without conceding priority (of material) or equality (of spiritual goods) to the neighbor who is "as" the self. Subjective self-love is a condition of agent-existence, but there can be a perverse assertion of the self-as-object that will distort and destroy agent-existence. Augustine's joyful explorations of the paradox never stoop to the pusillanimous thought that interests of self and neighbor may be judiciously balanced and apportioned. *All* must be self-love, for "human beings must also be told how to love, that is, how to love themselves so as to do themselves good," while *nothing* must be self-love, for "when it says 'all your heart, all your soul, all your mind,' it leaves no part of our life free from this obligation, no part free, as it were, to back out and enjoy some other thing; any other object of love that enters the mind should be swept towards the same goal as that to which the whole flood of our love is directed."[8]

To think of the self as a claimant among other claimants, and of self-love as an interest in competition with others' interests, is to leave Augustine's paradox behind and enter the modern world of the rights-possessing self. When the debate over self-love resurfaced in the seventeenth and eighteenth centuries, this was the concept that dominated it. Joseph Butler's musing wonderment "not that men have so great regard to their own good or interest . . . for they have not enough," may seem to bring the Augustinian paradox back before us, but a moment's further reading shows that everything has

---

7. Augustine, *Confessions* 10.40.

8. Augustine, *De doctrina Christiana*, 1.25, 22. On this question see my *The Problem of Self-Love in St. Augustine* (Eugene: Wipf & Stock, 2006²).

changed: "but that they have so little to the good of others," he goes on, making a difference between an interest in our own good and an interest in others' good which Augustine could never have countenanced. Self-love, for Butler, is distinct from other impulses of action, a "cool" affection, as he liked to call it. He thinks it only a "strange affectation" to represent "the whole of life as nothing but one continued exercise of self-love," for on his terms that representation could mean only one thing, Epicurean hedonism.[9] Those who could not share Butler's confidence that Epicureanism could be avoided by a balance of self and others, meanwhile, had no recourse but the extravagant thesis that one might attain indifference to one's own good, even lose interest in one's own salvation.[10] What earth tremor had disturbed the grammar of self-love and thrown the Augustinian paradox out of kilter?

The first shifting of the ground occurred in the scholastic age, when Aristotle's dictum that all things seek to prolong their own existence drew down good self-love within the magnetic field of self-protection. At that point no materialist reduction was implied. The essential coinherence of material and spiritual existence, as the scholastics understood it, was a safeguard against such a thing. By conceiving that spiritual existence depended on communion with a holy God, they erected a bulwark against a purely worldly notion of self-protection, whether sensual, emotional, or intellectual. As the key anthropological premises fell away, however, and the pursuits and aversions of human nature began to be thought of as instinctive animal impulses, things looked very different. Take a version of the scholastic proposition, "Reason . . . postulates . . . that each man should love himself, and seek what is useful to him . . . and . . . endeavor to preserve his being," and combine it with the materialist premise that "the knowledge of good or evil is nothing else than the emotion of pleasure or pain, in so far as we are conscious of it," and it is evident that the conclusion will consecrate material self-interest — not sensual self-interest necessarily, but quite definitely the welfare of the unit as opposed to the universal. "No virtue can be conceived as prior to this virtue of endeavoring to preserve oneself" — so wrote Spinoza on behalf of the "new moral science" of the mid-seventeenth century.[11] The results,

9. Butler, *Sermons,* Preface, pp. 29-34.

10. Thus Fénelon, of whose position I have written briefly in *The Ways of Judgment* (Grand Rapids: Eerdmans, 2005), pp. 301-2. The root of his problem in seventeenth-century egoism is well demonstrated by Robert Spaemann, *Reflexion und Spontaneität: Studien über Fénelon* (Stuttgart: Klett-Cotta, 1990²).

11. Benedict de Spinoza, *Ethica ordine geometrico demonstrata* 4.8,18,22. Trans. A. Boyle (London: Dent, 1910), pp. 149, 154-55, 157.

garnered up by Adam Smith in his well-known theory of providence, sur-
vive like mammoth tusks fossilized in the rock strata of our contemporary
moral landscape.

A certain clarity is brought to the paradox of self-love if we look behind
Augustine's identification of faith with love of God, to identify the elementary forms of self-love, negative and positive, as faith and faithlessness: believing that we are addressed by God, and not believing it. The self comes
before our mind because we learn that we are ourselves the objects of God's
demanding and perfecting love. No love for any object could be grounded
other than on that divine love, of which we are (from our own point of view)
the first beloved. We cannot overlook where we stand; love of God and of
neighbor must not be absent-minded, but self-aware. Yet precisely because
God's love is the ground of our active self, it presents itself to us as a summons; it demands the effort of existence, and does not allow us to remain
where we are. The challenge to responsibility is always heard in it, taking
form as a word that opens up the world to intelligent action.

It is no adequate response to the paradox, then, to take the gift of self for
granted, forget it, and focus our whole attention elsewhere, as the advocates
of "self-forgetfulness" urged, who thronged the literature a century ago.[12] The
only meaning we could attribute to a gospel of self-forgetfulness would be
that the agent must wrap the gift of self in a napkin and bury it, rather than
venturing on the exchange of life. Augustine's elaboration of the reflexive
self was prompted precisely by the need to underpin the moral imperative
at the root of his conversion. To assume a commanding point of view on the
world from which all else appeared to us, but we did not appear to ourselves,
would indeed be the false self-love that presumed on its ontological security.

The Objectified Self

There is a second stage in the logic by which the self finds itself in the world.
If the elementary motions of self-love are best characterized as faith and
faithlessness, the world of the self's observation and understanding now
reflects the self back to itself as one object of love among other objects.

In my first naïve wonder at the world I fail to notice that the pair of
eyes through which I see it are themselves part of the world I see. I see
cities, mountains, books, and people, questions and answers, problems and

---

12. For example, Kenneth Kirk, *The Vision of God* (London: Longmans, Green, 1931).

triumphs, but I do not see the eyes with which I see these things. But as I interrogate each thing about its connections to other things, I come across myself. I find I am a piece of the world's events. I trace the connections I see back to the eyes through which I see them: Do I see what others see? What do I fail to see? Do I change what I see when I see it? What is it in the world that brings about my sight of it? And so I come to understand that my observation, too, is a thing observed, and not excluded from the judgment God pronounced on all that he had made, that it was very good. My gaze rests on myself with what tradition calls *amor complacentiae,* "love of complacence" — not on myself *as agent,* but on myself as a thing among other things. "Love what God made in you," Augustine tells us repeatedly.

As I locate myself in God's world, I observe others like me. For to understand a thing — any thing — is to know it as one of a kind, and to understand oneself is to know the kind, or kinds, to which one belongs. Self-love is love of a kind — not a "species" in the reductive biological sense, defined by animal characteristics alone, but a kind constituted through self-awareness and agency. So there emerges into view the self's inevitable companion, the neighbor, the other member of the kind, always and from the beginning "as yourself." The self finds itself among other selves, set beside them in equality and reciprocity, the object of their gaze as they are the object of its. That moment of reflexive self-discovery in the gaze of others is a disconcerting one, typically accompanied by blushing. For whom, or for what, do we blush? For ourselves, certainly, but for ourselves as others see us, ourselves as we have only now learned to see ourselves, things-in-the-world, mortal creatures, other people's other people. At that moment of self-learning there is a possibility of loving ourselves, too, with what the tradition calls *amor benevolentiae,* "love of benevolence." "Have mercy on your own soul," Augustine liked to quote the Vulgate of Ecclesiasticus 30:24, "pleasing God."

Of this moment of reflexive self-awareness that defeats the temptation of solipsism much has been said. One thing that might seem unnecessary to say, but is not, is that it must be considered. We cannot arrive at ourselves by default. "Only be yourself!" the enthusers tell us, as though the whole trick of living were to give less attention to ourselves! But to see ourself *alongside* the neighbor, to see the neighbor *as* ourself, is no spontaneous observation but one requiring care and consideration. When Jesus warned, "everyone who exalts himself will be humbled, and he who humbles himself will be exalted" (Luke 14:11), he spoke, apparently, of two alternative mistakes and not only one, a false self-promotion and a false self-humiliation, both in need of correction. The reality that exposes false pretensions catches up with us, not only to throw us down from heights of importance we have arrogated to ourselves, but also to dig us up from bunkers of insignificance we have hollowed out for ourselves. Hiding like Saul among the baggage, we shall be dragged uncomfortably before those who expect something of us. Perhaps, after all, there is truth in the suggestion that the two failings join hands behind the curtain, that modest invisibility is not very different from boastful self-promotion. Whether publicizing oneself or shrinking from publicity, one hopes to avoid the candid gaze that sees through one's self-image. What is required is that we know ourselves as we are known. To refuse self-knowledge is to refuse to find ourselves in the world God loves, to refuse to love ourselves for the sake of God's love for us.

The moment of reflexive self-awareness has often been claimed as the decisive moment for morality, the threshold of moral sensibility.[13] What kind of threshold must it be, to have such significance? Not only a change in how we see *ourself,* to be sure, but in the way we see *the world* as a result of finding ourselves located within it. Yet we should not leap too quickly to suppose an outright shift from subjective to objective perception, from an "inside" point of view to an "outside" point of view. Thomas Nagel speaks of an "objective" viewpoint, in which we "raise our understanding to a new level (as) we examine that relation between the world and ourselves which is responsible for our prior understanding, and form a new conception that includes a more detached understanding of ourselves, of the world, and of the interaction between them."[14] Three elements go into this proposal, which are assumed to belong together: (i) two distinct ways of learning, "accumulating information" and "raising our understanding to a new level"; (ii) a reflexive moment in which we take our own viewpoint into the field of knowledge; (iii) the description of this moment as "detachment." Accepting that there is indeed a qualitative difference between acquiring knowledge and understanding, are the second and third elements sufficient to account for it?

"The natural place to begin," Nagel tells us, "is with our own position in the world," a sentence whose awkward construction betrays the problem.[15] "Begin with," or "begin from"? It is not at all "natural" (in the sense of "unreflective" or "untutored") to begin *with* our own position in the world. That we even have an "own position" is not something that naive first impressions

13. Cf. Robert Spaemann, *Persons,* trans. Oliver O'Donovan (Oxford: Oxford University Press, 2006), p. 184.

14. Thomas Nagel, *The View from Nowhere* (Oxford: Oxford University Press, 1986), p. 5.

15. Nagel, *The View from Nowhere,* p. 13.

will recognize. What we begin "with" is the world itself, offering itself to our wondering and uncritical gaze; what is "natural" is to take it at face value. To question the face value we need interrogative skills. To say "begin from," on the other hand, is to be guilty of nothing worse than ironic understatement, for it is not merely "natural," but quite inevitable, that whatever point of view we start from will be our own point of view. Then there can be no suggestion of "moving away" or leaving "the personal or merely human perspective further and further behind."[16] Here there is a confusion between perspectives and realities. It is easy to move away from thinking of personal *realities,* less easy to move away from personal *perspectives.* If, to grasp the sheer contingency of human existence, I train my mind to think of galaxies colliding and exploding in prehistoric space, I conceive those non-human and non-personal events from the perspective of my own scientific education, with an imagination shaped, no doubt, by such special effects as I have watched on video screens.

Behind this program we detect the notorious confrontation in political philosophy of liberalism, with its objective view of justice — "the perspective of eternity" Rawls called it — and the "situated" viewpoint of communitarianism. This opposition gave voice to deep-seated antinomies of thought, "subjective-objective," "inside-outside," difficult to elude but pregnant with self-refuting paradoxes. If the liberal is to take an objective view of the position he occupies, he must actually occupy it, for otherwise it is not his own position that he objectifies. If the communitarian declares that all points of view are "situated," what seems to have been proposed, despite his best intentions, is a universal claim from a universal perspective. What underlies these self-refutations is the assumption common to both sides that no "particular point of view" on the world can allow us a view of the world as a whole. This assumption has fallen victim to its spatial metaphors, and normalizes what in fact is a moment of philosophical dizziness, a loss of perspective on the I-world relation. Agency, venturing on the world, can for a shorter or a longer time lose touch with its God-given sense of self. Admiring the world and its goods, absorbed in the object of observation, it falls into self-forgetfulness, mislays the entry-point that God had given it, and then, appalled or delighted, comes upon itself as an object indistinguishable from all the others. But the dizziness passes. Subjects we are, subjects we shall remain, however objectively we see the world.

Let us propose instead that *every* particular point of view affords a view

16. Nagel, *The View from Nowhere,* p. 6.

of the whole, or, to be more modest, offers the promise of such a view. All perspectives are windows through which reality may be seen and studied. There is no "departure," no "distance," no "detachment" from the point of view in which our consciousness is born, which is, after all, the point of view of our bodies, which we cannot step outside. What there may be, however, is persistent attention to what lies behind the immediate representations of the world. We discover that the world is not merely a surface, not merely a series of images, but that there is a depth, "within and behind," which is also visible from our point of view, though not immediately so. The objective view can only be formed by one who occupies a subjective viewpoint. Its paradigm self-announcement is, "I realize that I have a particular point of view on this question and that other factors may weigh more heavily with other people, yet it still seems to me impossible to ignore, etc. etc."

The only way to attain objectivity is to take note of *more,* not to take note of *less* or to take *less note* of what one noted first. Objectivity may, in the storms of experience, be simulated by changes of mind: "I used to think justice worth striving for, but when I lost my court case it became clear that justice is merely the interest of the stronger!" Any fool can change his mind; the difficult thing is to enlarge it.

The observing self never renounces itself as a center, but it observes further beyond its untutored field of vision, embarking on a wider and more comprehensive exploration which makes it more, not less, a center. Does this conceptual cartography suggest that knowledge is like an empire, referring everything back from the frontier to the center that controls it? Again, the problem lies in the spatial analogies: "center" is a misleading notion if we think in terms of one universe of perception structured around one center. The discovery of the world is precisely the discovery of other "centers," other views on the world that are irreducibly different at point of entry, but are able to make contact and form a common field of reference with ours.

Other centers do not mean *no* centers, nor that my center is exchange-able for any other. A phrase one may sometimes hear used with a defensive or ironic tone conveys the suggestion of a loss of the self's necessity: "I happen to be . . . ." It is meant to prise open the range of possibilities: "Just because I *happen to be* X doesn't mean that I *cannot be* Y." But the thought it conveys is purely speculative; the self has disappeared into the neighbor's neighbor, who is *as* the neighbor as the neighbor is *as* the self, whose position and possibilities are indistinguishable from anyone else's possibilities. An "I" that has really passed through the boundlessness of the world and "found itself" at a particular time and place, can admit no "happening to be" what it is. Another person may "happen to be" something, but that third-person view is not available for first-person use. I have a unique and indissoluble relation to what I am.

The paradox of seeing myself as others see me, an object among objects and my neighbor's neighbor, is that I feel myself agent and object simultaneously. Contingency is a fact about the order of the world, and my own contingency is what makes me speculatively interchangeable with my neighbor. But when I find *myself* here and not there, now and not then, I experience my own position as a necessity. "If I had been born in another age" is an entertaining game that relieves me, for one pleasant moment, of the burden of existing as myself. But I am who I am, and when I am. I may have multiple and indeterminate possibilities; nothing is impossible except the impossible. Yet no discernment of possibilities can be more than a speculation until I have first understood and accepted the parameters that govern my actuality. Theoretically, everything about my being is contingent, and might have been otherwise; practically, everything about my being is necessary and must be embraced as such. So long as I think of myself theoretically, I have not advanced an inch beyond abstract reflection. My moment of self-recognition, then, does not take the form, "Here is another member of the species *homo sapiens!*" but "*This* member of the species *homo sapiens* is identical with the self that *I* am!" From that proposition we derive the genuinely important inference that "It is not similarity of others to myself that is in view, but the same incomparable uniqueness."[17] Or, not "I'm no more special than anyone else," but "everyone is as special as me."[18]

Other centers do not mean other universes. A plurality of centers of vision are effective precisely as they offer multiple points of access to a unified and common reality. The threshold is not crossed by knowing just one thing, but by conceiving and exploring the relations of things, setting our minds to seek a common wisdom that others, too, may seek from different starting-points. And so the self and the other are discerned as a community of inquiry in relation to a common object. Behind the "I" with which we wrestle so hard there is a "we" in whose vision we seek to participate. It is the mark of a serious search for wisdom not to be hung up on self-consciousness, but to "think judiciously" of ourselves (Rom. 12:3), which means to think of ourselves alongside others as members of a community.

17. Spaemann, *Persons,* p. 185.
18. *Letters of C. S. Lewis,* ed. W. H. Lewis (London: Geoffrey Bles, 1966), p. 242.

I and We

Modernity generated two rival myths-of-origin about the I and the we, both constructivist. According to the one the individual constructed society, according to the other society constructed the individual. Each took one pole of the dialectic for granted and problematized the other: what we call "individualism" is a theory of how society is generated, while "social behaviorism" is an account of individual self-consciousness. Contractarians interest themselves in politics, social behaviorists in psychology. A Christian belief which understands the agent-self as suspended on the call of God can settle with neither myth, for it takes neither of the poles for granted. Agency conferred by God, whether singular or plural, cannot be relegated to a presupposition. Arising from God's call, it is a focus of questioning, and no questions may be begged, not even whether it is singular or plural. It must be sought after, prayed for, and appropriated with new thanksgivings for deliverance, both in its individual expression, as "person," and in its communitarian form, as "community."

The two myths displayed their constructivist character in the difficulty both had in locating freedom. It was the tragedy of the late-twentieth-century reassertion of the individual, loosely called "neoliberalism," that it hoped to secure freedom by entrenching the free individual at the foundations of everything, only to find that it had denied itself a way of describing and elaborating the *conditions* of individual freedom. Its rhetoric reduced freedom to a mathematical point, a private energy lying behind all social forms, an undifferentiated impulse with no lived dimensions. If talk of freedom is to have substance, it must imagine how it can be exercised in a sustainable social order. It cannot realize freedom through protology any more than Marxism could through eschatology. Neoliberalism ended up with a curious looking-glass version of the Marxist utopia: instead of the state withering away to leave society, society withered away to leave the state, which now, however, rested on nothing more than an aggregation of supposed individual preferences. Our contemporary difficulty in shoring up the authority of governments against the voracious appetites of their consumer-electorates springs from the neoliberal legacy, which cut solid social ground from under government's feet.

It was never a sufficient reply that there would be no point in being free unless one were "free for" something. That did not settle the legitimate anxiety that freedom might be hijacked: "freedom for" could veil a totalitarian project. When rival claimants to freedom pursue rival goals, the defense of freedom means social conditions in which the ground of each claim may be made apparent. To be free requires understanding. So the correct reply was that freedom could only be evoked by a comprehensible good. Freedom requires goals; it needs to fulfill itself in and through fulfilling them. But to be equipped with material goals, it requires also a formal goal, which is its own vocation. To be "free for" any thing is to be "satisfied in" that thing, which implies a measure that can correlate the agent-self with its goals. That measure cannot be derived circularly from the goals themselves; something lies behind them, something calls free agency to be true to itself in attaining *these* goals. There must be a further horizon to freedom, something which freedom to pursue these goals is itself freedom "for." That further horizon is social. Cooperation itself is a goal, which explains how we find satisfaction in cooperating even with those whose immediate goals are different from our own. Individual freedom shrinks if it lacks the capacity to imagine itself part of a wider common agency. It must look for the Kingdom of God.

The acting self needs depth and dimension, a reflexivity to see itself in a social context, carrying within its self-knowledge a knowledge of the world beyond itself. Everything turns on what the self, in its "inner space," contains. The pinpoint self reduced to a single impulse, *homo oeconomicus,* is simply not equipped to exercise freedom. The free self must be richly related, capable of satisfaction in its undertakings, and so reflexive, an agency that can "appropriate" itself. That is what the Reformers' thesis of the priority of faith intended with its denial that any agency can please God if it has not been received from God. The content of the self, giving agency its purchase on the world, is the call of God that leads the self out into existence, responsive to the gifts and purposes of God for his world.

In the opposite myth, that of the socially constructed self, it might seem that such an elaborated and receptive self was on offer, but the appearance is deceptive. Its interest, as we have said, lies in accounting for the individual; society is viewed not as an agent in its own right, but as an "organism" out of which agency and selfhood are spun. Agency is therefore a product, but this reduces it to a function that leaves no room for the agent's own conception of it. In representing thought as a subjective experience accompanying social processes, the myth cannot avoid making redundant whatever it is we *think* we are doing when we act. The supposed social rationality of thought never meets up with its intentional content; the way the mind frames the world is treated as an irrelevance. But that means that freedom has no place in action, for we certainly have no freedom if we do not know what is up with us when we think we are up to something.

The thesis of the social construction of the self is best taken as a thesis about how the individual self is morally matured through the interplay of self and society. From the classic text of Mead we may learn some useful, if pedestrian, lessons of this sort: that socialization is not only a question of adapting ourselves to society but of finding ways to adapt society to ourselves; that being in touch with social reality need not suppress originality; that we may laugh when someone falls over, but should be sympathetic if he has hurt himself.[19] From one angle and another freedom takes form as a capacity to act within the exchanges of symbolic communication. But whose is this freedom? To what can we ascribe such capacity to act? Mead answers the problem in terms of his well-known distinction of "the I" and "the me," the "I" responding to stimuli, the "me" located within the field of stimuli, the "I" subjective, the "me" objectified, and so on.[20] But since with the passage of time the "I" passes into the "me," not vice versa, and since it is the "me," not the "I," that absorbs the attitudes of others into the self, it seems that the "I" is simply an aspect of the self which got forgotten in the original thesis that the self was constructed socially. The "I" enters as a *deus ex machina*, lowered onto the stage of the social self precisely to supply what it lacked, which is to say, freedom.

What is missing is a "we" — not an "us," an object of engagement, the social aspect of the objectified me, but a genuine subject-we, the *accompanying condition* of the freedom of an "I." To be free is not merely to *have* an agent's point of view on the world, but to *share* one. A point of view on the world, indeed, can only be had by being shared. The active self is plural as well as singular, and that from its very inception. It cannot think of itself without a neighbor, except by reducing itself to a passive receptor of impressions; as soon as it recalls its agency, it reaches for shared perspectives. Agency operates in the field of common meanings and purposes, of communication and participation.

How are we to locate and describe this common field? The temptation is to take it for granted, to refer to "we" without any reflective discipline, so that "we" becomes an indefinite "one" (as in the French *on*), the self and its outlook projected across the universe in a speculative colonization of society: "we don't . . . (believe in miracles, punish offenders, think the soul is immortal, or whatever) these days." The question, "Who is we?" may always be put,

---

19. G. H. Mead, *Mind, Self, and Society* (Chicago: University of Chicago Press, 1934), p. 206.

20. Mead, *Mind, Self, and Society,* pp. 196-200.

not merely as a debating ploy, but as a matter of truthful self-knowledge. And the answer may be given that the "we" is the heavenly city we await, anticipated in the communities we now engage in, which find a common perspective on some things some of the time. It may be summed up by saying that God's gift of other people is not "society," an objective whole of which we can take a view, but "a community," in which we may participate. Community is a communication: not an empty container, but a field of shared space and context, which can be explored and characterized. The active self, from its first calling forth, must participate in such a field, and owes it the tribute of loving understanding.

Mankind

To have the neighbor "as yourself" is a matter of equality, recognizing likeness of needs and aspirations, and it is a matter of reciprocity, recognizing the "alongsideness" of mutual recognition and community. But these are purely formal notions if we abstract them from the order of creation in which they acquire substance. "The neighbor as myself" must be like me and alongside me in some determinate respect. Christian understanding, speaking with the voice of a humanism made possible by monotheism, has said that my neighbor is my equal *as mankind.*

"Anthropocentrism" is something to disapprove of these days. After a long period in when the moral high ground was occupied by a nihilism that called itself, implausibly, "humanism," a swing of philosophical fashion brought about a general loss of nerve over the human race. The sin of "speciesism" was added to the indefinitely expanding catalogue of unjust discriminations. But practical reason must be anthropocentric in one sense of the word, at least, since the human agent, in conceiving the world as a sphere of action, necessarily takes him- or herself as the baseline. An objective nonparticipational point of view on the universe of goods is not accessible — not, at any rate, to us. We see ourselves "in the middle" of the cosmic order, as in the eighth Psalm, with the angels above us and the animals below us, a bridge between spiritual and material worlds. That is the view that opens up to us as we engage with the world practically. Reflective enough to understand that there may in principle be other views, we must also be reflective enough to understand why no such other views could ever be our own. God and the angels may see a universe in which man is not central, but among us such an imagination is no more than a speculative "what-if?" — the suspending of human self-knowledge and experience. Nothing is achieved for other kinds of creature by doubting man's conception of his place, for such a doubt does not encourage careful attention to other creatures, but only expresses an uneasy preoccupation with man's power to modify himself. Post-humanism is anti-humanism, and anti-humanism is another variety of anthropocentrism. There are better forms of anthropocentrism, forms which allow more humility before the complex wonder of non-human creation and more responsibility for how we treat it. The Book of Job, for example, explores the animal kingdom's independence of mankind precisely by calling Job to answer before his, and its, creator.

If we refuse to speak of a human kind, we shall certainly not be able to speak to any purpose of equality. Without a "kind" in which all humans participate the idea of the neighbor as a moral equal has no purchase. It may seem, however, that since human nature must be understood in a many-layered way, as physical, sensitive, animal, rational, and so on, equality and reciprocity could be founded in some competency characteristic of humanity, a competency that humans may possibly share with other genera and species — a "rational nature," perhaps, as Kant speculated, or (more popular with those who believe they have overcome "the essence of man") a sensitivity to pain, since "the same things as cause me to suffer cause him to suffer."[21] But as Spaemann well insisted, it is not regard for a common competency that entails the recognition of equality, but fellow-membership of a community. Community is communication, and communication needs its nature and powers, to be sure, but it subsists in the act of mutual recognition and acceptance, possible among human beings by virtue of the power of speech, and it is this that constitutes their relations as those of equal participation. Equality as we have learned it in the Western moral tradition is co-humanity. As love ordered by knowledge is due to itself, so it is due to the community where ordered love is conceived and communicated, and is due to that community from itself. Ordered love is not ordered in respect of a floating feature which we can recognize and admire separately in each particular instance — due to her because she has it, due to me because I have it, due to this porpoise if, and to the extent that, this porpoise has it. Ordered love is not so distributed. It is what we communicate in the mutual recognition of members of the human community. We owe equal love to each other because we communicate with each other in something we share together equally, if we have it at all.

21. R. M. Hare, *Freedom and Reason* (Oxford: Clarendon, 1963), p. 222.

If the idea of equality is cut off from that of co-humanity, two consequences follow for our moral thinking. First, a jungle of new and unsus-
pected duties springs up in our path. Mainly new duties to animals, in the
first instance; there is an organization, we are told, campaigning for "fair
trials for dogs." But to stop at that point is unimaginative, for there is no good
reason, once the initial step is taken, to treat likenesses between human and
animal species more seriously than those between humans and non-animals.
Hume's sarcastic illustration of the sapling that "murders" its parent tree thus
returns as a genuine moral difficulty: why should arboreal parricide be less
weighty a crime than human parricide, or arboricide than zooicide? Let us
be quite clear: there are duties in respect of animals, and (why not?) of plants,
too. We can know enough about how different living species flourish and
suffer harm to know what kinds of use will foster their wellbeing and what
treatment of them is compatible with care for the world God made. When
we read of dolphins killed in dragnets, of battery hens denied the possibility
of walking on two legs, or of ancient forests felled to make housing estates,
we feel justified guilt on behalf of our race. But responsibility for these creatures is unilateral. We have no relations of *equality* with them, for there is
no reciprocity. We cannot without lunacy expect that equal regard be paid
to us by trees.

In the same way there could be no relations of equality with superior
beings such as angels. But what if we imagine a species wholly different
from us biologically (and so unavailable for intermarriage) and possessing
more or less comparable powers of reason, with which we could communicate fully and at will by speech? There is nothing intrinsically impossible
in this imagination, which has been widely explored in fiction.[22] Are we
not told these days that evolution proceeds by distant species developing
similar traits independently? As far as we know, of course, the imagination
is counter-factual, and therefore does not touch the assertion that duties of
equality and reciprocity are owing to all members, and only to members, of
our human kind. But if it were one day to prove factual, we should simply
conclude that the "kind" laying claim upon us was constituted not by one
biological species alone but by an intercommunicating *ensemble* of two or
more species. A kind it still would be, but one in which we participated on
equal terms with members of our own and of the other species. We might
call it by C. S. Lewis's invented name, *hnau,* or with Kant, "rational being"

22. For instance, and with serious philosophical intent, in C. S. Lewis's novel *Out of the
Silent Planet.*

— but the point either way would be that the *community* of kinds founded the duties of equality, not the regard we felt for rational powers as such or for speech as such.[23]

The other and more immediately threatening consequence is that the idea of equality no longer supports duties we believe we owe to other human beings. This is true especially of duties of "attributive justice" (to use Grotius's term), obligations to treat people in certain ways on the basis of special aptitudes or needs: scholarships for able students, jobs for competent applicants, milk for growing babies, materials and tools for willing workers, medical care for the sick and elderly, and so on. There are still those who pretend to believe that no child should be educated beyond a level to which every child can aspire to, a perverse egalitarianism based on the denial of human potential. Human equality is a matter of being equally human, and being human of itself demands a diversity of kinds of engagement. Humans variously endowed are equal before death, before social communication, and before judgment. Their lives, their capacity to occupy a place in society, their responsibility for what they do is of equal weight and makes equal demands on others in the face of all variations.[24] But precisely these foundational equalities allow for differences of social role and corresponding treatment which do not subjugate some human beings to the demands of others, but realize the full wealth and breadth of human powers. Attributive justice responds to variety with variety, treating different people differently in a way consistent with their equality but not directly derived from it. Differentiation is a principle underlying all cultural growth and enrichment, of persons and of societies. At this point, too, we need to know ourselves.

Doubt of Meaning

We return to the sin against the self, and take a third and a fourth sounding on the spectrum of forms of doubt, at points where we shrink in refusal from the call to be open to the meaning of the world God has given us.

There is a sin of *disparagement:* "Do not speak evil of one another,

23. On this cf. Spaemann, *Persons*, pp. 236-48, and especially p. 248: "Yet if there exist within the universe other natural species of living beings possessing an inner life of sentience, whose adult members usually command rationality and self-awareness, we would have to acknowledge *not only those instances but all instances* of that species to be persons."
24. See my remarks in *The Ways of Judgment*, pp. 31-51.

brethren!" (James 4:11). Penetratingly the apostle identifies this tendency to think ill of others with the rejection of meaning: "To speak evil of a brother or to judge a brother is to speak evil of, or judge, the law." The negative view of the person becomes, or from its inception always secretly is, a refusal of the universe of meaning, the law of God which forms the criterion of whatever is good or bad in his or her action. The task we are presented with is to understand that meaning better and conform our disposition to it, being always, even in our relation to those who cause us pain or disappointment, "doers of the law." What we may find painful or disappointing is comprehended there; it is a fault, but a fault in one whom it declares to be our "brother" and our "neighbor" — James does not pause to distinguish these terms. If we do not put ourselves in a position to see him or her as such, it is because we want to avoid having to accommodate in our understanding failings that cause us, perhaps quite rightly, pain and disappointment. It is simpler to see the *bête noire* through the lens of anger and frustration, a lens which inevitably distorts a very great deal of God's good ordering. What is said about individual persons must be said, too, about institutions, traditions, and practices. The "clean sweep" posture characteristic of the root-and-branch reformer is a refusal of whatever meaning these may offer us. True reform involves appreciating and preserving their meaning within the project of correction.

Disparagement may spring from anger, but it is not an expression *of* anger, not, that is, of anger as a passion. We shall have to say more about the passions at a later stage, but may observe in general terms that they involve an energy which supports action — ill-considered action sometimes, perhaps, but not necessarily so, and, if not ill-considered, the more effective for being energetic. In general, the passions pass from us when they have done their work for us, and when they have passed they usually leave us free of their influence. Anger for a short time — until sunset, as the apostle briskly suggests (Eph. 4:26) — may help us over the shock of injury. It can open the way within our thoughts for an active pursuit of just reckoning and just reaction, which will draw us away from the one-sided grief of an injured plaintiff to a fuller understanding of the wrong that was done, and may lead us in the end to the most positive action imaginable in the face of wrong, which is clear-headed, unsentimental forgiveness. So it may help us to recover our capacity for action. Yet once the fire of anger has died, it may leave behind a deposit, a smoldering pile of cinders. Here is the anger C. S. Lewis described as "the anesthetic of the mind," which continues to find comfort in holding someone to blame for the hurt received.[25] Like other anesthetics, this cold anger can be addictive. The illusion that we may go on occupying the "moral high ground," simply by reminding ourselves and others of our injuries, is not an unpleasant one, and may do something to assuage the sense of humiliation and betrayal. It is not surprising that we try to build a permanent home upon our little eminence of outrage. What keeps us there is what keeps the hypochondriac in bed, the self-doubt and uncertainty of our ability to live effectively. Rather than seek for the purpose of God to overcome evil with good, we justify ourselves by refusing to accept responsibility for our failure to recover. We put ourselves in the position of holding the world perpetually in the wrong against us.

And so it may come about that generalized resentment or disparagement is our substitute structure of meaning, the sole basis on which we are capable of understanding the world. All we encounter comes to be interpreted through this filter. We dare not dispense with it, for fault-finding is our only purchase on ourselves and our agency, and we do not know what would be left of us without it. There are plentiful examples of how this influences the formation of political identities into the friend-enemy consciousness, so wearisomely familiar in international relations, and into the "victim mentality" which has become in our generation the ugly stock-in-trade of every social enthusiasm. The local anesthetic of the mind is the general anesthetic of the political community. But what is true of public engagements may be true of private engagements, too. And we should not neglect to note, if only in passing, that resentment often proves the paralysis of art. Art, in whatever medium, as the artefactual representation of humanity to itself, must, by whatever canons are appropriate to the medium, be truthful. The revelatory power of suffering that appealed so strongly to the Romantic movement — no bad theme, to be sure, for any artist — spun a coarse strand of self-pity that wove its way into much of the most admired literature and music of the nineteenth and early twentieth centuries. Self-pity is impotence, and in art, too, impotence found a welcome among those who could not distinguish the clenched fist raised against heaven from seriousness of purpose.

We make a fourth and final sounding, briefly and merely to open up a train of thought we shall have occasion to pursue when we consider sins against the world and time. Less plaintive, more self-knowing, and more

25. C. S. Lewis, *Poems,* ed. W. H. Lewis (London: Geoffrey Bles, 1964), p. 125: "You have what sorrow always longs to find, Someone to blame, some enemy in chief; Anger's the anaesthetic of the mind, It does men good, it fumes away their grief."

ironic, and to that extent more habituated and entrenched, *moral detach-ment* takes refuge from life and action in the observer's stance, watching the world go by and expecting nothing from it. The ironic stance may appear to be the very opposite of withdrawal from meaning, but in reality it lies just one step beyond the negativity of disparagement. Where the negative view of the world asserts the righteousness of the self against all objective meaning and value, detachment withdraws the interest of the self entirely from the fray. Its acceptance of whatever may come is won at the price of self-disqualification from agent-involvement. A sense that the world can do nothing that will make a difference to the self is the reverse of a decision that the self can do nothing that will make a difference to the world. The posture can declare itself as cynical indifference; alternatively, it can declare itself as idealistic criticism, mounting such passionate and principled moral objections to every possible course of action that there are cogent reasons for attempting nothing. The idealist is not actually very different from the cynic. Neither is at a loss for an opinion on what is going on.

Balthasar once proposed that the essence of sin was *gnosis*.[26] Intellectual perspectives bounded by observational science afford the ideal cultural form for an age that is at once cynical and idealist. When reason refuses its fulfillment as *practical* reason, when it entrenches itself in abstract and quasi-scientific schemas of explanation and description, it withholds itself from life. Kant, too, knew that the road of natural necessity was more traveled than the footpath of freedom.[27] Balthasar's reference to the *social* sciences in this context should not be taken to suppose that these disciplines of learning, undertaken with a clear appreciation of their function and competence, have nothing to tell us about human affairs. They are, after all, simply part of the disciplined observations we make of one another, and practical reason can

26. Balthasar, "Neun Sätze," p. 82: "The demonic expresses itself above all in a loveless, self-glorifying gnosis that claims to be as coextensive as the agape that works God's will. . . . Since it will not accept the personal, concrete norm, it portrays sin as mere guilt, the result of a violation of a law or an idea, and it endeavors increasingly to exculpate it through psychology, sociology and other similar means." Trans. Graham Harrison in Joseph Cardinal Ratzinger, Heinz Schurman, Hans Urs von Balthasar, *Principles of Christian Morality* (San Francisco: Ignatius, 1986), p. 88.

27. Immanuel Kant, *Grundlegung zur Metaphysik der Sitten* (*AA* 4:455): "At this parting of the ways reason for speculative purposes finds the road of natural necessity much more traveled and more usable than that of freedom; yet for practical purposes the footpath of freedom is the only one on which it is possible to make use of our reason in our conduct." Trans. Mary Gregor, *Practical Philosophy*, Cambridge Edition of the Works of Immanuel Kant (Cambridge: Cambridge University Press, 1996), p. 63.

always make use of disciplined observations. The target of criticism, rather, is resort to the social-scientific mindset as a default position, a knowing posture that affords a retreat from the demands of moral reflection and deliberation. As students incapable of an ordered train of thought offer universities the "research" they have put together by questionnaire and statistic, the bewitchment of scientism tightens its grip on the mind of those who are not, and never will be, scientists. To think about human behavior without asking how we humans shall behave is to install the point of view of a surveyor of opinions in substitute for that of a responsible agent. It is the deepest and most intransigent denial of the self's calling, the refusal, as the existentialists liked to say, to exist.

CHAPTER 4

The Good of Man

Self-communicating Good

Speculatively, we may look on our species and its interests as infinitesimally unimportant, no more than a minor disturbance on the edge of the great galactic system. Practically, that point of view is unsustainable. Attending to the world as the theater of the life we are given to live, human agents place human existence center-stage. Even ecologists of the deepest green dye, returning from their searching visions of nature in which humans are more of an irritant than a decoration, come to rest in urgent appeals for the reconstruction of human attitudes. "He has shown you, *adam,* what is good!" (Mic. 6:8). Creation is good, the works of the Lord are good, and out of them appears a good of *adam,* a human existence which flourishes in relation to all other goods, not excluding that original goodness which is God himself.

Good is "shown," because good is objective. It is not the projection of our purposes, a way of talking about what we propose to ourselves to do or to acquire. It is not the reflective equilibrium of our feelings of wellbeing. The good that follows upon either of these subjective conditions can only be a secondary good. For the subjective conditions themselves are intentional: they focus upon the objective good that elicits them and makes them possible. We form purposes only because we recognize that there are goods to be aimed at; we feel well because there is an objective state of flourishing for the psychosomatic organism of the type we are. Along such lines as these R. M. Adams distinguishes goods of "welfare" and "utility" from goods of "excellence."[1] A good of welfare depends on the subject's feeling well; an animal in the zoo with every advantage to hand that it lacked in the wild is not well off if it feels displaced and anxious. A utility-good depends on the satisfaction it actually gives to users; a software program is not "useful" unless it finds its market among those who do in fact make use of it. Only excellence is good whether or not it is appreciated. It is "worthy of love and admiration" independently of what we think of it. A beautiful work of art is beautiful among philistines. It stands before us for what it is in itself, not for what we may make of it. The verb that denotes our response to the objective claim of good is "admire."

But to say that the work of art is excellent *independently* of our response does not mean that its beauty *has nothing to do* with our response. It invites us to admire it. Beauty comes first, admiration second, and that order is all-important, but beauty is open to admiration by whoever is capable of admiring it. It would not be beauty if it were not so; that which is good in itself is good for all. There is a risk that in stressing independence we conceive our relation to the good as *disinterested.* Either we think that we have no interest in the good we admire, or we think that the good has no interest in being admired. Adams's otherwise admirable treatment of the theme avoids the first of these two false conclusions: our interest in wellbeing, he thinks, creates an interest in admiring excellence.[2] But it does not avoid the second.

On the one hand he posits an "eros" that "pursues excellence," on the other an excellence that seems to turn its face away from the pursuit, looking upwards rather than downwards. Following Plato he holds that excellence is resemblance to God, who is the transcendent excellence. All things are excellent to the extent that they manifest godlikeness.[3] The concern of the excellent is with excellence. Excellent things appreciate God to a greater or lesser degree, and imitate him; God appreciates excellent things inasmuch as they imitate him. And that seems to be the only thing that is said about God's relation to what is less excellent than he. What is missing is a notion of *self-communication* on the part of the excellent-good, which is one reason why the relation between God and not-God in Adams's account never achieves the clear contours of creation. When things are good, they are so not by communication from above, but by imitation from below.

1. Robert Merrihew Adams, *Finite and Infinite Goods: A Framework for Ethics* (New York: Oxford University Press, 2002), pp. 13, 42.

2. Adams, *Finite and Infinite Goods,* p. 28: "It is an important part of the semantically indicated role of the good to be the object of motivated pursuit."

3. Adams, *Finite and Infinite Goods,* pp. 28-38.

Let us state the point in this way: the good is *essentially self-communicating,* open to participation by all. It has an "interest" (not to stretch that word very far) in being accessible, though no *need* to be. To speak of an "objective good" is to say not merely that it is independent of our interest, but that it is creative of it. To speak of a "transcendent good" is to speak of what presents itself supremely to our interest. "He has shown you," the prophet's saying can arguably be translated, "what is the good *of man.*" There is a referential difference between the good in itself and the good of man, for the good of man is dependent and responsive, consisting of doing justice, loving kindness, and walking humbly. But man's good and God's good alike subsist in his self-communication. The original good enables and sustains the dependent good, forming it, requiring it, and accompanying its humble walk. The original good offers itself to participation, not indifferent to our good, and, as there is no other good like it, it is the *subsisting reality* of our good, whether we know it or not.

Love of the World

But our good is not all the good there is. The good of man, the human bearing which consists in justice, mercy, and humility before God, is only a part of the universe of goods displayed for our admiration. It is the part that most immediately weighs upon us, to be sure, the point at which our admiration involves participation, but there are creatures we can observe merely to wonder at them, as Job wondered at the exotic bestiary displayed to his imagination, learning the differences between one creature and another and between the creatures and their creator. Mankind we cannot observe in that way. In all the variety of created wonders that meet our gaze we are required to find ourselves affectively and cognitively.

The created world gives shape to our existence as agents: that is what we mean specifically by calling the totality of things "the world," referring not only to singular objects, but to events, experiences, opportunities, restrictions, all, in fact, that determines our freedom positively and negatively. The Greek word for "world," *cosmos* (unlike the Hebrew *tebel,* which suggests foundations and underpinnings), carries suggestions of outward appearance and show.[4] It points not simply to everything there is, but quite specifically to its manner of appearing to us; it points to reality as filtered through the

---

4. The related adjective κόσμιος means "honorable," and the verb κοσμέω, "to decorate."

communications that give us access to it. The "world" is what is not ourselves, out there as opposed to in here; but it is non-self *as the self perceives it;* it is "my world" or "our world." In saying "world," then, we have not quite said "reality."

And so we can be told, "Love not the world!" (1 John 2:15), while at the same time we are told that God *did* love it (John 3:16), and the paradox is far from verbal, but turns on the different ways in which the world can be conceived. In the New Testament we find repeated references to "this" world, our common world, directly opposing it to God as a rival object of affection: "Do you not know that friendship with the world is enmity with God?" (James 4:4). A "world" constructed by agreements on what to see and what not to see opposes God's intentions, as when "the world hates you . . . it hated me first" (John 15:18, as often in the Johannine literature). Paul is "crucified to the world and the world to me" (Gal. 2:20), the world being what we characteristically value as opposed to the object of a true "boast," which is the cross of Christ. By vindicating righteous obedience Christ has "overcome the world" (John 16:33). Yet this opposition is just one moment in a drama of redemption. It is not eternal, but points to a history of the one world which God made and will deliver from the evil spirit that possesses it. It is the history of God's love for the world and the mission of his Son as "the light of the world," "the Savior of the world," and "giving life to the world." It is God, we may say, who is so in possession of the truth of the world that he *can* love it, without distortion or falsification, for its salvation. But for us to love the world is to constrain the real world within the dimensions of our restricted conception, and so to betray it.

When we are told, then, not to love "the world, nor that which is in the world" (1 John 2:15), the double object, world as a whole and world-part, focuses the problem of correct imagination. There is nothing accessible to our imagination that is not "in" the world, really speaking, God himself included. But is the world that is on offer, ready-formed for our subjective imaginations, real? The elements of which we form it are close to hand: "what the flesh desires, what the eyes desire, what the vulgar world boasts of."[5] However much we try to expand our mind to see things from the point of

---

5. Alternative senses of βίος (literally "life") as "wealth" and "vulgar world" are well evidenced in Liddle and Scott's *Greek-English Lexicon* (Oxford: Clarendon, 1940⁹). The former translation, preferred by Bauer, Arndt, and Gingrich on the basis of papyri parallels, is followed by most modern English translations. But it requires the genitive to be objective in the third phrase, while in the first two phrases it can only be subjective. On the larger scale of things the difference of interpretation is not weighty.

view of eternity, what we see and love will not be what really is, but a *simu-lacrum*. The phrases are carefully balanced, each consisting of a verbal noun and a subjective genitive: "what the flesh desires, what the eyes desire, what the vulgar world boasts of." "Love of the world" is formed of spontaneous responses to phenomena eliciting instinctive energies ("flesh"), immediate perceptions ("eyes"), and social solidarities ("vulgar world"). In each of these we have to do with what is presented as an object of desire or pride, either immediately by the senses, or proximately by the rumor of tradition, realities said to come to us "from the world," rather than "from the Father." The weight we give them is derived from their elemental role in forming our world, their capacity to dominate our constructive imagination. "Love of the world," in this deprecatory sense, then, is a framework of meaning shaped by individual and social spontaneities, an object limited by partial perception — "partial," both as self-interested and as incomplete. These same realities may come to be valued differently as we trace them to their origin in the Father's creative gift. Let us be clear at any rate that it is not the senses or the social tradition *as such* that we should distrust, but the uncritical relation in which we stand to them, allowing them to be the immediate parameters of value and determinants of meaning. Desire should serve, not shape, our comprehensive view of reality; "boasting" should ground itself on reality, not on consensus.[6] The "love of the Father" is the only point of reference from which we can grasp the realities desire and tradition point us to in their inner truth. Hence the fundamental opposition between these two loves: to love anything as "from the world" is to exclude loving it as "from the Father." It is a matter of where we draw the grounds of our appreciation from.

The implication of loving a world of desire and tradition, the apostle holds, is that our construction is not proof against the passage of time. "The world is passing, and so is the desire that belongs to it." Not only the immediate sense-impressions and mediated perceptions of tradition, but the world constructed upon them, shares the passing character of time. The created order is an order in time, and time passes — immanently (for that is how time is time) and eschatologically (for creation's time is under God's final judgment). Though one may say, viewing the world as the Creator's throne, that "the world is established, it shall never be moved" (Ps. 93:1), its permanence is not a necessary attribute but a function of the sustaining rule

---

6. The Greek of the New Testament distinguishes a possibly good boast from a presumptuous and over-confident one: in 1 John 2:16 it is ἀλαζονεία, as distinct from καύχημα and its related terms, used frequently in the New Testament epistles.

of God. Nothing that the world shows up, no object of desire or boasting, can endure unless God preserves it. When Paul says that the "pattern" of the world passes away (1 Cor. 7:31), he marks the difference between the immediate course of the world ("the present age" of 2 Tim. 4:10) and the ultimate purpose God has for it. How, then, can we avoid a purely ephemeral love of an ephemeral world, unstable, disconsolate, unappreciative, unfulfilled in response to the beauties and goods of creation but focused on what is not the case, which is the proper business of desire? "He that does the Father's will abides for ever." The will that has brought the world into being, and will sustain and redeem it, rules our responses to the world's phenomena. To fix our love and action upon the object of God's will is to engage in the world of God's creation *really*, and not in fantasy.

The preachers used to speak of "using the world," in which they included the "use" of suffering and disappointment. It is an old and now easily misunderstood mode of speech, which deserves to be relearned. Manifestly, "use" did not mean "exploit." Exploitation, as Augustine knew, is "abuse," employing a thing for what it is not, in order to serve some end that has nothing to do with it. Hannah Arendt's memorable example of the high-heeled shoe which may be put to service as a hammer without *being* a hammer, is an excellent illustration of exploitation. It cannot be good for the shoe as shoe, and is hardly efficient for hammering. Use involves recognition and appreciation, unfolding and exposing the potential of its object to serve the created order. To use the grasses of the field *for* grain to nourish us, to use the force and flow of accumulated water *for* energy, these undertakings reveal goods that belong essentially to grass and flowing water — not the only one in either case (what of the loveliness of waving grass in the evening breeze, the musical chuckle of the stream over stones?) but real and immanent goods, to be ignorant of which would be to be ignorant of grass and water. To use the pages of a theological book for toilet paper, on the other hand, as Gladstone discovered that his sister had done, is to *conceal* the significance of what they are, which is theology.[7]

This is all familiar ground to those acquainted with Martin Heidegger's great contribution to the understanding of modernity through technology.[8] Technology is a mode of approaching the world which has the power both

---

7. Philip Magnus, *Gladstone: A Biography* (London: John Murray, 1954), p. 84.
8. Especially in the essays, "Die Frage nach der Technik" and "Die Wende," trans. William Lovitt in *The Question Concerning Technology and Other Essays* (New York: Harper & Row, 1977).

to reveal and to conceal. Because it reveals so much, it conceals the fact that it also conceals. It discloses its object by "summoning it out" *(Herausfordern)* rather than "bringing it forth" *(Hervorbringen),* by "setting it up" *(Gestell)* rather than "setting it out" *(Darstellung);* it conceives it as a "store of resources" *(Bestand)* rather than as what it is in itself. And thus it exposes us to that "forgetting of being" which is the great danger of human existence. The sense of danger surrounding technological advance, the constantly contested nature of its progress, brings back to us a memory we are incapable of retaining by any other means, the memory of what we have forgotten.

To "use" things well is to reveal them for experience. "Experience is of what things are, not merely that they are," Jean-Yves Lacoste writes.[9] To experience "what" is to experience the *kind* of thing; to experience the kind is to experience the relation to other things, how like them, how unlike, how positioned before them or after them, its dependence, its independence of them, the service it renders them, the service it is rendered. It is, in short, to "order" a thing within a universe of possible and actual kinds of things and events. And as kinds are ordered, so are goods; no good is good solely in relation to its own kind, but in relation to other kinds, too, and so in relation to other goods. Goods are never "goods of" solely, but also "goods for." The lush green growth which means the health of grass is a good *of* the grass, but a good, too, *for* the sheep that graze it. Not a good *of* the sheep; their excellence lies not in greenness but in plump wooliness, but the excellence of the grass assists the excellence of the sheep. To be sure, goods inherent in inanimate objects are "goods for" without being "goods of": the hardness of granite is a good for us as we lay the foundations of a building, not a good "of" the rock — not in any sense, at least, that would make granite inherently superior to sandstone. When we have said that granite is better to build on and sandstone to carve in, we have said everything there is to say about that difference, but when we say that a well-fed dog is better for walking, a starved dog for frightening off intruders, we have not. A dog is a center of life and growth, as a blade of grass is, or a human being, and may flourish or fail to flourish; a starved dog is not a flourishing dog, however useful for certain purposes. By artifice we may devise instruments even with rational qualities that are "goods for" us without being "goods of" the instrument, e.g., computer memory, which is not the "good of" a computer in the way that memory is a "good of" a human being. But to know the kind of any thing is to know what "goods of" and what "goods for" constitute it.

9. *La phénoménalité de Dieu* (Paris: Cerf, 2008), p. 58.

To order is to account for how a thing is "for the sake of" *(propter)* other things. What is implied in that expression, "the sake of"? It is easier to say what is not implied. An act of *preference* is not implied. Preference is exercised over equipossible and still unrealized goods; it is a decision to realize one good at the cost of realizing another. It orders not *propter quid* but *pro quo,* not reflecting the relations of goods, but electing one. Nor is *instrumentalizing* implied. To make one good an instrument for the pursuit of another does not reflect the relations of goods, since an instrument is viewed not as the good it is, but reductively, in terms of its service to another good, and is therefore the pure case of exploitation. Loving one good "for the sake of" another is an act of discernment, which seeks out the ontological relation of the two and gives it a reflective expression in act. It answers a rational question about *what is important* about something, that we should love it. Not just "important to me, as it happens," but, as we say, "really important." The importance of things resides in their capacity to represent and reveal other things. The world of goods is joined up, and when we see one, we see others through that one. The one has a meaning in itself, justifying a particular action to realize it; at the same time it mediates a wider meaning, justifying us in devoting our lives to exploring and branching out from it. I may justify a visit to the city by the prospect of a pleasurable evening in a good restaurant, and nobody would think further explanation was required. But if I mentioned the restaurant as my sole reason for *living my life* in the city, I would be asked how it could be so important to me. Possible answers can be imagined — I have a business stake in it, I write books about cuisine, I have a love-affair with a waitress — but these simply show how the restaurant links me to a wider fabric of meaning, connects me with other and more encompassing goods. The human search for meaning moves from level to level seeking a more comprehensive meaning that justifies more, and the ordering of goods is an account of those levels of comprehensiveness.

The Order of Love

Here we must recall the great Augustinian principle that our experience of anything, the experience at once of "what it is" and "what good it is," is necessarily both affective and cognitive. The answer to the question, "What is to be known here?" cannot be disentangled from the answer to the question, "What is to be loved here?" Augustine's thesis did not stand on its own. It rested on the theological foundation that God himself was love, reaching out to reality that was not himself, and that all creation was ordered to the service of God and the human creation to love him. It had as a corollary that all human engagements with the world, foolish or wise, active or speculative, are manifestations of love. This thesis resonates through the history of Western theology and philosophy, and in the twentieth century came to mark the line of division between the philosophical tradition of the English-speaking world, with its tendency to divide affect from cognition, and that of Europe, which upheld the Augustinian claim for unity.

Popular theology likes the Augustinian claim, or what it understands of it. It likes to be told that the heart of everything is love, and that everything we suffer as evil will ultimately be disclosed as a strategy of love. It likes being told that when we love anything or anybody, we are a little bit godlike. What it does not like, though it is clearly entailed, is the idea of corrupt love corresponding to corrupt knowledge. It does not like sharing love with wickedness, admitting that it is capable of cruelty and brutality. It would like to classify the wicked as "loveless" and rule them out of the Kingdom of Heaven once for all, while it includes all lovers by implication. All of which avoids the force of what Augustine has to tell us about the naturalness of love, in the image of God though it may be, and its involvement with the worst as well as the best of human nature. There is a great deal to be said about love as self-sacrifice, love as the lifeblood of the church, love as the presence of God in the world, and love as the "more excellent way." But if love frames human actions from above, describing their highest limit and pointing beyond them to an end they would never envisage, so it frames human action from below, describing the line of departure for every engagement with the world and its contents.

That is why this exposition of faith, love, and hope engages with love not once, but twice. Love belongs with the variety of ends that human action may pursue; it belongs with the end to which God has purposed to bring all human action.[10] Love follows good as its formal object. God saw what he had made, and it was very good, and if anything God made is very good, then it is very loveable, even when it should not be loved or when something else should be loved more. Love spreads its energies as wide as knowledge itself. The question, "Of what kind is this?" always raises the question, "of what good is this?" Or, better, "What is the good that this is?" Every kind of being is a good, a distinct way of successfully being, as opposed to a simple failure to be.

---

10. So John Donne, in "Holy Sonnet 16," sees the "two wills" of law and grace as both summed up in love: "Thy lawes abridgement, and thy last command Is all but love."

Given the complexity of relations in which any given object of knowledge stands, we must impose a filter on any inquiry: *these* likenesses and *these* sequences, not others, are what engage our interest just now. Such selective investigations and interpretations have often proved a key to new discoveries, not only in the natural sciences but in the humanities, too. Investigative methods which select from reality are like probes reaching into caverns where common daylight does not shine. The only problem with them is that we may forget what they are and what they do, imagining that the information they bring back is truer, in some way, than what we perceive directly with our five senses. Among possible selective investigations are those that screen out relations of goodness, and trace sequences of events on a purely "factic" basis, isolated from the evidence of feelings and the consideration of goods and values. In so doing we discover interesting factual relations we would not otherwise have known about, but we may also lose sight of essential realities.

Consider potato blight, as someone has suggested, not as a *sickness of* potatoes, but as something that *feeds on* potatoes. The bacillus can be seen to occupy the same relation to its nourishment as the pigs do, or, indeed, as we do ourselves. Here is an analogy that is perfectly possible to pursue, and the student of microorganisms can, perhaps, tell us how it may be enlightening to pursue it. But that does not make this would-be value-free account of potato blight *superior* to one that remembers that potatoes, too, like other life-forms, can be well or sick. (We can speak of it only as "would-be" value-free, because "feeding" and "nourishment" are not value-free categories, and the whole appeal of the analogy depends on cashing their value: the blight has an appetite just like your child's!) The broader the range of phenomena we take note of, the easier it is to suppose that we describe reality as it "really" is, and that value has been set aside as an illusion. Such suppositions are not innocent. They cater to a very general human desire to have the universe delivered up to understanding without being asked to make commitments. In our time it is characterized by the appeal to a generalized notion of objective science, relying on measurements rather than feelings, which will forever relieve us of the need to make affective judgments of good and ill. The allure of the value-free is not hard to feel. But it is evidence of original sin. Those who make of science a modern priesthood — few of these are good scientists, since the practice of science encourages awareness of the reductive nature of experimental inquiry and consciousness of the virtues and values that underlie it — are the modern gnostics, the successors of those who liked to boast of the deep secrets of Satan.

Here, then, is an important distinction between different ways of know-ing, between (let us say crudely, since we lack the convenient distinction between *savoir* and *connaître* in French) "science" and "wisdom." Wisdom can never ignore what science can establish, but since its project is essen-tially holistic, it is necessarily affective, too. To conceive the pattern of the whole is to find cause for joy, the most profound and serious joy there can be. Correspondingly, to find serious cause for joy requires of us an effort to comprehend the pattern of the whole, for joy, as was known long ago by Plato, must be learned. Some goods are apparent and invite immediate affective response; they present themselves to us as goods *for us.* But many are hidden from our immediate grasp, and cannot be known until we have understood what they are goods *of,* and goods *for.* Only then can we begin to appreciate them as goods, in some manner and form, *also* for us — which is to say, to love them. Our knowledge and love of people often takes this course: those whom we most enjoy on first acquaintance disappoint us, and those whom we view with initial distrust turn out to be admirable members of their communities, whom we can learn to appreciate.

Suppose I am preparing to visit a country for the first time — let us say, Australia: I must set about forming a picture of "what it is like" in order to adopt the appropriate practical dispositions. I imagine a climate something like Southern Europe, an urban environment like North America, a popular culture reminiscent by turns of Britain, Ireland, and the Far East. And this imaginative knowledge carries with it affective and practical predispositions. I pack insect repellent and sunblock cream because I am afraid of the heat, and I study the finer points of wine and Thai curries because I appreciate the goods of food and drink. But I also try to learn of its history and higher culture: what its founding communities, aboriginal and immigrant, contrib-uted at the beginning, what they have received since, how its people comport themselves, what they worship, what they have heard and proclaimed of the Gospel. To know what Australia is like is not only to know how many miles it is from Sydney to Perth, but to have the right affective orientations to the continent and its inhabitants, to learn to value what most deserves valuing there, to fear what most deserves fearing. Without some such conception there is no answer to the question, "Where are you going?" That is how we participate in the whole we call "Australia," though none of us has actually seen Australia whole, but only small fragments of it.

And what can be said about Australia can be repeated *mutatis mutandis* of "the world." It commands something more within us than a bare cogni-tive capacity to register what is shown us. There is a secret to be entered, a meaning to be appropriated, an affinity to the agent-self we ourselves have been given to be, a promise that we are fitted for active existence within it. In finding the world given as a total field of knowledge, we find it to be an object of affective appreciation as a whole, not merely a container for specialized objects of appreciation. When the world's reality speaks to us, it speaks to us with a claim: knowable and loveable in itself, it is the context for knowledge and love of ourselves, of all other reality and of God. This is the claim made upon us by "Wisdom," the paradigm of realities that cannot be loved without being known or known without being loved. It tells us, "Take my instruction instead of silver, and knowledge rather than choice gold, for wisdom is better than jewels and all that you may desire cannot compare with her" (Prov. 8:10-11).

The unity of knowledge and love is a primordial unity-in-duality in our rational constitution, one we cannot possibly peer behind. It is not a simple sequence of cause and effect, getting to love what we have first come to know, or getting to know what we have first come to love. Failures of love and knowledge, similarly, are bound inseparably together. We speak of "false love," an affection misdirected to an object falsely conceived. We speak of "uncommitted" knowledge, which fails to appreciate its object. False love and uncommitted knowledge are not defective simply because they are incomplete. All our knowledge and love is incomplete; there is no total purchase on any reality in the world, only a partial coming to grips with it, which may, however, promise further discovery and encounter. But we may close down the possibility of further discovery, deciding that we have known enough of a thing. Such preemptive closure (which is what a "decision" is, strictly speaking) may be necessary for a range of practical purposes, simply in order to act. But a decision can leave us open and ready to go back and learn more. We can make it in the knowledge that our *status quaestionis* is a practical expedient, not the last word on reality. Or we can embed ourselves in the knowledge we have attained, making it, rather than its object, the focus of our love. And that is the love of the world that we are warned of.

Sin against the World

The refusal of the call of Wisdom is described by the biblical wisdom writers as *folly*. It is a sin that is possible only to those who were born to know and love, a failure to know what we love, and to love what we know, rightly. It is not a failure of natural capacity to know, but a failure to deploy that natural capacity well. There is a large number of things that every human being with a modicum of reason purports to know, and since such supposed knowledge is constantly put to practical use, much of it must be true on its own terms. Yet our knowledge of the world is not merely a matter of acquiring such items of knowledge. *How* we know them is the question. When Ethics asks this "how?" of knowledge, it is not asking the same question as epistemology, which also asks how we know. Epistemology has no concept of folly; its "how?" concerns the validity of our knowledge, "whether" we really know, and, if we do, whether we know that we know. Ethics addresses a different "how?" to knowledge, a question of our affective disposition in the construction of our world: how our many items of knowledge are formed into a truth of the world we can live by.

It is a truism that there are some things of which we are innocently and harmlessly ignorant. There is a difference between errors that "matter" and errors that do not. The contingent and isolated fact does not matter. If I forget the name of a town or confuse it with the name of another, the mistake may, by chance, prove costly if I drive in the wrong direction, but it does not touch the way in which I know the world as a whole. But wrongly joined-up facts, however particular they may be, can become mistakes in living my life. The scholastics had a famous illustration about a man who sleeps with a woman mistakenly believing her to be his wife; it is hard to imagine how this mistake could be wholly innocent, and impossible to think of it as inconsequential. False generalities are even worse. A mistaken supposition, for example, that all men are violent or all women irrational, will divert the course of our relations away from where it needs to run, cutting us off from truth and compounding falsehood.

Folly cannot be set down to *lack of good will*. Here, more than anywhere in the field of morality, the voluntarist thesis that the only good thing in the world or out of it is a good will, looks bankrupt. We who have just one chance at life, must get certain things right. If we don't, the question whether it was "our fault" is a meaningless one. Folly is an objective failure to live in a right relation to the world; by disbelieving some truths and believing some falsehoods we shall fail as human beings. Yet an earnest desire to know the truth of things does not, Christians believe, go unrewarded. If it is true that we are all entrammeled in error, it is also true that essential truths are made known to us by God, whether by natural or supernatural means. That is a statement of faith, of course, but it follows from the faith that God is self-revealing and wills mankind's salvation.

How, then, shall we describe the subjective aspect of "folly," the state of mind corresponding to objective error? An answer suggests itself: folly is the lapse of sustained attention. The love which holds the truth of the world for its object has become intermittent and fitful. This answer has to face an objection: though some errors are the outcome of inconsiderate and hasty attention, others result from persistent thought. The theoretical mind is by no means innocent. Yet we should not abandon our answer at the first check. Does not theory, too, fall victim to inattention? Must not love which holds the truth of the world as its object arm itself against theoretical bedazzlements? Let us recall two points that are by no means new to us. First, faith works through love, and love is the outworking of faith in the world, the self's emergence into the world from its origin in God's summons. Loving attention to the world thus clothes the self in worldly concreteness, situating it within the world it enters. Secondly, the truth of the self in the world is as a neighbored self, alongside another who is "like" self. Sustained attention to the truth of the world grasps hold of this elementary relation of self to neighbor.

Our moral imaginaries are formed through social communications, the process of synchronic tradition. Communications are sustained and qualified through receiving, retaining, questioning, and transmitting understanding. Heidegger, in his shrewd analysis of the "groundlessness" of "chatter," where "things are so because one says so," seemed to regard sociality itself as the danger, but here he displayed the pessimistic fatalism too characteristic of him.[11] Social communications require each one of us to be a neighbor to the other — neither a mere echo to the other, nor dictating what he or she shall think and say, but making the effort to offer what we may call "dialogical resistance." The point of view of the I emerges from what has been received from the We, and is fed back into the We again. "Dialogical resistance" is best understood as a kind of filter of individual discernment, allowing society's communications, as they pass through the minds and thoughts of its members, to be purified and refined, proved and confirmed. It is the universal condition of human thinking. "Our lips are our own," as the wicked say (Ps. 12:4), but when it comes to the words and thoughts they frame, our lips live on their imports. Failure of attention is failure of dialogical resistance, a failure to play the part that is irreplaceably ours in receiving, retaining, questioning, and transmitting. The failure to know the world is a social failure.

To engage in the common task of knowing is to recognize the authority

11. *Being and Time* 35, trans. John Macquarrie and Edward Robinson (Oxford: Blackwell, 1962), pp. 211-14.

that human communications have over us. Authority is recognized only by free moral subjects, who can, in the particular instance, recognize it or not recognize it; the generally misleading claim that authority is conferred by recognition claims its moment of truth at this point. But recognition is not without grounds. To recognize authority is to discover that it is grounded in reality. We recognize only what we think true, or authorized by truth. That is as true of politics — "They tell things the way they are," people say of their favorite political leaders — as it is of every sphere in which communication takes place. The disclosure of a fragment of reality that shines through something said or done commands our attention and belief, and so shapes our action. To recognize authority is to discern a reality accessed through what is communicated among us.

With folly, as with doubt, we shall take soundings across a spectrum. As at each point a false love of the world is paralleled by a false love of the self, so the various forms of folly are marked by forms of dread arising from self-dissonance, the inability to reconcile ourselves with the world as we understand it. Our first two samples lie before us at this point, the third and fourth to follow later.

(a) We speak in the first place of *inconsiderateness,* a lightheaded version of folly. The inconsiderate person acts on the world as it appears, and does not subject the appearance to reflection. Inconsiderateness is not pure immediacy. If one sees someone fall and rushes to the place, or if one ducks one's head as an object flies through the air, there is no space for reflection. But inconsiderateness is reflective to a certain degree. It imagines a *world,* which it constructs out of bits and pieces of experience, but the pieces have not been interrogated and ordered. The imagination has not undergone a communicative probing and confirmation. It remains as it is received, fresh with the dew of new affection.

Inconsiderateness is a failure to proceed towards self-contextualization. The spontaneous self projects its own world as, in Falstaff's famous phrase, "mine oyster." The tourists who crowd off their buses to beat the pavements of the great European cultural centers, led by polyglot guides holding their flags of identification aloft on the point of an umbrella, gaze at those who have business in those streets, the buildings which house them, the traffic which brings them to and from work, with unparticipating fascination, as though at interactive images on a screen. They could step into the path of a tram, expecting it to melt on contact. In absorbing and contemplating a world that confronts them as new, they cannot place themselves realistically within it.

We may call this form of inconsiderateness "complacency," using the final "y" to distinguish it from the "complacence," or *amor complacentiae*, which forms an important moment in admiration and worship. For the complacent person morality is a matter of occupying a point of view. The world and its affairs evoke affective knowledge, but it leads to no responsible thought about action. As from a seat in the theater or the football stadium it views the world and its affairs and enjoys the sense of being on the edge of them, as in Lucretius's famous example of those who watch a shipwreck from the cliff. Anger, sorrow, delight, amusement, all blend together to give us our world-experience, and we would not willingly be without any of them. We like to live life to the full, affectively, and pour our sense of agency into our tears and laughter, our manifold appreciations of the ebb and flow of events. These are allowed to play themselves out before us but are never held up to interrogation; they pose no questions as to their implication for the living of our lives, for the living of our lives has come to seem no more than simply the responses we make to them. Our knowledge of the world has, as it were, swallowed us up. Our satisfaction lies in deploying it, watching it, reflecting and commenting on it.

A poem by Rilke contrasts the fig, which fruits early in spring without blossoming, to trees which bloom luxuriantly and fruit disappointingly. The human race, too, produces only a rare man of action, he observes. For the most part "we tarry, ah! we are admired for our blossom! When finally we enter the belated inwardness of fruiting, it is a disappointment. They are few whose impulse to act mounts to such strength that they are ready, fully primed in their hearts, when the diversion of blossoming, like a mild evening breeze, stirs their young lips and eyelids."[12] The temptation is sketched erotically, but the eros in question is not sex; it is the love of beauty itself, the object of poetry, wisdom, and the affections as a whole. The "heroes" are those who "outrun their own smile," the smile of admiration that we lavish on the beauty that delays us. We ought, of course, to be cautious of the romantic glorification of action, plunging us, as the poet knows, towards danger and death. Action without thought and wisdom is not worth the name. Yet there

---

12. "Duino Elegies" 6:

> *Wir aber verweilen,*
> *ach, uns rühmt es zu blühn, und ins verspätete Innre*
> *unserer endlichen Frucht gehn wir verraten hinein.*
> *Wenigen steigt so stark der Andrang des Handelns,*
> *daß sie schon anstehn und glühn in der Fülle des Herzens,*
> *wenn die Verführung zum Blühn wie gelinderte Nachtluft*
> *ihnen die Jugend des Munds, ihnen die Lider berührt.*

is truth in this warning of a temptation to delay. Admiration absorbed in its object, positive or negative, is a position of innocent unselfconsciousness. It is attracted by works of art and objects of aesthetic appreciation, by drama, song, and sport, but it spreads its seduction wider than these formalized moments of pausing and looking on, which, precisely because they are formal, do not entrench on the sphere of our responsibilities. "Coming down from" the concert, the film, or the football match and setting about our business enriched by whatever rapture we have experienced there is a negotiation to be managed between imagination and practical reason. We can use up our strength in admiration, and fail to develop our admiration into grounds of action.

To a view that is wholly that of an onlooker, all that occurs begins eventually to assume a two-dimensional and tedious character. Spontaneity is paid for by boredom, and boredom by loss of resourcefulness. The human intelligence has only a limited capacity for simple admiration and wonder. "It's *déjà vu!*" we cry in response to each new challenge, to a snowfall, to disappointment in love, to a missed train. Emotional reactions of fear, anger, or resignation are indistinguishable in the one case from the next. And that is why the boundaries of immediacy are policed by dread. For as *reflective* knowledge, however short-winded its reflection, inconsiderateness cannot avoid knowing that its point of view is limited. It cannot escape the suspicion that the world it imagines is not all there is, and that something lies concealed from sight beyond its horizon. And since it does not reach out to inquire about it, the unknown becomes a threatening penumbra to the known, a foreign country of unnamable and irreconcilably strange counter-realities. This most immanent form of love of the world has dread as its constant accompaniment. We see it in young children, for whom loving one thing necessarily means hating another: a favorite teacher, a favorite food is always defined by reference to their opposites, the feared teacher, the loathed food.

(b) In reaction to the inconsiderate folly is the folly that would be wise — wiser than it was, wiser than the next person, wiser than the common run. There is a folly of *opinion,* which finds satisfaction, as the proverb says, not in understanding but in expressing one's mind (Prov. 18:2). Unlike the inconsiderate folly, this has exposed itself to the dialectic of social interrogation. But driven by a dread of having nothing to contribute to the social exchange, it allows society's exchanges to direct it, rather than the realities that they should be communicating. "Where we are now" becomes the sole measure of truth — always "we," never "I," for the voice is that of the immanent collective, not of a formed judgment. Here is the "simple" of the Prov-

erbs, who "believes everything" (14:15), and here is the "scoffer," who "does not like to be reproved" (15:12), the suggestible and the counter-suggestible, one echoing the current views and the other reacting against them, both wholly creatures of them, forming no judgment and offering no dialogical resistance. Opinion gains no coherence, and so has no prospect of growth. It is neither accumulative nor critical but reactive, a series of discontinued beginnings. A self too weak to interrogate or argue with the successive new reports of reality that reach it makes no contribution to communications by reporting its own experience or questioning others' reports. The mind is lively enough — images of the world and its doings are constantly formed and re-formed — but it is no more than a screen onto which public reflections are projected. Change of mind is no proof of independent thought; shifting assumptions are part of the music of time, and the leap from good principles to bad is as easily accomplished as the leap from bad principles to good. Forgetfulness can be as powerful an intellectual stimulant as discovery, but the change may be effected without probing or refining, without testing or interpretation.

The dialectic itself follows predictable currents. The phenomenon is familiar enough in politics: we assert things we know nothing about simply because those who deny them are those we habitually contradict. We speak of "moral attitudes" as "on the left" or "on the right." We cannot recall too often that these polarized postures are no more than habitual responses to the noise of discourse going on around us. They are not formed points of view about any reality, whether war, abortion, gay rights, labor unions, or anything else. Led by the Pied Pipers of the media we plunge into the caverns of imagination, framing our views on how the world may be put to rights and never giving thought to the fact that the world we are shown is a carefully constructed representation which demands interrogation. And so the reactions we form to it are no less "aesthetic" than those that respond to objects of immediate interest or beauty. The passions aroused by the news have a purely representative character, like those aroused by tragedy on the stage. Sharpening our arrows of opinion and firing them off at actors they will never reach, pronouncing judgments that involve us in no actual responsibility, we go through the motions of playing a part in the great communicative drama and so work off surplus active impulses before turning to the tasks that actually lie before us. We may, perhaps, feel more resolute about those tasks as a result of the exercise, but this is not the result of anything we have learned.

When from time to time we become aware that certain points of view have become fashionable, we should sense danger. We should know that complexities will be elided, so that even truths, when only partially grasped, will yield cruel and unjust implications. We should know that love of truth is corrupted (as Trollope's John Bold found) when focused on a narrow campaign. And we double our guard against the need of politics (not only democratic politics, but that, too) to rally the active forces of mass judgment around narrowly conceived agenda. "Is Saul also among the prophets?" they asked incredulously. One whose task it was to weld scattered tribes into a competent military union could have little space in his soul for the disturbing questions or unpopular challenges of the true prophet, but he could exploit its passionate urgency and authority to command. It is the fate of the politician to concentrate on programs of action that can ignite and unite passions. But the quantitative massing of judgments is inhospitable to exploration, and so betrays the truths it purports to champion. The best such politics can aim for is that someone with good judgment should mitigate the common passions; the problem of mass democracy is that simply arousing them becomes so all-consuming and competitive a business that no one with good judgment has much success at it. To take the commonest of experiences: a circular mailing arrives, telling of some shocking event or state of affairs, and a lobbying postcard is enclosed with a one-line message we are to send to our Member of Parliament or the Prime Minister. We are not told to inquire further into the situation; we are not told to refrain from judgment until we are in a position to make up our minds on the rival accounts that are given of it. We are encouraged, in fact, to model our behavior on what we most disapprove of in professional politicians, bending our ear to the latest lobbyist. To do otherwise, we are warned, is to be complacent. Ignorant passion is thus taken to be the special line of political amateurs, and we are encouraged to indulge it, leaving it to our cunning but indolent masters to work out what is to be done with it. They, meanwhile, declare their great respect for our ill-informed agitations, illustrating too trenchantly the old saying of John of Salisbury that whom it is permitted to slay, it is permitted to flatter.

Virtue

We return from the way we form our knowledge of *the world* to the way we find *ourselves* within the world. How, and where, do we see the good of *adam*? We see it in the lives of other men and women, wherever they are lived with such effect that we can appreciate them. Other human beings confront us as models; we have an interest in their achievements and sufferings, which are in some sense our own and invite us to make them our own.

It is in this connection that we speak of *virtue*. What is good for *adam* is also right for *adam*, and yet the sequence of good and right must be articulated clearly, not allowed to hurry on precipitately to obligations and decisions. To speak of virtue is to highlight the good as distinct from the right.[13] It is not first set before us as an object to attain, but as a model to admire. Something of this kind was intended by Jonathan Edwards's description of virtue as a kind of beauty.[14] Admiration opens us to the demands of human existence in general, but cannot teach us what will be demanded *of us*. We see goodness revealed in humanity as it is lived around us, we observe what human living and acting have been permitted to be, and we learn to delight in it. That is a condition, but only one condition, for our effective agency.

Delight in human virtue forearms us against too narrow an understanding of our own responsibilities, a preoccupation with decision-making that shrinks the moral field to a sequence of raw "situations," moral vacuums that suck our action into them by the claims they lay upon us. To see how a human life may take shape as a totality under the grace of God puts the decisions in perspective, the bad ones as well as the good ones. It allows us, moreover, to envisage ourselves as part of a moral community, in which other people's attainments, and not only our own, contribute to the good of what we do. This delivers us from the Levinasian nightmare of a moral "Other" who does nothing but lay claims upon us and take us hostage by those claims. We do indeed encounter our neighbors as laying claim on our service, but we also encounter them as those whose performance of human life has been accomplished without our help, and sometimes accomplished beautifully. Virtue is the service our human neighbors render us as guides and examples, helping us envisage our lives by living their own effectively, making sense for us of the moral idea of an achieved character, which in turn makes sense of the theological idea of the imparting of Christ's righteousness.

13. As was rightly observed by Robert Merrihew Adams, *A Theory of Virtue: Excellence in Being for the Good* (Oxford: Oxford University Press, 2006), p. 9: "Virtue is best understood as a kind of goodness rather than rightness."

14. The opening words of his Second Dissertation, "The Nature of True Virtue," run: "Whatever controversies and variety of opinions there are about the nature of virtue, yet all (excepting some skeptics who deny any real difference between virtue and vice) mean by it something *beautiful*, or rather some kind of *beauty* or excellency." *The Works of Jonathan Edwards*, vol. 8: *Ethical Writings*, ed. Paul Ramsey (New Haven: Yale University Press, 1989), p. 539.

In a well-organized discussion of Ethics, then, human virtue will have a definite place, alongside and complementing decision and action. Most ancient and early-modern discussions managed this bifocal perspective effortlessly. They deployed the language of the virtues widely, but not exclusively. There was no dedicated "virtue-ethic." Virtues provided the headings under which were ranged generic principles of deliberation: rules of exchange and contract under "justice," the obligation of promise-keeping under "faithfulness," and so on. Recent advocates of virtue-ethics, on the other hand, have more often than not championed virtue as a comprehensive approach to Ethics, hoping to correct a false preoccupation with deliberation. In doing so they have often claimed the wrong things for virtue. The deliberative approach, they have thought, was abstract and objective, virtue-ethics concrete and subjective. Decision-making distracted attention from who we are that act, whereas virtue could be relied on to purvey the "agent-perspective," and so on. But if agent-perspective and subjectivity mean seeing a given course of action from the point of view of the one who must decide and act, for whom the outcome of that decision is still indeterminate, that is exactly what talk of virtue cannot include. Its attention falls on the goodness the world has *already* seen and known. It shows us nothing that still lies, projected and undetermined, ahead of us. Virtue is not a law, not an "ideal," not any form of deliberative norm; it has no reference to a particular time and context we are assigned to live and act in, for what *we* are given to do or be is not revealed in what *others* have done and been. Talk about virtue is always third-person talk, observers' talk about deeds that have already taken determinate form.

Virtue belongs therefore to the content of tradition, the way in which our understanding of the world is formed; it has been a major theme in visual art and a constant structural element in narrative art. The work of tradition is the service by which "each one shall teach his neighbor and each his brother, saying 'Know the Lord!'" (Jer. 31:34). To know the Lord is to know what the Lord has done, the world he has made, the good he has set before mankind to realize. Our neighbors' service to us is to communicate the promise of our perfection contained within the course of the world and its history. Tradition involves representation: someone exists before me in a manner that communicates to me a secret promise of myself; someone is empowered to speak to me *of* myself and my destiny. But not empowered to speak to me directly, but only suggestively and indirectly, by speaking of human life in the world as it has been lived and is known. As the prophet knew, tradition must be superseded by direct knowledge.

There is another representation of humanity that we must put alongside that of virtue: the representation of human suffering. The two lie very close together in fact. Suffering is not a failure or degradation of man, which would make it a vice; it is an endurance of affliction, and the good of man is displayed through endurance, too. What we see in the suffering fellow-man is humanity crying out for a good it lacks, not humanity extinguished. Suffering is not a virtue, but it is, nevertheless, something accomplished, whether well or badly. A "Martyrdom of Saint Sebastian" may portray the suffering of death and the virtue of patience in one image, yet even where reflective patience is lacking, the struggle with oppression, pain, and death is still an accomplishment that may inspire us. "She fought bravely to the last!" the nurses report admiringly. The famous parable in Matthew 25 does not, as is sometimes said, invite us to see *Christ* in those who suffer; it tells us, in fact, that we shall not see Christ himself suffering, only our fellow-humans. Yet the humanity of those who suffer is the same humanity that Christ wore. That is the truth given to faith, the eschatological disclosure that frames and supports our recognition of the suffering fellow-human evangelically.

As with virtue, so with suffering: we can misunderstand what we are shown. We must be alert to the iconic character of representation, its reliance on formulae. The knowledge of ourselves that it offers us may be distorted in the way we appropriate it. The saint's moral achievement is not given for our slavish imitation; the sufferer's endurance is not given for our outrage. To treat them as though they were, is to make of them a tyranny quite as terrible as that of the uninstructed conscience. They are given us to open our eyes to the hidden dimensions of what we see about us, to interpret the good of man in ways that our convention-governed glance would otherwise pass over. These representative saints and sufferers offer us a kind of friendship at a distance — living their lives as we must live ours, but making us know that the world which contained such achievements and experiences invites and demands a serious effort on our part to inhabit it well. They are not to be imitated; they are to be loved, and learned from.

Since that friendship is offered us concretely through individual lives, those who encouraged the revival of virtue-ethics in recent decades were quite correct to turn at the same time to narrative. To grasp the meaning of an achievement or an experience we have to narrate it. But narrative is a discipline and an art. It requires a reflective moral culture, and the more serious the moral reflection in the culture, the more complex the art of narrating moral achievement becomes. The classic way in which the theme of virtue was pursued in Christian tradition was through biographies of saints, official and unofficial, focusing on their inner relation to God's calling. The emphasis on inner experience and personal ascetic discipline gave rise to a style of narrative which proved to be of critical importance for the West, influencing the rise of the modern novel as a comparable form of moral education for a mass public. Without this type of subtly inquiring narrative, uncovering the relational and spiritual springs from which the achievements flowed, tracing the growth of character, the overcoming of obstacles, the reconciliation of tensions, admiration of virtue could only focus on large effects, conforming to ancient wonder-narratives about Herculean heroes, or their Renaissance equivalents, the successful wielders of political power.

This should make it clear why talk of "virtue" quickly turns into talk of "virtues" in the plural. In using the singular noun we identify virtue as a historical moment, an extraordinary accomplishment in the life of an individual, unique and unrepeatable and therefore, of course, undifferentiated, since one unique departure from common patterns of behavior is, paradoxically, like another. In using the plural noun we recognize that there are forms and types, possibilities that can be known as such and differentiated. Francis of Assisi and Jeanne d'Arc both display "virtue," but resemble each other hardly at all, and nobody we admire from among our present-day contemporaries is likely to resemble either of them. Yet we can admire them both, distinguishing their contrasting virtues, and observing how each was of service to the social needs of their respective times and settings.

It is a point too little noticed in Ethics that the very language we use to name our virtues changes constantly. Each age creates a vocabulary of virtues (and vices) corresponding to the distinctiveness of its experience. Saint Thomas was aware of this, and so, together with each of the classical seven virtues, he discussed a range of contemporary virtue terms which he thought of as "parts" of the principal virtues. Our own age values "decisiveness," "flexibility," "competence," "decency," and, sometimes, "mateyness"; and if decisiveness is not a thousand miles from prudence, nor flexibility from justice, and if competence has something to do with fortitude, and decency with temperance, they are not *precisely* what was meant by those time-honored terms, but reflect ways in which the constituents of successful living have been reconceived in new contexts. When we encounter the virtue vocabulary of previous ages — "condescension," "honor," "deference," and so on — we tend to find it stilted and a little comic, as we do with their styles of dress. Our smirks betray a not unpleasant embarrassment at the changeableness of things, commonly exploited by the makers of historical period drama on television and film, who like to present bad characters as mockably dated, and heroes and heroines as modern before their time. Yet there is continuity enough to make past forms of badness and goodness recognizable for what they were, and "mateyness," after all, is in a direct line of descent from "condescension"!

There is another kind of pattern for human action, known long ago by Aristotle and often associated with virtue. We speak of "practices" to identify types of performance aimed at a specific good, involving operations deployed in various sequences to achieve various effects. An operation applicable to many possible practical undertakings, like cocking an ear to catch a slight sound, is not a practice. An action consisting of a sequence of operations in an invariable or an indifferent order, like plowing and sowing a field, is not a practice. Playing the piano and farming are practices. We can become skillful in them — not only in the sense that we can learn to do them efficiently, as one who has plowed and sowed all his life may get through a field at twice the rate his neighbors do — but in being able to deploy our knowledge of the operations intelligently and selectively, controlling the effect by varying pace, manner, or order, making wise decisions on what is needed when — what crop to grow on what field, what fingering will allow the melody to be heard over the accompaniment, and so on. "Dill must not be threshed with a threshing-sledge . . . but beaten out with a rod . . . Grain is crushed, but not too long or too finely . . . Even this knowledge comes from the Lord of Hosts, whose counsel is wonderful" (Isa. 28:28-29).

Practices are mastered by acquired skills, or "habits." The habit was, as Saint Thomas defined it, "the completion of a power," i.e., the extension of a capacity in time and effect by the learning of its operations. Acquired skills are plural; being master of one does not mean being master of all. But it has seemed to some that we may perhaps envisage a life as a whole as requiring a skill in deploying skills, and human virtue as a master-practice which, enabling us to know what is appropriate when, allows a creative approach to tasks that would otherwise be routine and slavish. Stanley Hauerwas has invited us to admire the disciplined skill of the bricklayer as an illustration of a morality acquired by training.[15] A skilled pilot who brought his plane and passengers to safe landing on the surface of the Hudson River captured the imagination of N. T. Wright as a model of acquired virtue.[16] What makes this thought attractive is that by stressing the intuitive and habituated nature of virtue, it offers a way of talking about excellence not simply as *acting* in

---

15. "How We Lay Bricks and Make Disciples," in *After Christendom?* (Nashville: Abingdon, 1991), pp. 93-111.

16. *Virtue Reborn* (London: SPCK, 2010).

a certain way, but *being* in a certain way. Saint Thomas spoke of the habit as an "abiding form immanent in the subject."[17] It carries the question of how we live back behind the act to the agent-self, and so delivers us from the fear of being bogged down in the externalities of practical thinking. "He is not a Jew who is one outwardly" (Rom. 2:28). And yet a skill is a habit learned in a tradition of performing the *same* operations in the *same* context again and again. It belongs peculiarly to limited performances, which afford scope for virtuosity precisely by their repetitive and predictable character. The piano contains the same number of keys laid out in the same way and producing sounds at the same frequency intervals by the same percussive mechanism. Were it not so, no pianist could develop a technique so fine that the keyboard seemed almost an extension of the hands. The pilot's skill is formed by endless repetition, using the same controls to get predictable responses in every condition of wind, visibility, and traffic. What makes these performances open to the display of skill is exactly what makes them different from living life as a whole: the expert is *on top of* the performance, and so extracts from it the ultimate that it is capable of yielding. Life is not like that. There is no range of repeated operations that give us all the necessary skills for it. The musician of life is expected, as it were, to pick up a different instrument each day and make music with mouth, lips, feet, and fingers, through holes in pipes, bows, and fretboards as well as keys. Those who purport to master the business of living confine themselves to narrow ranges of stock reactions to stock situations, failing to appreciate the sheer adaptiveness that life requires — something, perhaps, like Tolstoy's Alexis Karenin, whose virtues of tolerance, forgiveness, and official integrity are perfectly real, but who cannot extend himself to engage imaginatively with the situation of his wife's adultery. How should a successful civil servant respond to the loss of his wife's affection? How should an active manager comport himself when he has had a stroke, or a devoted mother when her children have died? These are not things to be learned *and then* practiced, as controlling a plane or playing a piano can be learned and then practiced. The "renewal of the mind" has to do with widening the horizons of understanding beyond the *praxis* and its habits, learning something by finding the unthought-of immediately demanded of one.

As there are patterns and types of all intelligible things, so there are patterns and types of human activities, of forms of human goodness such as courage, humility, wisdom, and compassion, and of the more specific forms

17. *Quaestiones disputatae de virtutibus* 1.1.

of human excellence developed by skills. There is enjoyment to be had in opening the imagination to these patterns, and observing them clash with the opposing patterns of malice, stupidity, and indifference, unskillfulness, and bungling. But the imagination tells me nothing of what forms I shall myself be called upon to imitate and perfect. The differentiated nature of the virtues reflects the differentiated character of the world and its events. The reason we do not all develop the same virtues is that we do not all suffer the same things. So moral reason cannot terminate in the acquisition of a virtue or a skill. It can begin, but not end, with reading biographies and novels, watching period dramas and admiring bricklayers or pilots. The figures I love and admire may turn out to be those least like myself, their qualities least like the ones I may perhaps come to represent to others. Contingencies of genetic inheritance, social environment, circumstance and opportunity shape my possibilities of excellence and failure. I must ask not only about the world of virtue and vice presented to me in narrative, but also about my time, and the particular opportunities for action it affords me.

This makes us uneasy; we fear it breaches human solidarity, we suppose we should all experience and do the same. Public communications fill our minds with uniform images and stimuli, a picture of one-size-fits-all virtue which does nicely for the indiscriminable citizens of a democracy. Yet even the most uniform public morality could not overcome variations of sheer contingency. We shall be what our future serves up to us, which will be different in each case. But what our future serves up to us will not be a blind fate, but an opportunity to glorify God, an occasion for life and action. That, at any rate, is the vast claim made on behalf of divine providence, a claim without which, perhaps, we might see no reason at all to devote further thought to what we are to do.

Prejudice

A self that merely observes and a self swept along by the ebb and flow of opinion: from these two failures of dialogical resistance spring the two forms of folly we have identified so far. But the social dialogue may be let down, too, by thoughtful and theoretically freighted communications. Our third sounding in the sin against the world takes us to the other pole, to a stiff-necked defensiveness which refuses the communication that human virtue offers, taking form as *prejudice*.

Prejudice may be thought of as knowledge on guard against the flux of immediacy, knowledge that is structured to sustain continuity in our sense of ourselves. It takes its departure from cognitive satisfaction — not only the satisfaction we find in the object known, but satisfaction in our knowing it. As there are places that evoke a sense of affinity in us — the way the stream sounds, or the gorse flowers, or the road curves round the side of the hill — , so there are truths which create around us an atmosphere in which we feel we can flourish. In such experiences of loving knowledge there lie greater earthly joys than any others. Imagination blossoms at the promise of a world we can inhabit. Taking hold of a truth like a cat stretching its claws, comfortable in its skin even when its object is no more than a ball of wool, reflexivity situates the self in the circle of its own knowledge — not viciously, for there is no knowing, as there is no loving, that is not self-aware — but perilously. The awareness of the self within the loved and known can shrink the imagined world to the dimensions of what is gratifying and reinforcing, confined to the circles where we have found our comfort zone, and on guard against whatever might point beyond it. The prejudiced inquirer is one whose interrogation has ceased to be led by its object. Thomas Aquinas has some penetrating observations about a *stupor,* or fear, aroused by "the unheard of," which stops us making judgments and asking questions.[18]

Prejudice has had its defenders of late, and they are not without arguments.[19] All claims must be tested for coherence, held up against knowledge we have already achieved or suppose we have; to that extent all claims must be subject to the point of view from which we have come to look upon the world. We have to select what we pay attention to, or we would go mad with the vast multiplicity of claims on our attention; our selection will inevitably be shaped by what we *have* paid attention to, and learned to find profitable in the past. We cannot constantly look upon the world as for the first time, nor would we learn much if we did. A point of view is not to be cast off like a caterpillar-skin for a butterfly existence that flutters everywhere and nowhere. Breezy and robust educationalists a generation or two ago used to rejoice at shaking students' beliefs, somehow believing they were making

18. *Summa Theologiae* 1-2.41.4: "*stupens timet et in praesenti iudicare et in futuro inquirere. Unde admiratio est principium philosophandi, sed stupor est philosophicae considerationis impedimentum.*"

19. This followed the influential lead of Hans-Georg Gadamer, as, for example, in his 1966 essay, "The Universality of the Hermeneutic Problem," in *Philosophical Hermeneutics,* trans. D. E. Linge (Berkeley: University of California Press, 1976), p. 9: "It is not so much our judgments as it is our prejudices that constitute our being. . . . Prejudices are biases of our openness to the world. They are simply conditions whereby we experience something."

them fitter for intellectual growth, but they were wrong; they merely de-skilled them for learning, and frightened them off inquiry. Losing hold on the world and seeing reality melt before one's eyes leaves one in no condition to learn anything. To learn is to integrate, and nothing can be integrated with a *tabula rasa*.

It would be better, perhaps, not to use the word "prejudice," for what is actually a necessary moment in the process of rational appropriation, the marshaling of presumptions that bear upon the truth of new claims. The offer of new insight cannot be tested and validated without questioning, and in order to frame questions we must draw on our acquired understandings. In locating these resources we lean on the instinctive presumptions that serve as landmarks to signal important perceptions lying below the surface of our memory. Yet how we frame those questions is all-important. We may frame them with an interest in what the new insight may be worth, or merely with a view to neutralizing it. We must start with a point of view, to be sure, but we may also come to acquire a point of view *on* our point of view. Objectivity consists in knowing oneself as knower, mapping one's point of view upon the world, understanding its strengths and limitations — not abandoning it, for that would be no more than an exchange of one stubborn point of view for another, but enlarging it.

At the heart of prejudiced knowledge is a refusal to accept the communication offered by human virtue. The capacity of another to do something well is what invites us to think reflectively upon our understandings. The virtue of another does not mean that he or she understands more than we do, but it may very well mean that there is something we have not understood. "How can one be so rational and still think this or that?" "How can one be so patient under affliction and have such little hope?" These are questions that presumption can frame either hopefully — there may be more to learn about rationality and patience — or dismissively. Prejudice is a refusal to receive the human communication, to learn from what our fellows can show us. That is what distinguishes it from real conviction, ready to venture forth from its affirmations to see what light they shed on the unknown.

The form of dread that guards the borders of our prejudice is *indignation*. Indignation differs from anger, as offence to the truth differs from offence to person or property, and that is why indignation may sometimes rightly claim the higher moral ground, for it may, indeed, find itself championing truth. Precisely because it has this important role, indignation cannot simply be avoided. The Psalter, as we know, is full of it, because the truth of God's good government is its main concern. Yet indignation may be inflamed into contempt of the world. The opposition between a private world of self-understanding and a universal world of public meaning can grow so sharp that destruction appears to be the only resolution that can vindicate the one against the other. The young jihadis who destroy themselves to show despite to a world that confronts them in arrogant indifference to the meaning they know how to live within, act out of love, to be sure. But it is a love that cannot receive and evaluate communications of good from the universal world of daily experience.

The only positive route to resolution of a well-justified indignation is wider and fuller appreciation of the providence by which God governs the universe. From Job to John of Patmos the indignant mind has been enabled to rise above its indignation to see the works of providence on a broader scale. Yet this must draw the indignant worshiper to recognize God's government of *his* affairs, too, precisely as an element of world-government. "Thou dost set them in slippery places" cannot be the last word; it must lead to "Thou holdest me by my right hand" (Ps. 73:18, 23). Providence is not a theory that explains some events by predicting others, but a disclosure of the greater things of which God is capable.[20] The gratification of seeing the moral order vindicated may not be snatched at too quickly; it must wait for God's reconciliation of the whole.

We flinch, and rightly, at the solemn predictions of Joseph de Maistre, the lonely exile discoursing through the summer nights at St. Petersburg upon the future of that storm of blood and terror which had spread from Paris to engulf his Savoy homeland and returned in double fury to the city again, of the coming defeat of revolution and the restoration of monarchy as God's assured ordering of the world.[21] His personal circumstances could have excused a waspish tone; the trouble is that he was so calm and lofty. His search for security in the vision of providential government became a way of standing back from the moral fate of the human race. And that is why his predictions, so strikingly fulfilled in detail, were so wholly wrong-headed in their longer tendency. The only acts of God he could imagine were those that recalled the past.

Complacent indignation, complacent because within the grand providential scene spread before its eyes it has assigned itself a secure position,

20. Note the fine remarks of Barth in *Kirchliche Dogmatik* III/3 §48. [= *Church Dogmatics* III, *The Doctrine of Creation,* Part 3, trans. G. Bromiley, R. J. Ehrlich (Edinburgh: T & T Clark, 1961), pp. 18-26.]

21. Joseph de Maistre, *Les Soirées de Saint Petersbourg,* in *Oeuvres,* ed. P. Glaudes (Paris: Bouquins, 2007), pp. 401-785.

indignant because it has clung to the self-reflexive moment and postponed the return to worldly action, is decisively exposed by Jesus' comment on a slaughter in Galilee and the collapse of a tower in Jerusalem: "Do you think that they were worse sinners than other Galileans . . . or more liable than other residents of Jerusalem? No, I tell you, unless you repent, you shall all perish likewise!" (Luke 13:2-5). What is *not* said here is that to see calamity as a judgment is mistaken. That would only be to reinforce the comfort zone, to make a reassuring world-picture even more reassuring. The point is, rather, that those who understand how calamity works judgment in this world must understand, too, that it is *their* world, and they are caught up in it. When someone close to us suffers a calamity, a difference opens up in our situations which pushes us away, even while we wish to rush forward with support. Because the calamity affects us nearly but differently, we find we have to struggle for perspective on our own account — the dilemma of Job's friends. And precisely for that reason we may step back, trying to bring what is opening up before us under control, instead of stepping forward to "weep with those that weep" (Rom. 12:15), risking the truth of ourselves in the truth of another's sorrow. There are, to be sure, moments in which we may take satisfaction in the evident justice of providence, but these are strictly qualified. We may stand on a high peak and marvel at the mountain ranges spreading for miles before us, watching in fascination as a storm lashes the sides of a distant valley while we remain in full sunlight — a fine geography lesson, and nothing amiss with it. But if we do not realize that the valley so afflicted is the one in which our own home lies, and recall that our roof has a tendency to leak, we are fools.

CHAPTER 5

Wisdom and Time

The Call of Wisdom

"Does not wisdom call?" asked the poet (Prov. 8:1). Nothing we have yet seen of love and knowledge and their mutual implication has equipped us to understand why it should. Our knowings and our lovings might be seen as simple facts about our relation to ends and kinds: we know what is good and we know what is what. But the order of value — the ends "for which" and the complex structure of "kinds" — does not exhaust the representation of reality. All that exists in the world conforms to the specific kind and end appointed it by God, not only for its essence, but also for its time. The world that offers us kinds and goods within a time over which they are distributed is hospitable to possibility. Possibility arises with time, and is conceived and realized only by creatures extended in time. The call of wisdom, then, is the call of the world's temporal openness to knowledge, a call addressed to our powers of living through time. If that first call by which God commands our agency takes form in instantaneous movement as we cry, "Here I come!" this call extends that moment into world and time, revealing us to ourselves as susceptible of realization and growth within a temporally distended world.

The reality of the world must thus not only be known and loved, but learned and sought. The call to learn the world is, of course, a call of God; it echoes the creator's will for us as expressed in his creation. But — here again is the difference from that first call — God's call reaches us only *through* the created world and as we are participators in it. It is addressed to "man," the bearer of God's image, entrusted with worldly dominion in knowing and loving, but it reaches us as the call of Wisdom, who was, in the ancient poem, first of the creator's acts and stood beside him like a master-workman (Prov. 8:22, 30). Whatever Christological extrapolation we may legitimately make from that, we must not miss the most obvious truth, that created order itself is not without a voice, but has the resources to call us.

The call of wisdom is an existential condition, not an episode. What sense, then, can be made of the blessing pronounced (Prov. 3:13) on one who *finds* wisdom? To "find" it is to attain a decisive purchase, to achieve a position where it is at one's disposal. The poet of wisdom summons us to "turn in" to Wisdom's house, to eat and drink of our hostess's provisions (9:5). There is a point of arrival to be looked forward to, a point of purchase on the world's order. If Wisdom always presents herself on the horizon of possibility, our arrivals cannot be final, but we should not make the mistake of skeptics in every age, supposing that if we cannot know with finality, we cannot know at all. That would be to impose an abstract ideal as a condition of our knowledge, a condition irrelevant to our temporal situation, making the knowledge actually available to us disappear. Knowledge is offered us, knowledge suited to our pilgrim condition. Were we invited only to endless inconclusive speculative questionings, wisdom would be of no practical importance to us, for success in life and action depends on our knowing where we are when we form purposes. But though the road of wisdom stretches indefinitely far, the hostelries beside it are frequent and well-provisioned. The knowledge "found" on the way of pilgrimage is neither ignorance nor speculation. It is valid within its own conditions, makes real contact with reality, allows us to attend to what is of ultimate and penultimate importance. God has "put eternity into man's mind," as Qoheleth declared (Eccles. 3:11).

Understanding is what Charles Taylor christened an "imaginary" — not meaning that it is fictional, but that objective reality is held in our minds in a manner that we never immediately perceive it. We do not have a front and rear view of a house at one time; we look first from this side, then from that, and yet this does not stop us imagining the house as a whole with reasonable clarity. The mind is not restricted to a succession of perceptions like a cursor tracing readings on graph paper. It forms representations of interlocking relations that constitute a whole. False steps may be taken by the imaginative intelligence, but these do not invalidate its work as a whole. To any contact with reality the imagination is a necessary intermediary. It may do its part with greater or lesser success, more carefully or more indifferently, and we may doubt what it tells us in this case or that. But we cannot doubt *it*.

We find, in order to seek again. Further pursuits, further searches will lead to further "turnings in" to Wisdom's house. We cannot settle down in our ideational constructions, just as we cannot make our home in a wayside inn. We achieve a grasp on the world as a whole, but the world as a whole does not remain quiescent in our grasp, but slips away and calls us to look further for it. But it is not fruitless, this framing of imaginative pictures, this venturing of theories and articulation of doctrines. Each finding leaves us with something further to help us with further pursuit. There is no ground here for anti-credal or anti-dogmatic postures, nor for the idle notion of a *tabula rasa,* beginning the whole inquiry after wisdom from the beginning again. Here, if anywhere, the language of "progress," so easily abused, is in place: where we can get to depends on where we have come from, both we ourselves and others into whose tradition of inquiry we have entered. Progress in knowledge is consistent growth in understanding, expansion of the scope of what we see and of our competence to see it. It is not accumulative and not deductive. We do not simply pick up more and more pieces of knowledge, but integrate what we learn with what we have known already. Neither do we simply draw consequences from a conception fully formed from the beginning. The framework of order can only be imagined as the framework for new concrete perceptions, and new perceptions can only be interpreted within a framework of order that unifies and situates them.

It may seem that progress leads from subjectivity to objectivity: emerging into the wide world like a butterfly fighting free of its chrysalis, we shake off the self-centered perspective and begin to see things as they really are. But this is a misconception. Objectivity and subjectivity are necessarily co-present in knowledge. On the one hand, pure subjectivity is not knowledge; it is only feelings of pain, joy, and so on. The most self-referential knowledge we can imagine must encounter an object, even one no more remote than a mother's breast. On the other, the idea of an objectivity won by leaving subjectivity behind is a chimera. Knowledge becomes no truer, only more superficial, if it discards subjective awareness. The favorite paradigm of objective knowledge, experimental science, is not in fact attained by the investigators' forgetting themselves, but by their being more sharply aware of their own intrusion upon the object studied, so that they allow for the effect this must have on what they see. Progress in wisdom advances in objectivity and subjectivity together. Someone who has learned, as the saying is, "to get in touch with her feelings" has learned something objective as well as something subjective, something about the modes of perception given to human beings as well as something about her own affective perceptions. Someone who has learned to keep a distance on conflicts that do not concern him has learned something about self-control, not only about other people quarreling.

There are, nevertheless, qualitative distinctions that may mark a progress towards wisdom. One is when we begin to reflect in an ordered way on *relations* among facts and events. All knowledge assumes relations — causality, contingency, succession, necessary implication, generic likeness and difference, etc. — but not all knowledge systematically questions them. For ordinary uses knowledge is content with just those relations that give form to facts of practical significance: if I know that certain symptoms give warning of the onset of an asthma attack, I can leave it to the specialist to wonder how genetic and environmental factors coincide in the causation of asthma. The systematic interrogation of relations may be seen as the distinctive function of science (in its widest construction). But among the relations that connect phenomena there is one that does not emerge immediately as presented to us in the world, but requires a reflective interrogation to notice and describe: the relation of knower to known. It is when that relation and its conditions are explored that we begin to reflect also upon ourselves, as knowing subject and known object simultaneously. "How is this known?" becomes "What may we know?" and so holds up to critical exploration the viewpoint from which we survey the world. Systematic reflection on this relation is what peculiarly distinguishes philosophy.

Seeking

We turn from finding to seeking. If wisdom's call can be a call *to knowledge,* how can knowledge be offered to us *as a call?* We cannot know what it is that we are still only called to know. It does not solve this problem to say that to know is also to love. For the mutual implication of love and knowledge conceives the object of the one and the other as the same object. Such a love — which we have characterized as "admiration" — stretches us only as far as knowledge goes, and no further. But now we encounter a love that seems to stretch out ahead, beyond knowledge. What is it that we love in responding to a call to know what we do not know? An answer may be reached through two concepts, both identifying variant forms of love, which describe, as it were, concentric circles around the question: desire and eros.

With time there figure in our view events of beginning and ceasing, things made to be where they were not, and unmade where they were. Desire we might describe as the love of possibility, love's focus upon anticipated future time, attending to what is possible but not yet actual. Desire does not know the future as it will transpire, but it comprehends a certain dynamic interplay of possibilities that gives anticipatory shape to a thought of the future. Yet because the possibilities are many times more numerous than what is actualized, and incompatible possibilities constantly occupy the imagination together, desires, too, may be multiple and inconsistent. We desire glory and we desire a quiet life; we desire wealth and we desire freedom from material responsibility; we desire intimate relations and we desire to be alone. That is why desire is the form of love most characterized by disturbance, since every possibility has counter-possibilities attached. Time is disturbing to our love of the world's good order.[1] And disturbance yields to sorrow when alternative possibilities overwhelm and extinguish the possibility we love. The element of sorrow was what made the Stoics take offense at desire; the wise man, they thought, had only "will-acts." It was a profound mistake. Sorrowing love before unrealized possibility is an essential element of our agency in time. It has a role in moral reflection on the world, preparing us for deliberation which will identify the one possibility that points the way to action.

Desire is the opening of love to time's distribution of created goods. Viewed atemporally, the world is the best of all possible worlds, the ensemble of all the good that God makes and does. Viewed temporally, these goods are no longer, or not yet, or not all at once. The tension between a conceived perfection of God's work and its distributed actualization, the distinction, as it is misleadingly called, between the "ideal" and the "real," is signaled by desire. In this nothing is yet said about a "fallen world." The distribution of goods over time does not mean that the world is *not* the best of all possible worlds, merely that the excellence of the temporal world is not a simultaneity, but allows for the play of succession and possibility. The natural order as we encounter it at its simplest has a cyclical character, undoing and remaking, manifesting itself diffracted through seasons and generations. "Fair daffodils, we weep to see you fade away so soon!" we sigh, well aware in fact that a world where daffodils never faded would be a chaotic world, not the ordered world of God's creation. Desires are plural and differentiated. We move from one to the next, and the satisfactions compensate by and large for the disappointments. The sorrow that accompanies desire is aroused by finitude, not by evil, and in itself it is not evil, but open to anticipated consolation. After

---

1. On which see the searching discussion of Jean-Yves Lacoste, *Être en Danger* (Paris: Cerf, 2011), pp. 283-301.

the daffodils there are the azaleas. Disturbance and striving, the sense of things coming and things going, belongs entirely to being alive.

Bringing moral reflection to bear on the evaluation of our desires, we distinguish good from bad, selfish from unselfish. But whether they are one or the other, they are ours, and they make us aware of ourselves as temporal beings, disposing us to an anticipated future. They do not make us agents, for the satisfactions they look for may have nothing to do with action, but simply with events: a fine day, a buoyant stock market, or whatever. Many are banal and obvious, tied to the warp and woof of the material and social setting of human life; what we desire is what hundreds of millions of others desire, what human beings can hardly help desiring. Just for this reason desires are a temptation. They make us average, indistinguishable, and so divert us from the path of faith and obedience and trap us in those anxieties — what shall we eat? what shall we drink? what shall we put on? — which Jesus commands us not to entertain. What we desire, we think good, but we can be deceived, desiring evil while thinking it good. Even unambiguous goods may not be the *right* things to desire, right for us, that is, here and now. God is more ambitious for us than we are for ourselves. He did not redeem us to make us indistinguishable and average. And so we need to pray, with the Easter Collect, that he will put into our minds "*good* desires."

It was one of the many confusions of that once-fashionable typology of love which contrasted outgoing agape with self-referential eros, that the simple naturalness of desire was lost sight of, swallowed up in erotic love. Eros is a specially heightened case of desire. Much desire, including much that is passionately felt, is not in the least erotic. Political desires, for example, had better not be entangled with eros, which can only confuse the perception of justice. The distinction between desire in general and erotic desire in particular turns on the place that the self occupies in the object. Though all desire is *our* desire, and so has an indirect reflexive reference to what will satisfy us, the object of most desire is simply what will happen, not what will happen to us. Eros is different. Typically, the good it attends to is *present* good, one that appears to us now, but when the present good makes us aware of future possibilities for ourself, love acquires its erotic character as an inward opening to future self-realization.

Routinely reminding ourselves that eros is by no means always interpersonal, let alone sexual, let us recall some further propositions we have already touched on.[2] Love is the affective recognition of a good; a good is

2. *Self, World, and Time*, pp. 112-19.

recognized as good in itself and as good for other things, a contributory strand in the web of communication that constitutes created good; as a reflective knower of the world's good, I can find what is good for some other thing good "for me, too." On one side of this territory love excludes the bare recognition of utility. Utility may certainly be among the aspects of a good we recognize, but if we think *only* of its usefulness, we have not thought of it as good in itself. On the other side love excludes the total indifference to self, the supposed "pure love," which would require us to occupy a position outside the communicative web of created good. An object is not loved if its good is not allowed to bear on us. Only God as Absolute, we might say, could love without self-interest; but even that statement must be balanced by the corresponding one, that only God can act solely for his own glory.

Within the range these two limit-cases describe, we may love with a greater or lesser sense of the object's significance for our own being. That may be confined to the margins of our attention, or it may impose itself on us intensively. We may thus distinguish two different tones of love, not absolutely opposed but at different ends of a spectrum, one confidently absorbed in its object, the other weighted down with the feelings that its object arouses. We shall make no sense of this spectrum if we forget that love is cognitive as well as affective, that every love measures a relation, in which the loved object figures as one term, the loving subject as the other. Erotic love is marked by powerful self-awareness. It is not the only love that is so: there is also the love of gratitude, in which the self counts on its assured position as a gift of the beloved. In erotic love the self is filled with a sense of its possibilities, a consciousness of future self-development that may spring from encounter with the present good. Here is the object of that disturbing desire associated with eros, the desire for fuller self-expansion.[3] In erotic experience we discover our own future opened up to us by the recognition of the good. The object of our love is not ourselves, but the other. Yet the longing which accompanies love for the other is directed to a larger and fuller self: possibilities for constructive action, for creative performance, for enjoyment, for growth of various kinds. The horizon of erotic aspiration is to *live in relation to* the good that excites it, to expose itself to its influence and shaping power. Plato conceived it as the goal of eros "to give birth in beauty."[4]

It was another mistake to accuse eros of an inherent possessiveness.

3. The point is helpfully made by Ralph D. Ellis, *Eros in a Narcissistic Culture* (Dordrecht: Kluwer, 1996), in opposition to drive-reductive theory.

4. Plato, *Symposium* 206 b 7.

Among the various concrete desires eros may give rise to in any case, there may be a desire to possess, and this, like any other desire, may or may not be well conceived. If on my walks I see a large and beautiful historic house set in a fine park in quiet and beautiful countryside, I may feel a desire — hopeless, but strong enough to disturb — to own the house and live there. Three minutes' reflection on the maintenance costs, the incommodities of so much domestic space and parkland, the inaccessibility of the location, ought to persuade me quickly enough that this desire is mere confusion of mind. I could get no more real satisfaction from the house by owning it or occupying it than I do when it makes the highlight of a favorite walk. Having got the better of an absurd possessive desire, I may then retain an erotic love for the house, walking that way often, finding the best viewpoint, learning its features and its history, taking photographs, painting pictures, writing poems about it. The house may become a powerful good "for me, too" — as well, that is, as for other walkers in the vicinity, as well as for those whose interests fit them to live in it, as well as for those who will enjoy seeing my photographs. There is a difference, though: in me the good of the house has aroused an erotic creativity, while those in other relations to it find their satisfaction in less active ways. My recognition of the North and South Poles as "good for me, too" is not erotic: my imagination is satisfied with the vaguest picture of their icy wastes and a bar or two recollected from Vaughan Williams's *Sinfonia Antarctica*. I am grateful for the part the poles play in supporting the temperate climate I enjoy, but I have no desire to visit them.

Philosophical and literary tradition has long conceived eros as the typical response to beauty of every kind. Any object in which it is plausible to find an opening for self-expansion we may find beautiful, because beauty concretizes the awareness of created goods in a particular conjunction of sense and imagination. Erotic desire is famously felt for people, but not only for people. It is felt for places: "Country roads, take me home, to the place I belong." It is felt for images and narratives of times past: Sir Walter Scott was among the masters of the erotic in Western literature. Most important for the argument we have in hand, it is felt for wisdom and understanding. We may "boil with eagerness for wisdom," according to Augustine.[5] But as with all other forms of love, eros is qualified and accompanied by the other tones and moods that love commands. Love of wisdom includes the grasp of some definite body of knowledge, the laws of classical economics, the interpretation of the Epistle to the Romans, the mapping of the genome, or

---

5. Augustine, *Confessions* 6.11.18: *fervere coeperam studio sapientiae.*

whatever, in which our simple admiration for the object permits us to forget (though not to lose) ourselves. But it also implies an erotic sense of the vast and unmapped universe of reality, which continues to call us and make demands upon our understanding that we have yet to rise to. There is a "desire" for wisdom, for the possibilities it offers us of being larger-minded than we are. It is a tense situation metaphysically, erotic love with its imperfect vision, oscillating between the givenness of its object and the ungivenness of what the object promises. One moment we want to settle down with a representation of the world and treat it as final, the next we are tormented by what is lacking, snatched away from our desire to be fit for God's creation by importunate desires for "hidden knowledge," desires that turn us away from the world we have been given in disgust.

Ideology

It is the world we are given to know and love, not a representation of the world. Our imaginative representations are not the realities. As the wiser among the Thomists knew, a mental representation *is* a love of the world, not the *object* of that love. It is the real world we love, not the imagination.[6] If allowed to, reality will correct and renew our imaginations. What we have to guard against is a representation entrenched in our minds, a "subjective object" that stands between ourselves and reality, blocking the view. Here is that "love of the world" against which we are warned, as "what the flesh desires, what the eyes desire, what the vulgar world boasts of" (1 John 2:16). That is how the attribution of meaning is thrown open to the danger of idolatry. The worship of false gods does not begin with the innocent mental labor of framing theories, finding explanations and forming anticipations on the basis of them, but with what Gerhard Sauter nicely calls the "immeasurable and arrogant positing" of meaning.[7] Meaning must have a perceptual and question-generating character. The search for connections is an open search, and theoretical positions are subject to the censure of reality.[8]

6. Gabriel Vasquez, *Prima Secundae S. Thomae cum Commentariis ac Disputationibus* (1604) 1.1.2.2: *"illud esse objectivum, quod est bonum apprehensum esse objectum ipsum formale voluntatis, sicut color est objectum formale visus, ac si cum Logicis diceremus, conceptus objectivus, in quem fertur voluntas, est ratio formalis objecti."*

7. Gerhard Sauter, *The Question of Meaning*, trans. Geoffrey W. Bromiley (Grand Rapids: Eerdmans, 1995), p. 150.

8. Sauter, *The Question of Meaning*, pp. 151, 133.

Here, then, we make our fourth sounding in the sin against the world. There is an inversion of eros which exchanges the promise of the object for a form of truth comprehended within the practical demands of a public order. In a word, "ideology," which closes off inquiry in the interests of stable harmony, transgressing the limited capacity of any political order to determine wisdom. Political eros is dangerous because it focuses our aspiration to wisdom upon worldly structures that are necessarily imperfectible. It offers us a concrete answer to an existential question, and such an answer, if taken seriously and not as a kind of licensed insincerity (such as often surrounds political discourse), violates the human capacity to question and transcend. Political order is ordered to public judgment, which is a cutting off of questions, a closure of what could fruitfully be explored further.[9] Judgment is essential to secular life and public order. Like death, it must be viewed as one of the nonnegotiable conditions of mortal life. Like death, however, it cannot be viewed as a fulfillment; if we confuse the two, treating the negative as though it were positive, the penultimate as though it were ultimate, we inflict unbearable oppressions on ourselves and others.

Every age has had its deceptive gnosis. "The source of unchastity is the conception of idols," said the wise man (Wis. of Sol. 14:12), and ancient Judaism and Christianity generally criticized the corruption of knowledge for social uses through the category of "idolatry," the objectifying of the sacred through a cultic object. "Who is there that does not know," as Saint Luke reports the wily Ephesian town-clerk as saying, "that the city of the Ephesians is temple keeper of the great Artemis and of the sacred stone that fell from the sky? Seeing then that these things cannot be denied, you ought to be quiet and do nothing rash" (Acts 19:35-36). But even in a society of objectless, word-based religion it was apparent to Israel's prophets that such a pretense of knowledge could take hold. One of Jeremiah's most trenchant polemics (23:16-40) directs the critique of idolatry back upon the prophetic class itself, which propounds an optimistic political gnosis based on visions and dreams. "Am I a God at hand, says the Lord, and not a God afar off?" he asks, exactly reversing what we might expect, a proximity of God to prophetic knowledge and of prophetic knowledge to God's purposes. Unless we have reckoned first with the vast distance that separates God's sight from what we see, we shall not even recognize immediate revelation when it is given us. It would be oversimplifying, then, to attribute modern ideologies to the remnants of a Christian conviction that truth alone could gather all from

9. On this see *The Ways of Judgment* (Grand Rapids: Eerdmans, 2008), 18-30.

every place into the City of God. Christianity had learned from the Hebrew prophets that claims to truth were of many contested kinds, and the notion of a society held together by its *own* truth, independent of truths attested by saints and martyrs, and held together by a *truth of science* rather than a truth of common life, has some affinity with the ancient gnosticisms that it rejected. Yet it is probably true that by discounting the bonds of kindred and race as political constituents, Christianity left the modern age with an outright choice between faith and gnosis as a basis for society. The ideological society is fueled by its own dread of the freedom of faith, which it cannot distinguish from arbitrariness, preferring the illusory freedom that a mechanized world-order can confer.

When Heidegger spoke of the modern era as "the age of the world-picture," he had in mind the role of natural-scientific interpretations of reality. But the distance between the scientific and the political is, as his disciple Erich Voegelin understood, not great. A "scientific" world-picture structures thought around abstract hermeneutic keys, affording a unified and encompassing view of reality apt for social uses. "What the vulgar world boasts of" is a representation that seems beyond question, ensuring basic agreements and common endeavors. The endless political contests of late-modern democracy depend upon just such a world-picture, every government ministry, every opposition party lined up with its own team of scientists and statisticians. Yet if it is science that provides the ultimate justification for the world-picture of late-modernity, it is not science *as a practice of inquiry,* the forming and testing and improving on hypotheses, but science *as a dogmatic system,* offering us certainties we should never presume to question.

Repentance at the beginning of knowledge and the vision of God at the end are the conditions on which we may be protected from the force of eros in framing political ideologies. One sometimes hears ridicule heaped upon liberals who, while denouncing ideology and credal rigidity, fall into the pit they have dug and impose rigid doctrinal standards of their own. We have not criticized such ideological contortions successfully until we have exposed the character of ideology as such, which finds in doctrine the promise of political stability and expansion. Political reason cannot be insulated from the collective yearning for strength and security. The "liberal's dilemma," then, which is how to uphold truth definitely but modestly, is every serious person's dilemma, and specific to liberals only in that they are historically guardians of the memory of once having found the political-erotic deeply troubling. Renouncing Thrasymachean boasts of the interest of the stronger, they acknowledged the duty of political institutions to perform justice impartially. But truth under conditions of impartiality is a circle that cannot be squared, unless truth can adopt a missiology shaped by patience, respectful of the eschatological "not yet." In the harsh solvent of a materialist metaphysic, liberalism is a disappearing creed, overcome by tensions that it formerly knew how to balance within a framework of faith. In its place arises the late-modern idea of a public truth maintained by constitutional *fiat,* the secularism of a society that prides itself on "knowing the science." This route, first seriously explored in Western society by Lenin and his admirers, can never arrive at a liberal evaluation of truth, which was founded on the knowledge that the fear of the Lord was the beginning of wisdom.

No one in Christian antiquity articulated with more clarity than the young Athanasius the peculiar perils of collective doctrine.[10] Reluctant to concede a place even to such a systematizing exercise as credal theology, he allowed it solely as an apologetic aid; the interpretation of Scripture was alone enough to tell us all we needed to know about the shape of the universe. "Idolatry," i.e., polytheism in its variety of representations, was the form in which intellectual overreach presented itself to his age. But idolatry was not the original error, he thought, but the consequence of a more profound doctrinal falsehood, belief in the independent reality of evil. Once we conceived of a real existence apart from the good creation of God, there was no avoiding confusion of the unreal with the real. The human soul, no longer directed to its transcendent end, contemplation of the Word of God in whose image it was made, lacked criteria to judge reality by. The fate of an idolatry, then, even in an apparently reductive materialist form, was to invent unreal reality, assigning substance to what in fact had none. Even the soul's desires could be reified to become the objects of belief, an observation which suggests that Athanasius would hardly have been surprised by anything Freud might have taught him.

Yet when these warnings have all been heard, the satisfying whole, the totality that accords meaning to the variety of elements and the particular experiences within it, is not an imagination projected on the world by a Promethean self-aggrandizement or by slavish religion, but is offered us by the creator. God did not create a world of disjoined and unrelated moments, but one tied together as a whole in a multitude of ontological and temporal relationships. Symbolic representations of the whole may go astray, but we cannot do without them, for conceiving the whole is a power of mind with which our human nature is endowed, and it needs to be taught and learned

10. *Contra Gentes* 1-7.

well. Christianity, it has often been said, has its own "worldview," its account of the whole. Did not the great Karl Rahner occupy a university chair in "Christian Worldview"?[11] If we accept this terminology, we shall need to make the clearest distinction between the way in which such a conception functions and the socially cohesive function of the idolatries and ideologies of the world. The Gospel offers a central and normative focus of joy, the resurrection of Christ, which becomes a torch to illumine the goods of the world, a vantage point from which we can explore, discover, and appreciate all other objects of joy. And when false imaginations of the world are overcome from this vantage point, the world that God made is made new for us, and offers itself to new adventures of love and knowledge.

Augustine's sketchmap of the objects of love, based on Jesus' double love command, is extremely spare: the self with the neighbor alongside the self; below them the human body, to be used and loved for self and neighbor's sake; below the body, other worldly objects indifferent in themselves, not to be loved but to be used for self and neighbor's sake; above all, alone to be loved for his own sake and all else for his sake, God.[12] Complex relations that arise among spirits, bodies, and inanimate things are left out, and it can reasonably be asked where non-human animals belong. But its simplicity has an important critical function. The word of God, Saint Paul tells us, has "made the wisdom of the world foolish" (1 Cor. 1:20). Though the pattern invites elaboration, we are not to forget that such thinking is exploratory, and that beyond that elemental framework we have no privilege of holding this or that scientific or metaphysical construction of the world to be irreplaceable. "Now I know in part." If we presume to speak of a worldview formed in faith, it must be of something different in spirit and manner, not only in detail, from the intellectual pattern-making of society. The neo-Calvinist thinkers of the twentieth century who promoted the "Christian worldview" under the influence of the Dutch thinker Herman Dooyeweerd had the resources to express the independence of knowledge against civil pressure by emphasizing a plurality of spheres of knowledge held together transcendentally by Christ as the Lord of each, though it must be said that their preoccupation with the organization of sciences allowed too little place in their worldview for the love of the good. Operationally this vacuum of moral direction left

11. Though *Weltanschauung* would be better translated as "world-onlook." The German distinction between an *Anschauung* and a *Bild*, "picture" or "model," is sadly lost sight of in the standard English term, "worldview."

12. *De doctrina Christiana* 1:22-26.

room for the return of civil conformity in the form of a political pluralism with which the sovereignty of Christ had little to do.[13]

Should we prefer, then, to speak of a Christian "axiology," or "theory of value," which corresponds rather better to the doctrine of love in Augustine's *De Doctrina Christiana?* Against a theory of value in its proper place (which is within a science and specifically within the science of Ethics) there can be no objection, once ambiguities surrounding the use of the term "value" have been cleared up. "Axiology" is a possible description of what we are pursuing in this chapter. But theory is concerned with something that is not theory, and what a theory of value must be concerned with is the actual encounter of the moral agent with the ordered universe of goods. A good theory may help the moral agent, but only at one remove. And precisely here, of course, Ethics, as a practical undertaking, will be unlike any other science in what its theories must attend to. In most sciences the history of a discovery forms an appendix, at most, to an exposition of what has been discovered. Science comes to rest in the knowledge of what has come to be known. But moral knowledge is, as such, its discovery. The good is self-communicative, and the moment of receiving it is one with the good received; the opening of the eyes is the good to which the eyes are opened.

"Axiology," too, is a conception that fails to distinguish the center of knowledge from its theoretical and reflective periphery, a distinction of determinative importance for the Christian understanding of truth. For truth is the disclosure of God's works in Christ which, once shown to us, must hold us in worshiping love; to the reflective and theoretical periphery we can allow much greater play of investigative tentativeness and self-correction. This means that we proceed upon our practical ways without too weighty a theoretical baggage, cheerfully confident of making sense of whatever the world may present us with. Its inhabitants, intelligent, foolish, tiresome, delightful, or dangerous, are given back to us to love; its natural framework, the course of its history, the conditions it sets for our own life can be learned afresh, unafraid of new discoveries or technologies but only of the oldest of all human things, the rejection of God's gift which is self-destruction. Freed from distorted imaginations, love reclaims its right to question the world's structure and relations, beginning with the life of "the brethren," those on whom the light of the world has dawned, who foreshadow the Kingdom of

---

13. The happy juxtaposition of my article "Reflections on Pluralism" with that of Jonathan Chaplin, "The Concept of 'Civil Society' and Christian Social Pluralism," in the *Kuyper Center Review* 1 (2010): 1-33, presents the two sides of this disagreement.

Heaven that is to come within the world. Their way through the world must set the agenda for inquiry.

World and Time

In the middle of a song of praise, which holds up for our admiring attention what God has made and done and his sovereign governance of time, there is a sudden disruption: "Today if you will hear his voice, harden not your hearts!" (Ps. 95:7-8). We are summoned to our own unique moment, with its unique opportunity and its unique danger. The disruption lasts no more than a second. Before we can be ready to respond to it, our attention is turned back to objective realities once again. But now we read those realities differently: in the world, too, we encounter time, not the "today" that lies before us, but time laid out objectively as history: "Harden not your hearts, as happened at Strife, as on that day at Testing in the wilderness!" The position in which we find ourselves "today" is mirrored back to us from the record of history. The danger in which we stand today is shown us in the danger of others, "who," as the ancient commentator put it, "heard the glad invitation in the past, but did not enter" (Heb. 4:6).

With the awakening to a sense of self and self's opportunity, the perception of loss, which accompanies all knowledge of time, becomes a sense of danger. Loss of self, unlike the loss of daffodils, is radical loss. The prospects for the self, to which eros has summoned us, are not accommodated within the ordinary cycle of birth and death. Time viewed from within the pursuit of wisdom is not cyclical, but has one line and one outcome. The tensions thus generated are articulated unforgettably in the ninetieth Psalm. The vast amplitude of recurrent time, the poet complains, reduces our scope for life and action to insignificance. From generation to generation Adonai sustains his people; his own existence stretches back pre-cosmically, before mountains, earth, and ages; that of the people, while less extensive, covers many generations. But the tenure on life of individual men is brief out of all proportion to these expanses. They die and return to the nothingness they came from, their few scores of years consumed in a whimper. Overshadowed by death, never free of "labor and sorrow," their every step is dogged by the incongruity of their span of life to the eons of world-time. Yet, the poet dares to think, there is another time to be thought of, a time that permits us human beings to incline our hearts to wisdom, including our practical affairs. We may learn "to number our days," not in the sense of knowing in advance how many they will be, which is impossible, but by taking them one by one, receiving each day "in the morning." There is hope that Adonai will turn to us in his favor and give us *our own time,* as in world-time we have encountered his disregard. He must reach out to us, accommodate his own doings to our little scope: "Show thy servants thy work. Prosper thou the work of our hands!" We may remember and predict, wonder and grieve over time given to the world, which supports narrative and anticipation, surprise and predictability; but time *of our own* elicits resolve and action, eagerness for opportunity. The times of the world and of the self, though mutually illumining and interlocking, are by no means the same.

Once this division is introduced into our view of time, the tension of meaninglessness infects human affairs on a wider scale, too. "History," which originally meant "inquiry," proves in fact to be recalcitrant material for inquiry. Observation is relentlessly hemmed in by the point of view of our "now," so that we only see a small part of what has been done, while even that is not open to synoptic and comparative observation, as material and spatial objects are, but has to be narrated according to the sequence of succession. And narrative sequence can never dispense with the actions of free subjects — divine, angelic, human, and of whatever other free subjects within the animal world or out of it there may be — which enter the course of events out of nothing, refusing to be subject to the generic order of cause and effect. Narrated events are part of reality, "what there is," yet they violate the framework of laws and regularities. History bursts out of the woven fabric of natural regularities, leaving loose threads of indeterminacy hanging. That is what makes the idea of history so elusive of philosophy, and with philosophy, of adoration and praise. John of Patmos, following the reflections of Old Testament wisdom texts from Job to Psalm 73, found the "sealed scroll" of history, held in the hand of God at the heart of a joyfully ordered creation, a matter for tears (Rev. 5:4). Here, in the realities of history, we can speak of a "fallen" world, a world at odds with its own given logic.

How, then, can history be brought within the purview of wisdom? To love the world in its temporal dimensions requires a "time of our own," a historical narrative which gives us what we may call a "point of identification" with the elusive realities of past time. Knowledge of history cannot rise above time, taking it all in from a height as one might view a continent from space. The attempt to assume such a perspective is what leads to the progressivist "whig" and the cynical "nihilist" view of the present, those two views, despite their differences of mood, being closely akin. It requires an historically situated view. Identification is a lively sense of proximate context, an interest in the difference of nearness and farness. There is one among those much-bruited multiple Greek words for love that signals this historical point of identification, the "love of our own," the word *storgē*.[14] The natural order suggests that all men and women are equally our neighbors; historical perspective divides them into nearer and more distant, tells of loyalties that bind us to some in ways that we are not bound to others. Some human beings, not all, are our children or our parents; some, not all, are our fellow-citizens or next-door neighbors. Some have instructed us in what we do, some are our students and likely successors, while others have no practical enterprises in common with us. Our relations are thus ordered in concentric circles of proximity to our point of belonging. This ordering has always seemed problematic. We do not have to be very reflective to know that such a way of ordering relations by our situation in the world could never predict what God, who judges our relations impartially, will do or require. Yet the moral and philosophical scruple that continually reasserts universal nature against particular loyalties is ultimately impotent to give us concrete guidance. How could *we* judge our nearest connections with the impartiality of God? How could *we* live without particular loyalties, as he does? The relations of *storgē* are the path by which we humans enter the world and pass through it. Those who pretend to a universal view of things at their expense are always to some extent self-deceived, while those who simply posit those relations fall into arbitrary self-reference.

The Gospel identifies a historical moment, at which time and the good are reconciled: the resurrection of Jesus Christ, an event at the center of history which vindicates the created order and heals the rift between history and the good. "The fulfilling of the times" is a theme that no one can read the Scriptures of either Testament and ignore. It summons us to bring our different historical moments into relation with a central historical moment, our various community loyalties into relation with a focal community of obedience evoked by that moment. The Gospel answers the dilemma of nature and history with a word — not a philosophical or world-describing word, but a narrative, which finds sense not only in the shape of creation-order, but in events, too. It is the crowning task of wisdom to recognize the dilemma of world-order as susceptible of only such a resolution as this. The reason of wisdom cannot point like John the Baptist, but it can help us so to understand the unresolved shape of things that we are ready for John the Baptist when we meet him.

---

14. It is to C. S. Lewis, *The Four Loves* (London: Geoffrey Bles, 1960), that we owe the introduction of this term into the sterile opposition of agape and eros.

The great diptych of visions in the fourth and fifth chapters of Revelation presents history as the sealed scroll in the hand of God. It cannot be opened and read until Christ, the Lamb who was slain, establishes by his sacrifice the right to make sense of history as God makes sense of it. A long tradition of interpretation, insensitive to the logic with which John deploys his images, has read the tableaux following the breaking of the seals as visions *of the future.* But the scenes that play themselves out in the sixth chapter, as the Lamb opens the first six seals of the seven, are those familiar to us from all past history: war, famine, victimization. What John is shown, then, is not only "what shall happen hereafter," but also how *what has happened* shall appear in the light of what shall happen hereafter. To the question where in this narrative they stand who faithfully seek to plot their way through a world at once ordered and resistant to order, a complex answer is given: they stand "with him on Mount Zion," the place in history where his sacrifice has been made, and they "follow him wherever he leads" in his path through history (Rev. 14:1, 4). He is the Lamb *who was slain,* i.e., who has occupied his place in this history and whose place it was to undergo the most contradictory, the most overwhelming, and the most defeating of the probations of order history has ever posed. Their position is with him and yet after him. Their capacity to live in history, their vocation to endure history, is wholly determined by the fact that he lived in history and endured history before them, but "before" does not mean "historically remote from," but in identification and fellowship with them.[15]

The meaning of a historical identity expands as lines of connection are formed between that central moment of history and our own. Identity loses its parochial narrowness, and becomes the door through which we are given to enter our relation to the created universe. This self-identifying love we call, after the terminology of the New Testament, "discipleship." The disciple is, literally, a "learner," but at the same time, given the patterns of rabbinic learning current in Jesus' day, a "follower." The cognitive and affective are bound together in the life of the disciple who learns by following and follows by learning. At the central climax of the synoptic narrative Jesus turns to address "anyone who would follow after me" to "deny himself and take up his cross and follow me" (Mark 8:34). "Following" is an idea with more than one sense: it means following *with,* adhering to the master and being in his

15. For a fuller treatment see my "History and Politics in the Book of Revelation," in Oliver O'Donovan and Joan Lockwood O'Donovan, *Bonds of Imperfection* (Grand Rapids: Eerdmans, 2004), pp. 25-47.

company, and also following *after,* coming later, carrying on the work of teaching where it has been left off, extending his wisdom into the mission of a school. To follow "after" Christ is to be conformed in love to the moment of resolution that occurred in his death, to carry forward in our living the imprint of the living-to-die that he lived. The disciple is a figure who identifies with more than one time and place: a time and place to inhabit, another time and place to be centered upon. He or she has recognized a time and place in history, there and not elsewhere, then and not before or after, where the possibility of wisdom was decisively given. In understanding *this* moment in relation to *that* moment, in finding in *that* moment the key to *this* moment's meaning and purpose, the disciple has overcome what was most threatening and destructive about historical relations, their contingency and moral arbitrariness. The narrative of the Gospel has conferred moral sense upon the contingencies of time. The disciple has realized the meaning of time by belonging not simply to a *historical* community (in which one may be born, live, and die without asking any questions about the universal right), but to an *historically interpretative* community with its life rooted in that central moment. All doings and sufferings are located in relation to the disclosure of meaning that Christ's death effected for all who come after. The love of Christ directs historical loyalties, as the love of God "above" all things directs natural loves. The "ends" for the sake of which it pursues and discounts the things of the world are presented from a new point of view as an historical achievement.

Knowing our place in history, welcoming our place in history "for the sake of" that central point, generates new paradoxes about life in the world: "Whoever would gain his life will lose it. . . . For what does it profit a man to gain the whole world and forfeit his life?" (Mark 8:35-36). Gaining life is set in opposition to gaining the world. The life to be gained is not, simply and solely, the self as such, which is God's prior gift to us and does not need to be gained, but the fulfillment of the self in agency. We may try to fulfill ourselves solely in relation to the world of goods. We may thus "gain" the world, but since the world does not contain within itself the resolution of the paradoxes of history, we fail to fulfill ourselves and in that sense forfeit our lives. The gain we envisage in devoting ourselves to goods of sense, intellect, art, and industry, etc. leaves us in a purely immanent relation to the world, without the powers of action and the freedom that God would bestow upon us. Only by "following after" the one at the center of history can we accomplish ourselves effectively. An opposition thus appears between the value-order of the world as perceived ahistorically and the word that holds the center of the world's history: "Whoever is ashamed of me and of my words in this adulterous and sinful generation. . . ." Merely to affirm the created world's order of value is to ignore this opposition. To affirm Christ's death and resurrection is to acknowledge it, and to find it resolved in the rebirth of agency.

CHAPTER 6

Love and Testimony

The Analogy of Love

Jesus' summary of the law within the scope of the two loves, of God and neighbor, encouraged the Western tradition, following Augustine, to assume that whatever needed to be said about Ethics could and should be said in terms of love. This was correct if understood in one way, incorrect if understood in another. The correct understanding is that since there is nothing in heaven or earth that God has not made good, we can rest in the love of whatever reality presents itself to us, heavenly or earthly, demonic or angelic. The incorrect understanding is that any such love will *ipso facto* fulfill what God has commanded us to be and to do. Love is a spectrum of affective responses to God's works, from lowest to highest, from origin to destiny. But because it is so, it needs the dynamic impetus of faith and hope to move it upward through its range of objects, to prevent it from settling down to rest prematurely. Love can fail of its heavenly destiny; it can be false as well as true, just as the cognition that frames its object can be false as well as true. Love goes out to realities as they appear to us; faith and hope give ways of appearing to realities concealed from us. Love, therefore, has a pilgrim's path set before it, to which it is directed by faith and hope.

There is, to be sure, a paradox in attributing an ecstatic character to faith and hope, when ancient traditions have thought love to be ecstatic, drawing the subject out of self towards the other. The important point in the ecstatic conception, however, is not the relation to the other as such; it is that the other is not simply at hand to be appropriated, a familiar feature of the world on which the self leans for stability. The other draws the self out of itself. But love does not always draw the self out; the loving self can be wholly at home with its object. If it takes an ecstatic form, it is because it is turned by faith to a world beyond its own world, and by hope to a time beyond its own time; it is stretched out through the arc of reality from nearest to furthest. Heeding the invitation of wisdom to turn from the visible to the invisible, from the beauties that confront us to the hidden ends in which our active lives may finally come to rest, it undertakes a journey on which it acquires depth and complexity as it takes the measure of the unseen bearing in upon the seen.

It is possible for an orderly theology to treat a great deal under the heading of faith that we have discussed under the heading of love, not least the knowledge of God's saving work in history. But faith reaches out to the unseen, as hope does, so that any discussion of our knowledge of the world and its history that treats it under the heading of faith will be directed to answering a distinct question, how knowledge of the unseen is rationally grounded in knowledge of the seen. Wolfhart Pannenberg's discussion of faith, hope, and love (following the order in 1 Cor. 13:13) is a worthy example of this approach.[1] Some of the constraints it imposes are shown up vividly in his treatment of hope. Squeezed into nine pages (as against thirty-seven for faith and twenty-nine for love), hope has little to add, since its grasp of promise has been taken over by faith and its interest in the neighbor's future by benevolent love. The treatment of love itself tells us rather more. Saint John's declaration that "God is love" serves Pannenberg as a defining point of reference.[2] Love is thus sharply divided into two contrasted aspects corresponding to creator and creation, the love which flows out from God and returns to God in redemption, and the love which is derived from creation and has its end in creaturely aspirations. To mark this cleft between *amor benevolentiae* and *amor concupiscentiae*, Pannenberg adopts the pair of terms popularized by Anders Nygren, "agape" and "eros," only to be faced with the task of evading the almost Manichaean opposition in which Nygren set them. Pannenberg's handling is subtle and circumspect, as befits a thinker who knows how to look about him. It allows for an *imago filii* in "upthrusting" creaturely love, an "obscure form of the mutuality of love" between Father and Son.[3] But his organizing principle, beginning from "katabatic"

1. Wolfhart Pannenberg, *Systematische Theologie III* (Göttingen: Vandenhoek & Ruprecht, 1993), pp. 155-237. [= *Systematic Theology*, vol. 3, trans. Geoffrey Bromiley (Grand Rapids: Eerdmans, 1998), pp. 136-211.]

2. Pannenberg, *Systematische Theologie III*, pp. 206-7; Eng., p. 182.

3. Pannenberg, *Systematische Theologie III*, p. 220: "*Vielmehr wird man in der 'aufsteigenden' Tendenz des platonischen Eros eine, wenn auch entfernte, Entsprechung zur ebenfalls*

divine love and attempting to find a reflection of it in the doubtfulness of human love, does not encourage the saying of certain modest things, which Ethics, for its part, cannot leave unsaid.

(a) In the first place, it hardly acknowledges a great deal of love that is neither benevolent nor concupiscent but merely instinctive, woven into our elementary social forms and practices. The small boy loves his mother, the hobbit loves his pipe. It makes no sense to include these loves under the heading of love's "brokenness"; there is very much that is broken in human love, but instinctive ties that do not rise above the threshold of moral evaluation should not, as such, be regarded in that light. If we are to speak seriously of God's initiative in redeeming our loves through his love for us in Christ, we must have in view the whole arc of love from the most commonly instinctual to the most godlike and self-outpouring. It was the gift of George Herbert to exploit this arc by speaking of divine love in disconcertingly familiar ways, as in "Love bade me welcome," where God is represented as a genial host trying to make an underdressed and embarrassed dinner-guest feel at home.[4] The analogies this generates can carry a worrying hint of sentimentality if we allow ourselves to forget that love is a *range* of affective dispositions, not an undifferentiated one, and that no familiar love can be raised to participate in divine love without death and resurrection. Our convivialities must be crucified if the affections they express are to be hallowed. Yet the language of "love" is not to be set apart for exclusively heavenly use.

It is, to be sure, a serious question how the language of love is to be sufficiently differentiated, its variety and pluriformity allowed to emerge. Love is differentiated in many ways, better or worse depending on its object and differently emotionally attuned as its object is present or absent. But behind these differences there is a univocal reference to talk of love, which is the affective affinity that arises to bind us to states, objects, or persons which experience in the world can offer us (including God, as he comes to meet us in the world). The New Testament, which has much to say about love as the virtue of community, employs the Greek word *agapē,* unfamiliar to those who have studied Plato's great discussions of love in classical Greek, a point of vocabulary that led Nygren to make the great mistake of identifying the *word* with a distinct *kind* of love, outgoing and creative, to be contrasted

---

aufsteigenden Tendenz der biblischen Gottesliebe als der Liebe des Sohnes zum Vater anzuerkennen haben." Eng., p. 195.

4. George Herbert, *Collected Poems,* ed. F. E. Hutchinson (Oxford: Oxford University Press, 1941), p. 188. The poem bears the simple title "Love."

with an alternative word for an alternative kind, questing for self-fulfillment. But in the vocabulary of Hebrew-influenced Greek of the first century *agapē* means just "love," no more and no less. Biblical writers used *agapē* and not *erōs* for the same reason that we use "love" and not "charity," namely that in their linguistic community *erōs* was not idiomatic. They had distinctive things to say *about* love — what and whom we should love, the cognitive power of love in ordering one object in relation to another, the extent to which we may invest ourselves in our loves, the relation of love to other virtues, and supremely the nature of God as love and loving. But in different *kinds* of love they did not interest themselves for one moment.

There is, then, an importance in retaining the general term "love," with its comprehensive range, in our vocabulary. Some typical distinctions among types of love are inevitable, but these should be fluidly heuristic and preferably not binary. If Greek words are used to characterize them, they must be understood as modern terms of art, not reports of how Greek-speakers of the first century spoke. Even our modern use of "eros," too deeply entrenched to replace, does not correspond to how Plato spoke of *erōs*. In this exploration we have spoken so far of love as admiration, of desire (with eros as a sub-class), and of love as identification; there is nothing to prevent us from adding other forms to the list as the discussion requires.

(b) The second thing the katabatic approach overlooks is that love generates many emotional states to accompany it: fear, grief, delight, longing, etc. The demand to fit love into two contrasting categories goes with a reluctance to thematize the *emotions* as a manifestation distinct from love and expressive of it. These taken by themselves may or may not express the stable moral disposition that we take love to be. I can long for a beer if I am hot and thirsty enough, without any settled love for that beverage that might make me prefer it to wine in normal circumstances. Any love, on the other hand, may be, and should be, accompanied by a series of emotions which unfolds as circumstances develop: at one moment I fear my child's danger, at another I feel compassion for my child's weakness, at others again I desire my child's presence, delight in my child's triumph, am irritated at my child's faults, and so on, without my love for my child changing as such. At times I may feel nothing much at all, but I still love my child. "Love is not love, which alters when it alteration finds," but it would be a mistake to suppose that love "alters" when its mood changes.[5] The "ever-fixed mark that looks on tempests and is never shaken" is not *always* looking at tempests, but may sometimes see a

---

5. William Shakespeare, Sonnet 116.

sunrise, and would be altogether too fixed if it couldn't greet the sunrise with some lightening of its countenance. Tempests and sunrises come and go; love remains, but responds to changing circumstances with appropriate emotions.

The same range of emotions, more or less, may attach to hatred: I fear my enemy's triumph, desire his impotence to exert his powers, delight in his failure, am irritated by his boasting, and even pity his folly. Hatred, too, may be a stable moral disposition, for wisdom includes an understanding of what merits loathing as well as what merits enjoyment. These continuities should remind us of the importance of the ground that Christianity held against Manichaeism in the fourth and fifth centuries, the denial that evil was a "nature." Evils *befell* goods, or were *defective enactments* of goods; they were events or actions of disruption, destruction, and failure. Investing evil with ontological dignity may elicit a shudder of loathing which appears to take the moral difference seriously, but this shudder will at best be aesthetic repulsion, while at worst it may be accommodated dialectically into love. Those who make a habit of watching horror movies teach themselves to come to terms with it. Where evil is admitted on the ground floor as a fundamental determinant of existence, Moloch is worshiped. Israel's way of dealing with Moloch by mockery and demystification was the right way.

Yet Christian thinkers refused to brush aside the emotional responses appropriate to evil. In the largely Stoic doctrine of the emotions adopted and propounded by Cicero, the four passions, "elation" and "sorrow," "desire" and "fear," two responding to the present and two to the future, were treated as disturbances of a rational poise. Though three of them had corresponding rational forms, "joy," "will," and "caution," there was no rational form of sorrow. This doctrine greatly exasperated Christian thinkers, who pleaded for the value of sorrow, especially in grief for sin. Sorrow, too, was a way of loving and knowing the good, an affective recognition that the goods we experience are not final and permanent, but created and transitory reflections of a more final good that shines through them. If joy is vital awareness of created reality, sorrow is the vital awareness of its limits. Good grief contributed to self-knowledge, and prompted us to hear the call of wisdom.[6] Admiring love, then, takes the double form of joy at being and distress at its cessation. There is no place for an equal-and-opposite exertion of hatred for evil.

(c) There is a third thing that is not adequately said within a katabatic conception of love, which is that every love takes its value from its object. An account of love built on the contrast between divine and human is too

---

6. Cicero, *Tusculan Disputations* 4.5.10-11. Augustine, *City of God* 9.4-5; 14.8-9.

much concerned with subjects, too little with how those subjects recognize and understand each other and the world of their encounters objectively. An account of love divorced from an account of knowledge drags the good apart from cognition. "Good" then becomes a term applied without ground in reality, without criteria of recognition, as in the stronger forms of voluntarism. Love must be the affective cognition of reality, as false or true as its cognitive content. That is why revelation must be treated in connection with love, too: "He has shown you, *adam*, what is good" (Mic. 6:8). The good is communicated to us, and as it is communicated, so it is recognized and affirmed in being loved. To deal with the whole content of revelation under faith is to miss the lifegiving and love-inspiring nature of revelation, the presentation of truth as *beauty*.

The dramatic opening paragraphs of Balthasar's sprawling multi-volume Dogmatics remain a place to which any theology that knows itself will want to turn back, even if the foaming spate of words that forces through the narrows of his "Introduction" subsequently branches out too far and wide across the plains of history and art. To confront the *whole* truth, Balthasar tells us, of man and world and God, of the historical Gospel, church and Kingdom, "in the night of our present and the uncertainty of our future," one must choose a first word that will not need to be taken back and twisted into shape later on, one broad enough to nourish, clear enough to irradiate all the words that follow it. It is a word theology has marginalized, philosophy has postponed, the exact sciences have never had time for. The word is "beauty," the point of junction between the good and the true, the "primal phenomenon" underpinning the attractiveness of good and the cogency of truth. In its two aspects of "form" and "splendor," it is inherent order on the one hand, compelling radiance on the other.[7]

Leaving aside all that is puzzling in the project of a "theological aesthetics" as "fundamental theology," a Catholic answer to Barth's doctrine of revelation, we may confine ourselves to what is important for Ethics in this idea, not as the first word but at the point that it occupies in connection with love and in the context of the world. We should not confuse beauty with specifically *visual* perception. A supposed Protestant interest in putting the word above the image, or a supposed Catholic interest in putting visual, and perhaps tangible, perception above hearing, are equally irrelevant to the

---

7. Hans Urs von Balthasar, *Herrlichkeit I: Schau der Gestalt* (Einsiedeln: Johannes Verlag, 1964), pp. 15-18. [= *The Glory of the Lord I: Seeing the Form,* trans. Joseph Fessio and John Riches (Edinburgh: T & T Clark, 1982), pp. 17-20.]

claims made here. Beauty belongs to what is heard as well as what is seen, and (why not?) to what is touched, smelled, and tasted. What is spoken of as "form" and "splendor" does not impose a visual image on top of a more reflected multi-sensorial perception. The appreciation of beauty belongs to intelligence, which draws on the deliveries of hearing, sight, and the other senses freely and as they may be relevant to the sense of the whole. Metaphors of light signal the immediacy of intelligent perception, as metaphors of sound signal the possibilities of form extended over time: "That strain again! It has a dying fall."[8] Neither, on the other hand, should we confuse beauty with symbol. Symbolic representation sets appearance apart from what it signifies, but in beauty appearance and signification are one. "We 'behold' the form, but . . . it is not the detached form we behold, but the depth that looms up through it . . . and never so that we leave the (horizontal) form behind to plunge (vertically) into the naked depth."[9] There is no dividing form on the surface from meaning that lies beneath. To see something as a radiant form is to see it as *itself* the meaning it conveys — open to exploration, but not to translation.

The Testimony

When we love any kind of thing, we know it as a form of created order that illuminates us, allowing us to find ourselves and other things in our relation to it. When we love a particular thing, we know it as an instantiation of form that has been given in time and space. When we love a particular person, it is as an instance of the form we know, but this time in a unique subject of action, who expresses form by doing as well as being. And when we love Jesus as the Christ (the point of unity between love of God and love of neighbor) we find his life and teaching to be the form that the whole history of God's saving work displays.[10] We discover in him the representative moment in history that gathers the intelligibility of world and time into itself, and sets other happenings, however unintelligible or misunderstandable, in relation

8. Shakespeare, *Twelfth Night* 1.1.

9. Balthasar, *Herrlichkeit I*, p. 112: *"Wir 'erblicken' die Gestalt, aber . . . nicht nur die abgelöste Gestalt, sondern die an ihr aufscheinende Tiefe . . . nie so dass wir die (horizontale) Gestalt hinuter uns liessen, um (vertikal) in die nackte Tiefe zu tauchen."* Eng., p. 119.

10. Balthasar, *Herrlichkeit I*, p. 146: *"Dass Jesus Christus die zentrale Gestalt der Offenbarung ist, um die alle übrigen Momente der Heilsoffenbarung kristallisieren und sich angliedern, hat das christliche Denken von jeher gewusst und doch vielleicht in der Glaubenslehre nicht eindringlich genug beachtet."* Eng., p. 154.

to it. When we delight in him, we inherit the blessing the Old Covenant pronounces on those who delight in the law of the Lord, the words of the Lord, the ways of the Lord, the people, the city, the servant in whom the Lord delights.

He himself trains us to make these delights our own, and to pray for the fulfillment of the world and its history according to God's purposes: "Thy kingdom come, thy will be done!" History is the concern as much of the second of these two petitions as of the first. In Saint Luke's version of the prayer, indeed, there is just one petition, a prayer for the coming of God's visible and active reign over all things, the final reconciliation of the tension between history and the good. The opposition of "earth" and "heaven" makes it clear, however, that the sovereign rule of God supervenes not as an innovation on the world we know, but as a disclosure of what is and always and everywhere the truth. The temporal stage on which God's will is still to be performed historically is distinct from the temple of God's counsel where accomplishment is already present. The Lord of creation is the Lord of history. Heaven, unlike Valhalla, does not have to be built; it is where God is, and is there in its fullness. The frustration of God's counsels which the tensions of earthly history present is only provisional, for God's hidden counsels have effect, waiting the fulfillment of time to complete the joy of men and angels. So the petition for history is a petition for the world, not simply as we see it, but as it is yet to take form in the conjunction of earth and heaven, of man's existence and God's rule. In making this petition we lend our active selves to the service of the world's good fixed in the purposes of God.

Here again, we pray for the presence and work of the Holy Spirit, illuminating the form of the world and its destiny. "Enable with perpetual light the dullness of our blinded sight!" He who spoke by the prophets is to be our instructor still, teaching us "knowledge and the fear of the Lord" (Isa. 11:2). At this point in the Lord's Prayer there is no explicit prayer for our own action. That must await the petitions that follow. We ask him for the reconstruction and re-attunement of our moral imaginary, bringing the world before our eyes as created, redeemed, and destined for fulfillment. "Teach me your statutes!" the poet of the Long Psalm cried repeatedly (Ps. 119:12, 64, 68, 124, 135). "Statutes," *ḥuqqîm,* are things engraved or inscribed; what the poet asked to be taught is what is inscribed already in the order of God's work. As the poet's eyes are opened to this order, they take in also God's *niphla'ôth,* the astonishing deeds through which law erupts into history (v. 18), as the whole earth is filled with YHWH's loving-kindness (v. 64).

God has answered our prayer for the Spirit of illumination in his own testimony to the meaning of world and time. "Revelation" we call it, but the word is hardly rich enough to convey the depths of self-disclosure and commitment that God has accomplished. This testimony is given supremely and first in the *coming of Jesus.* All four Gospels tell of Jesus' coming to the bank of the Jordan where John was baptizing, of the Spirit like a dove descending, and of the heavenly witness, the very heart of the Epiphany, the appearing of God's kingdom. The testimony of the Father to the human existence that he bound to himself is answered by the lived testimony of the Son to the Father's faithfulness and by the witness of the outpoured Spirit to the Father's love of the Son, evoking in response the testimony of Israel through its last prophet. Interpretation arises out of interpretation, and testimony is given in response to testimony, but there is no infinite regress. What constituted this event as the appearing of the Kingdom of God? Three congruent elements: the fulfilling of the times, attested by John as the appointed witness; the presence of God in his Son, attested by Father and Spirit; and the redemption of Israel, attested by the Christ, identifying himself with his people's aspiration for the forgiveness of sins.

(a) The testimony began with baptism, a sign of the fulfillment of the times, linking all human ages to that central moment of history. Christians are baptized because Jesus came to the Jordan where John the Baptizer preached the fulfillment of the times. That history is our history; it molds all history to its shape. With the sign came the testimony of John, in whom law and prophecy reached their close, the appointed witness who was to recognize the Son who made the godhead known. There are recognitions we make because we have known them before and recognitions we make by inference from other things we know. In neither of those ways could Jesus be recognized as the Son of God. The recognition had to take place in one leap: the scene identified itself, opened the eyes that must see it. Its authority did not derive from anyone's prior judgment. "I did not know him," John the Baptist declared, yet, "I have seen" (John 1:31-34). The moment cohered, imposed itself upon his mind, the form, appearance, meaning, and authentication all at once. It is the only way that anybody could witness the self-disclosure of God, by letting it take hold and impose itself upon the understanding. Thought cannot lead us to that moment; it can, and must, run out from it.

In a rather witty play of words the Baptist says that the one who comes after him went before him, because he was — if we may reproduce it in English — his "foreman."[11] The "before" and "after" of sacred time are gathered

---

11. πρῶτός μου (John 1:30).

up in this overarching relation of sovereignty in which the Word of God is "first." John's witness is given to that "first" at the point of its disclosure. That is why it is irreplaceable; we cannot set ourselves free of what John, and only John, can tell us. Yet that relationship, inescapable and irreversible as all historical relationships are, is not the whole of the matter. There is a movement from faith to sight; sight outgrows its beginnings in dependence on another's witness, becoming the shape the mind gives to all new experience. It forms the love of Christ, who is present though the Baptist is past. Sight must be given us, as all the founding phenomena of our experience are given us, and to receive it we must attend to the testimony. Yet given to us it is, and given to us, too, that we may witness the disclosure of God.

(b) In the voice from heaven, addressing not the crowds nor the prophet but the Son alone, the world's creator drew the veil from his face: "You are my beloved Son, in you I delight." The Son was acknowledged by the Father, the Spirit alighted on the Son. God acknowledging, God attesting, God self-acknowledged, self-attested: in that figure John saw the glory of the Lord in Trinity, the one in whom divine sovereignty is vested, the one who is to draw humankind together in obedience.[12]

(c) And at this point we must beware of rushing ahead too fast. We should like to say that the *glory of man* came to appearance there, disclosed as the glory of God was disclosed. The divine presence shining on the world with new clarity called forth the human presence with new definition, the last Adam stepping authoritatively out into the world as the first Adam and Eve had shuffled out of Eden, broken and bowed. But before we speak of human glory, we must say that God fulfilled the promises to *Israel,* the people in which human existence attained a historical dimension, "appointing" or "anointing" Jesus of Nazareth as "the Christ." The redemption of Israel was attested by one identified with the people that turned from its sins to believe in the coming of God. The gathering of the crowds to John was a popular movement in the strictest sense, a people acting for itself, but not wildly or

---

12. "*Des Vaters Stimme ließ sich hören, Der Sohn, der uns mit Blut erkauft, Ward als ein wahrer Mensch getauft. Der Geist erschien im Bild der Tauben, Damit wir ohne Zweifel glauben, Es habe die Dreifaltigkeit Uns selbst die Taufe zubereit.*" The anonymous librettist of Bach's BWV 7, "*Christ unser Herr zum Jordan kam,*" here paraphrased an Epiphany sermon of Luther (*WA* 37.250). Bach's three-and-a-half-minute aria is without qualification the highest representation of this moment in any Western art-form, converting the light and the drama, the humanity and the Godhead, the Trinity and the unity, all into sound-patterns. See Matthew O'Donovan and Oliver O'Donovan, "Bach's Musical Treatment of Jesus' Baptism," *Communio: International Catholic Review* 32/1 (2005): 119-27.

carried by mass emotion into irrational courses. It sought to lay hold of the principles of a common life, the law of God; it came to receive instruction in the conduct of its the various spheres of business (Luke 3:10-15), and as it did so, it confessed the wrong of its practices, the untruthfulness of its current patterns of life. And from the heart of this people one emerged to "fulfill all righteousness" on its behalf (Matt. 3:15). The renewal sought *within* Israel corresponded with renewal effected *for* Israel. The people that would live under God's law was granted God's self-communication in covenant partnership, a Christ in whom the two sides of the partnership were each present.

As we did in Chapter Two, we look from the beginning to the end of Jesus' ministry, where we see him as "the faithful witness" in his trial before Caiaphas and Pilate (1 Tim. 6:13; Rev. 1:5; 3:14). His testimony consists not simply in what he speaks of, but in the circumstances and the manner in which he speaks of it. As he was silent at the scene of the baptism, so he is here, but this time the silence is broken with three sayings recorded in the Synoptics (there are two in Saint John) that interpret his testimony to his interrogators:

(a) "As against a thief you have come out with swords and staves to arrest me? Each day in the temple I sat teaching, and you did not lay hold on me" (Mark 14:48-9 and parallels). In the synoptic narrative this occurs at the moment of Jesus' arrest, following his refusal to offer resistance. It is his testimony to the disparity between truth and force, which the authorities have acknowledged by not arresting him in public. His silence will bear witness to the disparity. But if for the synoptic evangelists this is a preliminary to the substantive issues in the trial, which turn on his personal role in salvation history, for Saint John it is the very nub of the matter, dominating the dialogue with Pilate. It is as the *Word* of God that Jesus stands before his interrogators; their questions appeal to a communicative logic which their violence subverts. So John places this saying, shorn of its first sentence and expanded, in the trial before the high priest: "I have spoken openly to the world. Constantly I taught in the synagogue and the temple, where all the Judeans assemble, and said nothing in secret. Why ask me? Ask those who have heard me what I said! They know what I said." After an attendant strikes him, he continues: "If I spoke wrongly, witness to the wrong; if rightly, why do you strike me?" (John 18:20-23). Not only is the *publicity* of truth and discourse about truth at stake in this secret trial, a publicity that does not bend easily to the control of force, but so also is the logic of any serious inquiry into truth, which is conducted by "witness," including argument, questioning, and answering. Error in speech can be corrected only by truer speech. By that means God has made himself known, and by that means God holds open the possibility of public and common existence. The communication of truth commandeers its own space, for it is public communication, impossible to contain within conspiratorial corners or esoteric conventicles, and equally so within the *camera* of the interrogator.

(b) In response to the high priest's question, "Are you the Christ?" Jesus says "I am" (reported with variations), and continues: "And henceforth you shall see the Son of Man seated on the right hand of power and coming on the clouds of heaven" (Mark 14:62 and parallels).[13] The indirectness with which the high priest's question is answered throws all the light upon God's purposes for history. The question concerns what Jesus has taught about his role. It is answered by pointing to the fulfillment of God's promise. The times *are* fulfilled; history *has* its climax; the traditional prophetic vision of the coming of the Son of Man on the clouds, then, will take actual form. All who exercise provisional power must know that God will take it from them and bestow it on the representative whom he has chosen. And as these purposes are realized, so there is no more evading them. The "seeing" of the purposes is, in the end, inescapable.

(c) In reply to Pilate's question, "Are you the king of the Jews?" (upon which Saint John lays the weight of his trial scene) Jesus answers in the Synoptics only, "You say so" (Mark 15:2 and parallels).[14] An indirect response, again, but a positive one. God's purposes for the world and its history have at their heart the restoration of Israel. If the universal confrontation of truth and power is central for Saint John, the synoptists keep sight of the calling of Israel and national restoration. Precisely that, of course, was prominent in the accusations laid by the priests, which sought, with the political deviousness Saint John's irony makes so much of, to frighten Pilate with the specter of Israel's nationhood. Frightening to Roman power, embarrassing to Sadducean politics, the purposes of God for his people will be the content of Jesus' witness.

13. The two questions, "Are you the Christ?" and "Are you the king of the Jews?" are substantially the same question, but the one asked from within the circle of Jewish tradition and the other from outside it. For this reason John dispenses with the answer before Caiaphas and focuses attention on the confrontation with Pilate, which has the issue of truth and politics at its heart. For the synoptists, however, it is the witness of Jesus to the fulfilling of the times, the climax of history, John's account of which has been given earlier, in connection with the theme of the gathering of the nations (12:20ff.).

14. On the exchange between Jesus and Pilate see also my *Desire of the Nations* (Cambridge: Cambridge University Press, 1996), pp. 140-41.

Receiving the Testimony

The self-witness of God at the Jordan and Jesus' witness before the judgment of priests and rulers evoke concentric spheres of testimony from the Holy Spirit, repeating and affirming the testimony to and by Jesus, and extending it in one important respect, by telling of his resurrection from the dead. "Beginning from Jerusalem, you are witnesses of this" (Luke 24:47-48). The prayer for the disclosure of God's purposes is answered by a Spirit-filled community of witness "to the end of the earth" (Acts 1:8). A community is constituted by a communication. The communication of any specific thing, whether food, care, or human affection, is founded on a communication of meaning, the shared intelligence of the reality. In this great chain of communication all who believe are empowered to participate. It is the founding "work" of love to receive the communication and to share it with one another.

We participate by *receiving* the communication. Attending to what is said is our first concrete moral undertaking, the material form in which we exercise responsibility for self-disposal. "Take care how you hear!" warned Christ (Mark 4:24). Hearing admits us, for good or ill, to a community of thought. The thought may be false, the community destructive; that is the danger of hearing, the reason for taking care. But discernment is possible. We may give or withhold attention, we may "consider," we may "behold." As we pay attention to the report, so we take note not only of its content but of its form: its strong claims and modest silences, its logical progressions and its fault lines, its authorizing references and unsupported ventures. The form of the report is no mere envelope for the content; it is the dynamic structure that interprets it. By it we judge the report's coherence with reality.

To the task of hearing carefully we bring a distinctive practice, a kind of "hearing" which is not quickly taken captive to the clamor of voices. This is the reading of texts. In reading we set ourselves at a judicious distance from the immediate, we consider reports from another place and time, "examining the texts each day to see if these things were so" (Acts 17:11). Mere textuality is of itself, of course, no guarantee of considered reflection. There are texts so nearly and newly produced that the reader treads, as it were, on the writer's heels: the email darting to and fro, the hastily produced news report, ephemeral writing of every kind which reproduces and concentrates the riot of voices ringing in our ears, and in respect of these we may well join Socrates in complaining that writing is inferior to speaking, since it cannot answer intelligent questions but only pompously reiterate what it said before.[15] But the ephemeral text does not represent the distinctive strength of textual communication, which is its power to cover distance, to open up historical and local views not accessible to immediate exchange. Literary communication thrives on distance, for writing postpones the encounter with truth, allowing it the time to take place when the conditions are ready: "What was written in former times was written for our instruction" (Rom. 15:4). It is for this reason that the spread of literacy has been the most important and indispensable step of enlightenment, central to the spread of the Gospel, to be mentioned first in any account of Christian works in civilization.

In the very acts of writing and reading certain claims to authority are made and conceded. The authority of most texts is limited; it comes to an end as the text exhausts its communication and the reader's receptivity is turned to criticism. But the criteria for criticizing one text have been formed by reading other texts. The critical reader depends upon an implicit hierarchy of texts, some offering special resources of understanding to shed light on the strengths and weaknesses of others. Is not the whole enterprise of serious reading a prolonged search for a "first text," a "classic" that can measure all texts? And here we come face to face with the logic of a *canonical* text. Theology cannot discard that logic. In the nineteenth and twentieth centuries it dallied too long with the romantic affectation of despising textuality (while adding vastly to the number of texts in circulation!), and the aesthetic scorn for "bibliolatry" hampered its work for more than a century. In the Scriptures the church holds the written testimony of prophets and apostles attesting the work and words of God. The church owns the unique authority attaching to the innermost circle of testimony, the writings of the generation that "looked upon and touched with our hands the word of life" (1 John 1:1). Divine act and self-testimony come first, Scripture follows; there can be no inversion of that order. Yet if we would hear the divine act and self-testimony at all, it must be through the writers whose unique role it is to tell of them.

At a certain juncture in Israel's history — perhaps in the so-called "Deuteronomistic period" of the late seventh century BC — Israel's scribes and prophets were ablaze with excitement at the role of texts in forming a faithful community. The opening verses of the first Psalm announce the discovery: "Blessed is the man who walks not in the counsel of the wicked, nor stands

---

15. Plato, *Phaedrus* 275d.

in the way of sinners, nor sits in the seat of scoffers; but his delight is in the law of the Lord, and on his law he meditates day and night." Twice-daily reading shapes the career of the one who lives life well. Delicately the poet contrasts the reader's independence of mind, growing like a fruitful tree out of well-watered roots, with the slavish subjection to social forms of those whose culture is created laterally, who *walk* in the counsel of the wicked, *stand* in the way of sinners, *sit* in the seat of scoffers, taking practical advice from those who know their way around, observing current practice carefully, repeating *idées reçues*. For this poet the canonical text was a legal text, for in Israel law and literature were inextricably intertwined. Prophets and historians, the great literary producers of the era, were closely involved in the renewing and expounding of law. The ambition of the editors of the Deuteronomic code, whose labors to establish a decisive law-text left their mark all over the collection of laws they bequeathed, was that each Israelite home would have texts inscribed on the doorpost, each Israelite would carry texts around on hand and forehead and would learn to recite them, so becoming a living expression of the law, one "circumcised in the heart," not dependent, as they comment ironically, on legal counsel to be sought either from heaven or from overseas. "The word is very near you, in your mouth and in your heart" (Deut. 30:11-14).

In the New Testament writing and reading may seem by comparison to be relegated to the margins, and yet we find that those marginal references to them are in fact load-bearing pillars for the self-understanding of the church. Writing comes explicitly to notice in literary beginnings and endings where the authors speak of their own work, as in the introduction to the Gospel of Luke or the final words of the Gospel of John. To single out one such instance (Col. 4:10-18): in the concluding instruction to the church at Colossae to forward their letter to Laodicea and to have the letter to Laodicea read among themselves, what is at stake is nothing less than the catholicity of the church. Greetings from Paul and his circle acknowledge the Colossian assembly as an integral part of the world church and its mission; it in turn must send greetings to its neighbor, for the condition of being acknowledged is to acknowledge. In Laodicea there is a bishop called Nymphas, and in Colossae one called Archippus, who needs to be told to take his ministry more seriously. Bishop to bishop, church to church, servant of God to servant of God, the greetings of those who read the same apostolic texts confirm the intercommunicating structure of the apostolic churches. So the multiplying cells of the Christian community establish themselves as one holy, catholic, and apostolic church by shared reading.

It was no luxury for the early churches, this literary connection with the apostles; it is no luxury for us that we should hear words addressed by the apostles to the earliest communities and should enter into their communications. It is the condition of our own relation to the teaching of Jesus of Nazareth and the work of God in him. The canonical Scripture draws its authority from the central, normative strand in history, the coming of the Christ. The privileged book witnesses to privileged events. The "end of the ages" is not only the fulfillment of the promise of the text, but the fulfillment of the promise of history itself, the Christ-moment at which the secret of the world breaks surface in what God has done on earth through his Son. Reading of Scripture proceeds on the basis that *this* text has been received, with all its remoteness and all its nearness, with its immediate appeal and its strange distance, that it has been received from a source that cannot be ignored, and that it cannot simply be taken up in any way and from any point of view that happens to strike us, but must be read interrogatively by a community that looks to it for its identity. In the church's worship the lectern is at the center. No act is so fundamental to its catholic identity as reading. This is not to devalue preaching, singing, prayer, let alone sacramental act, all of which find their authorization through reading — and if we hesitate over that, we may be reassured by the good sense of Thomas Aquinas, for whom the word is the "form" of every sacrament.[16] And we may decently recall the Anglican Thomas, for whom the integrity of public reading was chief among the grounds for Reformation.[17]

These remarks on reading embrace in principle everything that needs to be said about interpretation. There is, to be sure, good reading and bad, careful reading and careless, and we must distinguish them. But in the play of words with which Hilary of Poitiers set up the relation of reading and interpretation, *non in legendo, sed intelligendo,* the opposition is far too sharp. Once a wedge of that size is driven between the two, we soon fall back into a stereotyped division between the Protestant "reader" and the Catholic "interpreter," the one suspected of idiosyncrasy, the other of authoritarianism. Whatever special roles and ministries the church may develop for interpre-

---

16. *Summa Theologiae* 3.60.6-8.

17. Thomas Cranmer's Preface to the 1549 *Book of Common Prayer* concentrates more or less exclusively on the need for a new lectionary, complaining that "commonly when any boke of the Bible was begon, before three or foure Chapters were read out, all the rest were unread" and insisting that "the readyng of holy scripture is so seet furthe, that all thynges shall bee doen in ordre, without breakying one piece therof from another." *The First and Second Prayer Books of King Edward VI,* ed. Douglas Harrison (London: Dent, 1910), p. 3.

tation — the pulpit, the academic commentary, theological reflection, the magisterium — the heart of the matter is that all readers are interpreters and interpretation is necessary for reading. Good interpretation never struggles *against* the text, reading, as the fashion is, "against the grain," deconstructing the textual surface and showing it up as a confidence trick. Good interpretation never tries to bargain with the text, forging a compromise between what it says and what we would like to hear from it. It never supplements the text, overlaying it with independent reflections that head off on their own devices, never invokes a higher wisdom to cover the text's nakedness. Interpretation is the cheerful acceptance of the text's offer of more than lies on its surface, its invitation to come inside, to attune ourselves to its resonances and its dynamics, its suggestions and its logic.

This may be illustrated with an example. The well-known story of how David was brought to the court of Saul, excited the king's jealousy, and was finally driven into exile appears on inspection to have at least three contributory strands, one attributing David's presence at court to the king's need for music, another highlighting his precocious warrior prowess, a third, with the figure of Samuel in the background, stressing the divine anointing. As the construction of the text appears more complex, so does the historical background of which it speaks. We observe that the first constitution of the monarchy in Israel coincides with the rise of an elite warrior-culture and the practice, otherwise unknown in Israel's narratives, of single combat. With this we connect new developments in the use of body armor, the result of improved metal-working techniques, which according to a passing note (1 Sam. 13:9) the tribes of Israel were slow to acquire. So the once-straightforward narrative reveals many interesting dimensions. At which point the excitement of discovery may lead us to make a bad mistake: we imagine we have *wrung* this historical information out of a reluctant text, and forget that everything we have learned was simply what the text showed us. No "method" of ours — none, at any rate, that can be trusted — has not been shaped by the text itself, its points of connection and transition, its juxtapositions, its haltings and hesitations, its ambiguities, its strands of consistent and confident narrative. The text has disclosed itself and its background. If we suppose we have defeated it in battle like some Goliath, we shall, no doubt, triumphantly cut off its head. We shall then be fools twice over: first in conceiving that our cunning overcame the text when the text overcame our naïve simplicity, second in not allowing the text to overcome our second simplicity, which is the pride we take in analysis to the neglect of a synthetic understanding of the text as a whole.

Confession

As we receive the testimony, so we are called to take a part in testifying — no new testimony, but the same testimony we receive, yet renewed as it is allowed to shape and illuminate our active lives. Here, then, is what Christians have in place of a "worldview": a message about the order of God's works which we may both receive and give, a testimony to receive and amplify as it is passed through the thought and experience that is given to us to live with. Renewed interest in Augustine has given the term "confession," in its broad sense, a wide currency of late in referring to this further testimony required of us. It serves the turn very well, provided we remember that confession is not a separate beginning — here the apostles fall silent and my voice takes up the tale — but a faithful repetition, extending or amplifying the testimony we have received.[18] We in our time take it up from the prophets, apostles, and evangelists that first confessed, and from the church that echoes their confession to us, learning to think and say for ourselves what has been thought and said before us on our behalf. We may rightly see baptism, as the later Barth did, as the foundational act of confession, though avoiding the individualism with which he worked that idea through. The church itself, recognizing the coming of the Kingdom of God in the baptism on the banks of the Jordan, invites each new member to join it in recognition by being baptized. Baptism, as a sacrament, is a communication of the word that leads to further and continuing communications of the word, and among other communications to theology, which brings its light to shed upon the world under the guidance of the word in Scripture. The idea that thinking for ourselves must always be a new beginning free of the influence of text and tradition would be a foolish one — as though thought could ever arise in the sealed hermetic chamber of our own mind! There is, of course, a moment for the individual at which the flame catches hold of the tinder, the new thinker "catches sight" of what is being shown him or her. But thinking is not a matter of stubbornly clinging to that moment or trying to repeat it over and over. Any ideologue or dabbler in ideas can do as much. Thinking integrates the illumination of the moment into humane understanding, makes it part of the world that is commonly known and lived in. Theology founds its thinking on the reading of Scripture, not thereby

18. See Charles Mathewes, *A Theology of Public Life* (Cambridge: Cambridge University Press, 2007), p. 87. The discussion of this theme by Wolfhart Pannenberg, *Systematische Theologie III*, pp. 129-41 (Eng., pp. 110-22) deserves careful attention.

restricting or inhibiting the texts that may instruct it or the subject matter that may occupy it, but referring the widest explorations back to the central authoritative narrative of God's dealings with mankind. Often this has been inadequately done, by those concerned to stay within the letter as well as by those concerned to escape the letter's constraints. Yet taking a broad view of the record of Western thought, so much of which has been explicitly Christian and implicitly theological, one can only be struck at how reflection on Scripture has consistently called forth discovery, and discovery consistently fed back into a deeper understanding of Scripture.

But it is better not to confuse matters by representing "confession" simply as a kind of scriptural interpretation. We need not resist the suggestion that " 'ethics' . . . [is] part of an act of interpretive response," if what is meant is that the testimony we give must be congruent with the testimony we have received.[19] But what the confession of thought and word is not, is a kind of *exposition.* Since authority not only commands but authorizes, in our thinking we take the testimony of prophets and apostles onto new ground. Without presuming to improve on it or to supplement it, we are granted a certain power of amplification, filling out the testimony with what it means to this moment of time, this place, this setting, in which we have been given to bear it. That is why theological understanding has the power to be "creative" — to use a seductive word — without compromise to the content of the testimony or the disciplines of handing it on. It is why, indeed, theological understanding has the power to govern *practical* thinking and generate moral theology. What confession speaks of is precisely what Jesus and the apostles spoke of, the coherence of the world and its history in bringing to perfection the works of God in Christ's resurrection. We are not invited to testify to our own struggles, thoughts, and relationships in place of that unique and irreplaceable content, but we can supply a distinctive point of view on it, won from the experience of living under the guidance of the Spirit in this context rather than that, surrounded by these people rather than those, confronted by these problems and questions and not others. Our testimony is a reflection of our active engagements, sometimes a confession of sin, sometimes a confession of thanks, but always a confession of praise, which we alone are in a position to give from just *this* point in world and time. There are narratives we alone can recount, ideas we alone can sort out, deeds and actors we alone can appreciate, but in those narratives, ideas, and appreciations we never for a moment depart from the content of the Spirit's

19. Mathewes, *A Theology of Public Life,* p. 102, and the whole section from p. 95.

testimony, the disclosure of the world's creator to Israel and the salvation of the world in Jesus Christ.

The continuing work of the Father accompanies the words of Jesus (John 14:10). And when we, in our time and place, repeat those words and make them the basis of our testimony, the Father works. The form our testimony takes is not speech alone, but also action — or, better, speech *as* action and action *as* speech. The self-explanation which we offer to whoever asks us is an act, and by it we bind the living of our lives to the truth we are given to tell with our lips or our word-processing software. The acts each day requires constitute a speech, a meaningful and contoured account of what it is to live, here in this place and time, under the guidance of the Spirit which the ascended Christ poured out upon his followers. Disciples do more than replicate and refer to Jesus' actions. The tireless activity of the creator and sustainer of heaven and earth accompanies their spoken action and acted speech. "Whoever has faith in me, will do what I do himself; and will do greater things than these, because I go to the Father" (John 14:12). There are mistaken ways of hearing that promise; we may clothe it in a mega-narrative of progress which fortifies us with the thought that where Jesus and the apostles were naive, we are advanced, where they were primitive, we are developed, where they were idealistic, we are bound to the harsh realities of experience, and so on. The ridicule of Kierkegaard silenced such pretensions for a generation or two, but the ridiculous comes back into fashion with its usual impertinence. The promise of "greater works" cannot be detached from its other half, "Whoever has faith in me, will do what I do." The extended adventures which constitute our service of love are measured by that norm, the works and words of Jesus, the perfected law which lies at the heart of Scripture. The man of the first-century Middle East has gone to the Father and rules at God's right hand, judging the ambiguous proposals of science, literature, culture, politics, economics, and sexuality, and we must be ruled and judged by his words and works, even while our works go beyond his.

The Moral Confession

At this point we speak of "confession" in the narrower sense which tradition has also given the term, as moral confession, and specifically confession of sin. Only at this point can we speak of that. When awareness of sin thrusts itself forward and demands to be heard first, it is not a confession of God's righteousness, merely of our self-loathing, or, perhaps, our sneaking self-admiration, those two tones being not as far apart as we might suppose them to be. But in confessing the form in which God's righteousness is shown us, we confess our own place as discreditable and discredited agents, whose failures to live and love in truth are shown up by what God has done. Stopped in our ways by God's self-testimony, we allow ourselves time and space for dismay at what we learn of ourselves, the folly of our ideas about the world and our attempts to negotiate it. We have to "turn in" to wisdom *out of* the marketplace and highways of folly, and to make that turn we shall have to come to an understanding as to why and how the marketplace and highways have been so foolish.

There is a reflective moment in the repentance of sin, going far beyond the bare admission, "We did wrong!" It searches out what wrong we did and how we did it, seeking to know why our acts have been incongruous with our self-understanding and intentions. We may assuage our need to know with easy stories: it was not we who did it, but others; circumstances forced it on us; a spell, an ill-omened presence or provocative ill will magicked us into performances in which we, too, were really victims. Or what we did was not incongruous, but, set in a different light, understandable and maybe in the circumstances commendable. The ways of projection and recrimination, excuse and evasion, are always open to us, and they are the more attractive because there will always be something (something!) to be said along those lines. Our agency *is* responsive to pressures brought to bear by others; the moral meaning of an act *is* open to a variety of interpretations. Such lines of thought cannot simply be blocked off. The decisive point, however, is whether self-inquiry is led by the question of our own responsibility, or whether that question is concealed and obscured. We may use the intellectual flurry of introspection to bury our self-knowledge in, and the price we pay for the funeral is no more terrible than becoming stupider and stupider, further and further out of touch with reality, more and more baffled by the world's perpetual wrong-footing of our intentions.

Analyzing our misdoings, narrating our wanderings, is therefore an important discipline of confession. Our acknowledgment of fault may, and should, be detailed and factual, though it can never be exhaustive or complete. It may, and should, take cognizance of the extent of our errors, which will often be greater than we would wish them, though sometimes not quite as great as we would like to boast. A careful narration has the salubrious effect of denying us the self-dramatization of a Miltonian Satan, just as it denies us other equally pretentious roles. We do not acknowledge our faults

rightly unless we appreciate the commonplace ineffectiveness and insignificance of all sin. To thank God that the harm that our fumbling blindness
inflicts, though by no means trivial, is not quite on the titanic scale — that,
too, is what it means to be humbled beneath the judgment of the Lord.

And so it is that by inquiring into my own performance and its mis-
chances, I learn the truth and applicability of *general* categories of human
failure. "I am a man of unclean lips, and I dwell in the midst of a people of
unclean lips" (Isa. 6:5). There is nothing self-excusatory about this. It does
not exculpate me that my lips are similar in their habit to my neighbors'; it
simply offers a more comprehensive account of my blame. My sense of being
a distinct and wholly independent agent in the world is, after all, a deception,
for all the time I am merely carried along by the prejudices and instincts of
the herd. My competence is correlated with those among whom I dwell, and
in facing certain truths about them, I face those truths about myself. Someone newly appointed to a post of responsibility is eager to make a mark. He
or she would like to "turn round" some culture of mediocrity in which affairs
are bogged down, but typically ends up imitating the ways of predecessors,
having been too little aware of how the office determined the way it was
discharged. I, too, am a bureaucrat! I, too, am driven by crude measures of
liability avoidance and financial efficiency! Only when I see myself in that
light may I also come to see the window of opportunity given me to get to
the heart of what the business is really about. We seek to understand the
generic nature of our failures, that our place of action in the world may be
given back to us with altered prospects.

It is the generic character of sin that makes confession of sin a communicative task, something we may owe to another and not merely brood on
within ourselves. "Confess your sins to one another and pray for one another
that you may be healed" (James 5:16). The mutuality of the exercise turns on
the discovery of *community* in sin, a discovery only possible, breaking free
of the separations and demarcations of judgment, when we know ourselves
to be a community of God's forgiving and restoring grace. This is the knowledge that makes *moral teaching* a central element of Christian community,
free of the suspicion of esotericism that accompanied the ancient search for
wisdom. There may indeed be distinctions between righteous and unrighteous within the community that confesses sins to one another: "the prayer
of a righteous man has great power in its effects." There may be distinctions
between teacher and learner in the sphere of obedient life. But these distinctions are relative: "Let not many become teachers, for you know that we who
teach shall be judged with greater strictness!" (James 3:1).

Moral teaching at its best addresses generic truths specifically, focusing on typical points of urgent need. Let us stay with the Letter of James, a work persistently underappreciated by theologians precisely because of its moral aims, which taste, to the palate used to the rich gravy of Pauline doctrine, "strawy." The author, though of the apostolic age, makes no claim to apostolic standing, for he has no revelation to unfold, no kerygmatic proclamation. The themes of Christology and redemption are notably absent. Yet of all the New Testament texts none follows so closely the teachings of Jesus of Nazareth, and especially the Sermon on the Mount. Its rhetorical style, recognizable within the pattern of ancient moral teaching, is unusual in the New Testament: well ordered in fact, and weaving its threads of thought close together, it creates an impression of casual disorder by not articulating connections, but throwing out observations in short, jerky utterances, easy to remember and quote, rich in metaphor and simile. By the classical technique of "diatribe," it externalizes the logic of practical thinking by invoking imagined objectors. It is focused on the paradigmatic human oppositions that generate moral need: rich and poor, sick and well, hesitant and confident. But it does not map the spheres of human responsibility descriptively (family, work, economic life, etc.), nor follow the Household Codes in their address to the "stations" of human society (masters, servants, wives, children, etc.). It is addressed throughout to all Christians everywhere in their most universal moral needs.

Moving in a circle, it ends where it begins with patience in the face of trial, physical and moral. From this it turns inward at first, analyzing temptation in terms of desire, then outward to the social character of morality, which occupies two long sections, one on equality, the other on speech. Society and individual are both in play in the fourth chapter, tracing conflict back to acquisitiveness, and finally attention is directed back to patience, focusing on how the individual can be held within the community in sickness. It comes to rest on what the author himself has been doing, the moral instruction that helps us overcome sin (5:19-20).

James's letter, as a moral treatise, begins where a doctrinal treatise would end. The verb *chairein*, "rejoice," appears for the first time in Romans at 12:12, the noun *chara*, "joy," at 14:17. But it is James's first word (1:2), for joy is the creature's natural assent to creation, the form of the rational agent's participation in the work of providence. It attests God's completed work and initiates our uncompleted work. But then the object of joy breaks up before our eyes, dispersed temporally and qualitatively into "varieties" of "occasions" that we "fall into." Created worldly good presents itself as diversity and succession, temporal variations that we experience threateningly, as "trials."[20] Joy and trial arise together, as in the Beatitudes, so here. Joy is the implication of recognizing the trial *as* a trial. But it is not given immediately to experience; it must be "reckoned," realized in the affective life through reflection. The sufferer must take a view of the suffering, learn to see it within the goodness of God's deeds. The trial must bring the sufferer to him- or herself, for it is in the gift of self-attainment that joy appears. The name of this self-attainment in time is patience, which must be allowed its "full effect" (1:4), all the time it needs to achieve its goal.

What if there is a shortfall at the beginning, a deficiency in the "wisdom" required to envisage the world and its events rightly? We may be caught in perplexity and bewilderment, not knowing what it is we confront. The wisdom asked for must be *our* wisdom, not another's; only so can it make our trial comprehensible to us. Where does it come from? James points immediately to the gift of God (1:5). Why immediately? Was there not much to be learned from Scripture, tradition, and community? Yes, but it is learned there *in answer to* prayer, not as a *precondition* for praying. Scripture, tradition, and community are God's answer to the passion of perplexity when it is forced back on his direct and uncensorious aid. Yet there is one thing God looks for, which is that we ask in faith. "Whatever you ask in prayer, believe that you have received it," Jesus said (Mark 11:24), and James sees this as prayer for practical wisdom. Unbelief is ambivalent, looking over the shoulder, leaping from every decision to its opposite (1:8).

James's examples are never casual, but take us to situations that typify the moral life. Faithful "consideration" is illustrated by poverty and wealth, the two presented in a surprisingly parallel manner: the poor believer and the rich believer can each make a "boast," for their trials are very similar: constant indigence, on the one hand, sudden financial ruin on the other. The rich must joyfully accept the transitory and unstable character of great resources, knowing that nothing better is to be expected from the flux of worldly wealth (1:10-11). That, of course, is only James's first comment on the slippery slope of wealth, which subsequently slides through acquisitive competition in 4:1-6 to end up in the mire of 5:1-6; but when he first encounters it, wealth is a "trial" which may be met considerately as well as inconsiderately.

Two other examples of inattentive action are anger and talkativeness (James 1:19-20). Anger, represented in a striking metaphor as a bodily emis-

---

20. James does not distinguish "trials" from "temptations," as English translators do. See further on p. 168 below.

sion — we *exude* hostility, it breaks out of us and streams down us — is unable to "work the righteousness of God," because it is not a deed but a passion. Not unlike it is the flood of uncontained words, pouring out ideas, advice, rebuke, denunciation, explanation, always one remove from action and to that extent uncontrolled. But what of life under the control of the word? Again, a double illustration, outward-turned and inward-turned: visiting orphans and widows in their affliction, keeping oneself untainted. The first is the church's practice of *diakonia,* care and support for the needy, the second its moral separation. Together they sketch the shape of true communications: things we have to be shared with others, things others have that we are bidden not to share.

James tells of a mirror into which we may look, and on seeing ourselves, act. He is himself such a mirror, showing us how we conceive and bring forth the works of faith, and how we misconceive them and fail to bring them forth. The usual caricature is, of course, uncomprehending: James is not an apostle *of action* in contrast to Paul the apostle *of hearing.* Faith, for James, is the root of action, proved in bringing action authentically to birth. The key is being "quick to hear" (1:11). We know, of course, that he warns us to "be doers of the word, not hearers only, self-deceived" (1:22), but there is more than one way of being self-deceived, and James is no less concerned about the temptations of Martha than those of Mary, hurrying on too quickly, not listening properly, being a "forgetful hearer." The forgetful hearer has forgotten "the implanted word" (1:21), which is "the law of liberty" (1:25) that sets us free from purely mechanical reactions and gives us the power to act for ourselves. The forgetful hearer has forgotten God's will "to beget us by the word of truth" (1:18), and has therefore forgotten his own face (1:24). James, the moral teacher, reminds us of our face, bringing us back from our wandering, saving us from death and "drawing a veil over the multitude of sins" that we have left strewn behind us along our path (5:20).

CHAPTER 7

Hope and Anticipation

The Future of Today

And so to that "today," when, "if you shall hear his voice, you must not harden your hearts" (Ps. 95:7-8). To exercise agency effectively we must consider the time we occupy, formed by what we have learned to love, following what has been achieved for us, yet hearing and making answer now, in this new and instant moment. This third step of practical reason is the decisive one — tautologically, since it brings all that has gone before to the test of decision. If we fail to engage with God's will on the day that it claims our obedience, we fall back on general evaluations and criticisms, and accomplish nothing. For criticism makes only a feint at self-disposal; it is reflexive thought, "starting aside like a broken bow" (Ps. 78:57) from the action looked for today, and turning back to yesterday. The thought we bring to today must be purposive. But "today" is not instantaneous. It is an opening, and as we engage with it, we are extended in time, bending our attention futurewards — but always to *this* future, not to the speculative future of tomorrow. What makes "today" different from a tomorrow or yesterday is that its future is open before us; it is freedom's moment to realize itself in decision and action.

We should not, then, be tempted by the present tense evoked by the word "today" to renounce an interest in the future. Some theologians, prompted, perhaps, by a well-known *Pensée* of Pascal, have warned us to forget the future in order to attend to doing and living in the present.[1] As

---

1. Blaise Pascal, *Pensées,* ed. Brunschvicg #172, ed. Lafuma #47: *"Nous ne pensons presque*

Oswald Bayer has put it, the "present given to us" is "pastless" and "future-less."[2] But when, we may ask, is that doing and living in the present to be done and lived? Before lunch? Before death? These times are ahead of us. "Now" cannot be the time of a performance, for a performance is extended through time and "now" has no extent. Time is measured by recollection and anticipation. So the future cannot be held at bay from practical reason. To frame a purpose is to look forward; to act on a purpose is to enter a future. Yet there is a just critique and a fitting warning: we should not be so beguiled by futures as to miss the note of present immediacy in the word "today" — "each day while it is still called 'today,' " as the apostle comments (Heb. 3:13). The future, because it is indeterminate, is a beckoning space into which our imagination quite naturally expands. There are a thousand futures which imagination can conjure up, and though they can sometimes be alarming, they can also be delightful to play with. The expansive exercise of imagination has its own proper part to play, but it is essentially specu-lative, and our thought will fail to make the transition from speculation to practicality if it does not shorten its focus from the open universe of inde-terminate futures to the determinations of the present future, the future of today rather than the futures of tomorrow. To frame a purpose is to engage with a future right ahead of us, a future tied to our moment of purpose as a boat is tied to the quay from which we step into it. This future, the future of today, we call the "opportunity."

What light has Ethics, as a reflective discipline, to shed upon the op-portunity? When we ask about goods — good things, good relations, good happenings, good promises — we open an extensive chapter of Ethics where there can be very much specialized detail, all of it in generic terms, the natu-ral terrain for a descriptive science. The good is good as such, whenever and for whomever, and Ethics can identify and organize areas of experience of the good, each with its tract of moral reflection, bioethics, political ethics, economic ethics, the ethics of truth-telling, and so on, subdivided, it may be, at seemingly endless length. World-description is indefinitely expansive. But a purpose is narrow and focused. Its object is *one* thing, and that one thing a *new* thing, an action that falls to us to perform, still unperformed and therefore not open to description other than in prospect. Moral think-

point au présent; et si nous y pensons, ce n'est que pour en prendre la lumière pour disposer de l'avenir."

2. *Zugesagte Gegenwart* (Tübingen: Mohr-Siebeck, 2007), pp. 1-6. Cf. Gerhard Sauter, *The Question of Meaning,* trans. G. Bromiley (Grand Rapids: Eerdmans, 1995), p. 27.

ing deliberates in order to form purposes, but Ethics cannot form purposes. What it can do is reflect on and describe the function and conditions of good deliberation. And if we say that the function of deliberation is to identify the opportunity, it is a work of ethical reflection to explore what constitutes an opportunity. In outline we may suggest that the opportune time is a time *in the world,* when the act will correspond truthfully to the conditions that obtain; it is a time *for the agent,* who may realize him- or herself according to God's calling; it is a time *of the future,* which opens a way to the realization of God's purposes.

For initial commentary on these three determinants we turn again to the petitions of the Lord's Prayer, the beginning and end of moral thinking, at the point where it addresses "this day." "This day" governs each of the three successive petitions which face the challenge of decision and action. Action, new and unique on each occasion that the prayer is uttered, lies at the unspoken center of these three petitions. What has to this point been a prayer for the effective disclosure of God in the world, becomes with the third petition a prayer for the "us" who first called God "our Father," and for the conditions of our action. And though that "us" is everybody (for we pray as Adam and Eve's descendants, asking that no person or community may perish of famine, that no sinners may be hardened against forgiveness, that no human action or policy may fail of God's purpose and be frustrated), it is also ourselves in particular, the children of God whose "today" lies open and in question as we pray. We are not angels or souls made perfect, to intercede for the needs of mankind from an infinite distance. Human need is focused prismatically through our own needs.

The third petition of the prayer, the first of this group of three, asks for the worldly conditions of action, the material resources necessary to it, and among these, representatively, for those that allow us the power to exert ourselves. To ask for bread "this day" is to pray for *new* bread, bread that "succeeds upon" bread, for even the material conditions have to be sought against the horizon of the new day.[3] They are not brought with us, stored up in readiness for the moment, but like wandering Israel's manna that bred maggots when kept overnight they must be asked and received as we have need of them. Already, then, attention is focused upon the opportune time.

---

3. The epithet ἐπιούσιον is commonly, and best, understood as meaning "successive," which, taken with "today" (Matthew) and "each day" (Luke) yields "daily." Origen's famous discussion (*On Prayer* 27), which gave currency to the interpretation "heavenly," is an example of the philological skill and exegetical stubbornness that made the first of the great patristic theologians the lopsided giant that he was.

Bread is part of the natural cycle of life: we eat and excrete, we sleep and wake, we inhale and exhale, we are born and die, we are predators and prey, we nourish our blood and bone on vegetable and animal life and bestow our blood and bone as food for microbes and mites; but rather than simply praying for the stability of the ecosystem and our place within it, nourished and giving nourishment, we are to pray that these perennially fluid conditions of our passing life may be met *this* day, that the life we receive and hand on may be lived *now,* that the Father on whom we have called and whose will is to be done on earth, may be glorified by us *today.*

The fourth petition asks for the condition of freedom. We who grasp at the opportunity of today must be set free from yesterday. The metaphor of "debt" speaks of liability from the past, something still owing to what we have been, blocking out the future horizon. New acts we project are weighed down by the need to justify ourselves; they fail of being the joyous risk upon God's future that they should be. Repentance alone cannot relieve us of the burden we have brought with us, for repentance, too, is oriented to the past. The obstruction may be unacknowledged sin, but it may also be acknowledged sin, kept alive in the memory by persistent self-examination. John Donne knew that repentance could simply perpetuate the wrong that gave rise to it, paralyzing us in unbelief:

> For long yet vehement griefe hath been
> Th' effect and cause, the punishment and sin.[4]

What is needed is a divine interruption of the scrupulous (but never completed) narration of past guilt and wrong. We are dismayed, and should be, at the relentless introspective torment of some early-modern spiritual diarists, of Bunyan, Brainerd, and Froude. Torment accompanies sin as the fever that accompanies infection, and self-accusation is its fevered groaning. But the tormented self-knowledge of repentance, however necessary as a preliminary, is not the true self-knowledge. It isolates us, and allows us to take an interest in ourselves as "chief of sinners." As we repent, we trace as carefully as we can the lineaments of our fault, deciding where we were in error and why, but if we pursue the exploration to the end, we discover our neighbor's sin jostling up against our own and learn that we are one of a kind. Up ahead, if we accept forgiveness, there will be individual vocation, personal distinctiveness, all that makes one human being wholesomely dif-

---

4. John Donne, Holy Sonnet 3, "O might those sighes and teares."

ferent from another, but our sin is the sin of the race. And so we come to baptism among the crowds, seeking forgiveness for self and neighbor alike, asking God to set sin and its torment aside. What we ask is simply a "letting go" *(aphesis),* bringing the long interrogation of the fever to a preemptive close. No forgiveness can possibly help us unless it forgives us the task of repenting, too.

The fifth petition asks for the condition of future time itself, a future for the future action, holding it within the ultimate future of God's purposes. The danger lies before us of an action without a future, an action that has been pointless and ineffective. "Deliver us from evil," the second of two clauses which appear in Matthew's but not Luke's version of the prayer, adds nothing new, but explicates the clause preceding it. For what is "evil" to me, if not the final frustration of my agency? "Temptation" *(peirasmos)* is a testing, not some passing external difficulty we might be expected to circumvent, but a testing of ourselves, our weakness, our potential for self-destructive betrayal of what we are called to be. It is for our good that God permits such testing, but it is not a good we can take the measure of and embrace; therefore it is not a good that we can *ask for,* knowing what we ask, but a providence that we can recognize in the event of our deliverance from it. Praying not to be led into testing we acknowledge the deadly threat that it presents. "Harden not your hearts . . . as in the day of testing in the wilderness" (Ps. 95:8). The danger of testing is precisely that we collude with the evil that challenges us. Evil takes shape in the world, and we can believe that in God's providence the world will be none the worse for it in the end, but if we *collude* with it, it brings our agency to nothing and we are incalculably the worse for it. And so "Lead us not" is the only petition in the prayer framed negatively, not because it is more important than the others absolutely, but because it is the most urgent for ourselves. We may read it alongside the parable of the two houses on the sand and on the rock that concludes the Sermon on the Mount (Matt. 7:24-27). The alternative outcomes of human life are set before us: the collapse of the enterprise of human living into impotent nothingness, and its survival, not as a result of its construction but of its situation. The collapse of the fragile world in which our human action is set and on which it depends, the dissolution of our common universe of meaning depriving us of the power of action, these are the terrible realities to which the word "temptation" points, and the reason to ask not to be led into it is that nothing less than we ourselves are at stake there.

Three Prospects

The future is the stretch of time defined for us by its indeterminacy and inscrutability. Our relation to the future is not like our relation to the past. We cannot join it up, turn it into history and narrate it. We see it in glimpses, reflected off surfaces, anticipated by extrapolation from present regularities, projected as we frame purposes, or conceived of the inmost aspiration of our nature to rest eternally. When we speak of God's foreknowledge or foreordination of the future, we assert faith in its coherence, notwithstanding its inaccessibility to our view. We may say, if we will, that in the knowledge of God the future "is" already, but its factual shape, what *will be* past history one day, is unknown to us, or we may say that there *is* no factual shape to the future, and that its coherence rests wholly in God's power to effect his purposes; the difference between these we may leave to the philosopher. For Ethics the important thing is that a coherent future is, implicitly if not explicitly, essential to coherent action. We need a future to which the future of our action is open, a future that will not simply swallow the action up as if it had never been.

It is a commonplace that hope, rooted in the aspirations of our nature, is a basic and perpetual endowment of human consciousness, an orientation to the future that we cannot be without:

> Hope springs eternal in the human breast.
> Man never *is,* but always *to be* blessed.[5]

Or, more prosaically: "Human life is in its essence hope; the experience of human life is realized in a perpetual interest and active anticipation of a better future, still unclear, which is what we call hope."[6] To this, however, an Ethics attentive to the Gospel will enter a reservation. Three different approaches to the future risk being confounded here.

(a) We have a perpetual *interest* in the future, born of our agency. We turn to the future implicitly in all existence, and we turn to it explicitly in deliberating our purposes for action. The "good works" of which we read (Eph. 2:10) that they are "prepared before that we should walk in them," are prepared *before our feet,* a path leading us into the future.[7] It is not an empty

---

5. Alexander Pope, *Essay on Man* 1.95.

6. Bernhard Welte, *Gott und das Nichts* (Frankfurt am Main: Verlag Josef Knecht, 2000), p. 121.

7. A predestinarian reading of "before" as "before the world" is unwarranted. We are God's

habit of speech when we refer to a major deliberative topic, such as how the Euro is to be reformed, as "the future of" the Euro.

(b) This deliberative interest can be given content only as it is helped by *anticipations,* founded inductively on what we know of the world and its regularities. Anticipations are imaginative projections drawn from the past horizon of the present and extending the orderly pattern of events into the future. They may or may not be interested or practical; they may simply be the speculative views of an onlooker. They may or may not be "unclear," for there are many degrees of clarity, but some, at least, have the all-but-certain luminosity of secure induction, as with the knowledge that the sun will rise tomorrow, a prediction defeatable only by the destruction of the planet (though bad weather may simulate it!). They may or may not have a better future in view; they may quite possibly have a worse, generating an "interest" expressible only as repugnance and dread.

(c) Only if we appreciate the character and limits of these two prospects can we achieve a clear focus on the third, which is hope. If we suppose that our purposes *create* the future or that our anticipations *predict* the future, we shall find no room for hope. Hope is based neither on purpose nor on evident anticipation. It comes to us most importantly when our resolutions fail and our anticipations are ominous. Only then are we entitled to speak of a "better future, still unclear." Hope is, as they say, "excessive," reaching outside the narrow corridor of anticipatory imagination to something unimaginable which, for lack of another word, it is likely to call "mercy," "deliverance," or some other quasi-religious name. Hoping is not something that we always, or even often, do. It is a moment that transcends the normal conditions of life by which we negotiate the future. In unruffled circumstances cheerful anticipation can light our way for the short term, but its light, generated from probabilities and regularities, can as easily be turned off as on. It is when it is turned off that we may see the pinpoint light of a star shining in the darkness.

Hope never knows its object fully, and it may be that some titanic spirits hope with nothing at all to pin their hope on, perfectly conscious of their ignorance. It is more common to try to anchor hope on some eked-out anticipation, however implausible. God does not abandon hope to either of these impotent resorts. He puts hope in our reach through his promise. Without the promise the ultimate future must be sheerly unknown, and therefore sheerly disruptive. Promise is not something we might anticipate on the basis

---

workmanship, the Apostle declares, formed in Christ Jesus with a view to the good works God has prepared the way (προητοίμασεν) for us to live by.

of regularities; "the kingdom of God is not coming with observation" (Luke 17:10). Promise offers no speculative finality, no final coherence to the fragmentary anticipations we can win from the present, no rational unfolding of time's concrete possibilities. It speaks of what cannot be foreseen, for the deep changes in the world when the lion shall lie down with the lamb. The object of hope, Saint Paul tells us, is what we do not see (Rom. 8:24). But if we hope, he goes on, we also expect and endure. This brings us back from the ultimate horizon of the future to the immediate future directly before our feet, a space illumined by hope in the promise and open for freedom to move into, even if it is no larger than a space for patience, which is also an exercise of freedom. Hope, to recall the famous mixed metaphor, is "the anchor within the veil" (Heb. 6:19). In offering us the one thing about the future we may trust, it allows us to act in the knowledge that, whatever is uncertain, the future holds the coming of the Son of Man. In that knowledge our purposes may be formed this side of the veil, as we seize an occasion to do something, however modest. Hope assures us that what we do in witness to God's faithfulness will be worth doing, will endure before the throne of judgment.

Critique of Anticipation

Anticipations of middle-distance future are thus sandwiched between a *further* future of hope and a *nearer* future of purpose. The future of anticipation, dreary with anxiety or buoyant with optimism as it may be, must be kept in its place. "Tomorrow" may be the name of a misplaced care, unsusceptible of our attention and yet dangerously fascinating (Matt. 6:34). To distinguish anticipation from hope, and to restrain within limits the power of anticipation over purpose, that is the focus of the critique we need.

We may be surprised at how largely such a critique figures in Jesus' own teaching about the ultimate future. It forms a unifying thread through the long and varied eschatological discourse in the twelfth chapter of Saint Luke's Gospel. This begins with a warning against "the leaven of the Pharisees," a "hypocrisy" against which Jesus would forearm the crowds who throng him in hope of learning how to live (vv. 1-3). What is that hypocrisy but the assumption that there is stability in the present order, confidence in predicting how the world is bound to go? Nothing is more focused on the present than a crowd. When public interest or collective sentiment dominates, the past and future of present reality, the narratives and prospects that give it meaning, are buried beneath the glaring immediacy of the present. The crowd, therefore, is a place where secrets are kept; to deal constantly with public discourse is to keep a reserve on what cannot be uttered in that medium. The anxious strivings of our time to achieve "transparency" witness to an uneasy knowledge of the disingenuousness of public dealings. But as the secret spreads and permeates beneath the surface of things, making the present unstable and the future disruptive, as the subterranean stream forces its way up to become a spring and the unspoken comes to be spoken, so the uneasy knowledge becomes a cause of shame. That much Jesus tells the crowds: to act wisely and to live well means treating present appearances and present anticipations as perfectly fragile.

Whereupon he turns to his intimate circle (vv. 4-7) and speaks of a power that commands the disruptive future. The present order pretends to have the future in its hand; it utters warnings and threats, tightening its grip upon the vulnerable life of the body. But these warnings are not the real future, only a projection of the present. Beyond the life of the body is a future where the buried secret makes its appearance, an unforgetting future that does not reduce realities to unimportance. Are they told, then, to *trust* the one who commands that future instead of *fearing* those whose future is no more than a projection? No, they are told to *fear* the real future, too. Fear is not an inappropriate reaction to a time that overthrows the present. Threatened as we find ourselves in the present, yet we have a stake there, even in the threats that menace us. The present is, after all, the scene of our life; those who threaten the body make us, at least, important to ourselves, and perhaps to them. But the future reduces us with them and their threats to oblivion. Before we can learn to *trust* what overthrows those threats, we must realize that our very existence may be of no future account.

What, then (vv. 8-12), is the thread that links the present to the future and allows us to hope rather than fear? There is a correspondence between "confession" and "denial" in the present and "confession" and "denial" in the future. God's purpose to bind the present and future together is articulated in the title "Son of Man." To look around us and to see among the hidden things of the present that Son of Man for whom and in whom the future is prepared, is to find our link to the future, the Ariadne's thread that guides us out of the labyrinth of present and present anticipation. And here the strong Christological positivism is subtly qualified by a balancing emphasis on the Holy Spirit. If we hunt for things hidden in the world, what if we are mistaken? What if we mistake the Son of Man, and condemn the one we ought to welcome? Even that situation is recoverable, for the way from present to future is a way we will be "taught," given words and responses to the threats of the present as we need them. The Spirit will guide us to confess the Son of Man in the end, if we are ready to be guided.

Called back to the crowd (vv. 13-21), to worldly controversies and public resolutions, by someone who wants him to arbitrate a will, Jesus refuses this useful
service to the public good, and follows his refusal harshly with a warning against
covetousness. Was the request, then, motivated solely by greed? Could there have
been no justice in the claim? Justice in possessions! The very Lockean ideal of human
society! In opposition to it Jesus pits *life*, not constructed out of "what we have,"
but, as the parable of the rich fool illustrates, entrusted as a deposit we must give
back, an appointment to appear before the Lord of the future. And so he turns to
the disciples again (vv. 22-31) to elaborate upon the life that is "more than food" and
the body, through which we live and act, that is "more than clothing." At this point
the future available to hope is distilled in the phrase, "his kingdom." The future is
thus converted from peril to a goal of aspiration, but only because it is in the hand
of the Lord of the present, who sustains and secures the orderly sequence of life in
the world, including its forgotten and unimportant things.

The discourse on the future has risen from warning and challenge to a climax,
where the ground of hope is laid out clearly. Then, as though to stress that hope, so
far from being a constant alignment, becomes a focus of attention only at key moments, it descends again to the warnings from which it began. The climax is reached
at verses 32-34, where Jesus declares that the Father has resolved to give his flock the
kingdom. Hope, springing up as excess over anticipation, finds its security in God's
promise. Who, then, is this "little flock" that is entitled to hope? It is indeterminate,
a community hidden from public society, held together by confession of God's purposes for the Son of Man, its practical reason oriented to the promised kingdom, its
resources wholly committed to pursuit of what is given to hope. Sale and investment,
the perpetual exchanges of worldly economic life, are the model for the great eschatological redirection of practical reason. At the center of the agent's gaze is "treasure."

And how does hope transform the immediate horizon? The answer is astonishingly spare (vv. 35-40): by demanding watchfulness. The parable of the servants who
stay up for their master's return is one that echoes through the teaching of Jesus. It is
a measure of the importance Luke assigns it that he recounts it twice here in different
forms, separated only by the accompanying parable of the householder and the thief.
The other Gospels offer no parallel to Luke's first version, with its curious indifference
to what the watchful servants are to do with their time and its extravagant promise
that a grateful master will reward them in the small hours of the morning. Mark's
version mentions a variety of duties, Matthew's the duty of the household steward
(Mark 13:33-37; Matt. 24:45-51), but here the servants do nothing at all but stand
around in their household clothes ready for their chores whenever the knock on the
door shall come. This striking adaptation highlights the *formal contentlessness* of the
practical task that is given us. No definite thing, or things, must be done in the light

of the promised future. The single category that embraces all the many things we *may* have to do is waiting, attending wholly and with concentration focused on what is *not yet* happening, so that whatever *is* happening is handled with a mind supremely bent on something else. That gaze into the distance, causing all intervening action, as it were, to disappear, is Luke's key to life lived hopefully.

But such a life can only be lived in danger. Since the form and time of the hope is so unrelated to our ordinary expectations, attention may flag, the thief may catch us out. And so Peter replies in some concern: the parable sounds troubling to those who have just been told that their Father will give them the kingdom. Is its warning, perhaps, not meant for them, but only for those who do not yet identify with the little flock? Jesus will not allow that, and so a second telling of the parable is offered (vv. 41-48), where, following Matthew's version, the domestic scene is full of tasks to be completed before the time runs out: the steward must have the staff in place, their needs met, every preparation complete. Here danger and hope accompany one another, as carelessness and watchfulness accompany one another, perennial possibilities in our enduring of time. The coming of the Son of Man is dangerous for the same reason that it gives us hope: it cannot be brought within the commerce of ordinary anticipation and calculation. It is "an hour you do not expect."

There follows a brief episode (vv. 49-53) on the role of the Christ in history: to introduce the end of time, to kindle the earth, to undergo a baptism, to bring division and not peace. "Peace" would be the confirmation of an order in which the present is determinative; the radical hope of the promise of God will not confirm that order. The Christ, too, must wait and watch, constrained in longing till the time of accomplishment comes. Whereupon Jesus turns back to the crowds (vv. 54-56) in a further accusation of hypocrisy. It is a curious one, since they seem to be criticized for not doing what it is clear cannot be done, which is knowing the time and the hour. This ironic charge is, of course, the key to the whole long passage: the hope of the end *cannot* be assimilated to the calculation of the weather. But to live life on the basis of anticipation is to behave as though the end *could* be viewed in that way; it is to ignore the destabilization of the present that God's future has introduced. And so, indeed, they are criticized for not recognizing "this moment of time," the present of action, the time which cannot be subsumed into anticipation, whose every possibility is held hostage by the ultimate future and *only* hope, endurance, and watching suffice for what is required.

The concluding parable (vv. 57-59) takes a last look at action as it is shaped in the immediate moment when set before the horizon of the end. It is a perpetual out-of-court settlement, a coming to terms, in which the last word hovers over us, not yet spoken. Is all concrete action compromise? We may say so, in that it has to be formed within the constraints of a time when anticipation counts for nothing and only what can be won from the moment is secure. Like the parable of the threatened steward who cut his deals before the auditors moved in, this little parable sets a high premium on the brief moment of freedom given us — not because it does not believe in the future, but because it takes the disturbing threat the future poses more seriously than normal reckonings do. Anticipation has no urgency; based on regularity, it deals with time by renewing and recycling our debts. But urgency is what the future really imposes on us.

It is not that we can repudiate anticipation, or do without it. We need a critical appreciation of its just role and limits. We may start, then, by eliminating a false objection to it, which may be prompted by a resistance to consequentialism. Anticipation does not propose a *factual knowledge* of the future, or of any moment in the future. If it proposed such a thing, it would cease to be useful to practical reason, since factual narrative of future events would entirely undercut the indeterminacy that freedom requires. A factually knowable future would suppose the necessitation of the future by the present, which in turn would suppose the necessitation of the present by the past. The condition of free agency is to know the future only partially and indirectly, through prophecy or conjecture, and it is said even of the Son, through whom God acts in history, that the day and the hour are not revealed to him. There can, of course, occur a moral pathology in which the purposes we presently form are imagined so vividly that they seem as necessary and as factual as the past. For Shakespeare's Macbeth (not to deprive the historical king of his vaguely recorded but honorable place in Scottish history!) the vivid imaginations evoked by the witches on the heath create the illusion of being an onlooker on his own projected crime:

> My thought, whose murder yet is but fantastical,
> Shakes so my single state of man, that function
> Is smother'd in surmise.[8]

Instead of asking, "What am I to do?" he asks, "What is going to happen?" and his normal awareness of himself as a free agent is suspended. The sense of freedom is often anxious, and in an extreme case we may indeed suppress it, seeking the comparative security of a view of ourselves as playthings of destiny. But it is not to this diseased state of mind that consequentialist the-

8. William Shakespeare, *Macbeth* 1.3.

ories of ethics propose to bring us. Most of our anticipations do not confuse fact and purpose in this fashion. We think of regularities between events and outcomes which, without a necessary implication of future by past, allow us to speak of *tendencies likely to produce* certain future outcomes. And it is tendencies, not outright predictions, on which rational people are tempted to rely too much in their deliberations.

Anticipations are based on tendencies and tendencies are aspects of *present* regularities. We observe many kinds of tendency and entertain many kinds of anticipation. Some are affective, shaped by love or fear; some are calculated precisely on the basis of proven laws of nature. There is so much order to observe in the world around us, so much to extrapolate from, that it is wonderfully easy to form anticipations. But they often contradict each other (we may fear two incompatible things at the same time), and are insuperably difficult to draw together into a view of future history as a whole. Dystopian or utopian total futures tell us more about the fears and hopes that produced them than about probable future states of the world. Yet predictions are marketed at astonishingly high prices. Why is that? It is because they offer us an important purchase on the tendencies of the present context of deliberation. All deliberation, in fact, depends on powers of anticipation to connect a projected end-of-action with the exertion needed to achieve it. It would be foolish, then, to protest against anticipation. It compels us to observe a cognitive discipline, to recognize a logic of events which experience suggests; it forbids a flight into Micawberish *insouciance* about reality. To the extent that reliable anticipations may be soberly possible, we ought to treat them as seriously as any other information we have. But we repeat: it is the logic of the *past-present* that anticipation retails to us, not of the future.

Without pretending to factual knowledge of the future, anticipations may lay claim to a definiteness of their own, a measure of probability. A tendency can be a strong one, and can have a clear direction. But the more we depend on anticipations for deliberating, the more definite we shall want them to be. If, in the manner of classical utilitarianism, we impose the moral burden of forming purposes *solely* upon anticipated outcomes and nothing else, we shall make the demand for definiteness very high indeed. The objection to this is simply that though anticipations are sometimes probable, in general they lack the definiteness to meet the demands we would make on them. Unfortunately, they also lack the definiteness to resist our demands. They are not definite about what they cannot be definite about, and that gives us our excuse to think them more serviceable to deliberation than they really can be. So we fall into a serious error about action itself, conceiving it as a kind of skilled *poiēsis,* a technically controlled operation to produce an outcome which we have designed. This is an illusory view of action, for the productive skills of a craftsman or manufacturer are specialized in relation to their material, and events cannot be determined technically as clay or wood or plastic can be. Within specialized productive contexts we can anticipate with some definiteness what follows from what, but we cannot extend that definiteness to the general run of things we do. Anticipation may thus invite exaggeration of its powers on the basis of selective evidence, yet, if we listen to it carefully, we may hear it murmur that the *most* predictable thing about the future of events is its capacity for surprising us, which means disappointing our best-formed expectations. Behind the small galaxy of planets with predictable courses, there is a vast outer space of unpredictability. When we act in a social context, supremely, we are in a context of freedom where anticipation is largely reduced to guesswork.

Fear of freedom can be at work here, encouraging the belief that we *know* things, especially about others' behavior, which in truth we only *wish.* From this can arise a further confusion of resolution and foresight, curiously inverting the phenomenon Shakespeare assigned to Macbeth. Of the nuclear strategists of the 1970s, who argued that massive deterrence would certainly keep the peace so long as everyone declared in tones of scientific objectivity that it was certain it would, or of the economists of the 1990s who predicted infinite runaway growth for as long as "confidence" was sustained by optimistic predictions, we might say that surmise was smothered in function. They asked "what are we to do?" when they should have asked, "what is going to happen?" They could not accept the *certain* anticipation that there could be *nothing certain* about how humans would behave in uncharted circumstances, and so they suppressed the certain uncertainty with a resolute determination to impose certainty where a reasonable judgment would not have it. Setting such plainly diseased examples of public reason aside, we need to grasp the general point that lies behind every anticipation, however sober: human behavior can be made predictable only by abstractions of thought. *Homo oeconomicus,* that entertaining cartoon character of economic theory, may be useful in hypothetical projections and abstract models for such isolated strands of the real world as scientists like to study. But so extensive and so definite are the predictions made for *Homo oeconomicus* that it can seem irresistible to think they reveal the future of *Homo sapiens,* too. Overextended reliance on anticipation creates a demand for definiteness, which feeds back into a pinched conception of human actions and interests.

The demand for definiteness may impact on our decisions in one of two different ways. There is, in the first place, a preference for the short-term focus. A regime dominated by anticipation is governed by predictability, and the capacity to predict confers power to decide. But that capacity depends on a narrowed focus on the *essentially* predictable, on processes that resemble mechanical processes. Because the most certain utilities are short-term mechanical utilities, there develops a prejudice in favor of the mechanical and short-term utility over the long-term and spiritual one. There is, however, an alternative corollary, which may flow precisely from dissatisfaction with that narrowed focus. If decisions are *not* limited to short-term technical operations, the wider exercise of prudence has to be represented *in the guise of* a predictable mechanical process. We must *pretend* to have a scientific statistical prediction, precisely in order to suit our generalized conception of what responsible decision-making ought to be. And so it is that in late-modern society there is a constant confusion of speculative anticipation with hard science. We act on predictions that we have no sufficient reason to believe. Speculative projections are taken at face value, simply because we have long since formed the habit of discussing social causes and effects as though they were mechanically determined, a habit formed to help cope with a world where definite predictions are the key to power. We have created a regulative discourse of deliberation in which everything must give grounds for anticipating everything else, since, if it did not, we would apparently be left in a moral vacuum. If consequences are the only justification of policies, a habit of doubting the inevitability of consequences has a threatening, even an anti-social appearance. It is not that bureaucracy makes us think in utilitarian ways, but that utilitarianism makes us govern ourselves bureaucratically. The bureaucracy is an apparatus set up to entitle us to make confident predictions in every field of social policy, because confident predictions are what we have decided we need in order to justify our actions.

Hope and Anticipation

Reflective thought can handle impossibilities, can imagine "other worlds" which serve us as hypotheses to focus on the real world. Anticipation, on the other hand, deals only with the possible. Hope, too, moves in the sphere of the possible. But the possibilities are not of the same order, and this poses a temptation: to confuse the multitude of concrete possibilities arising from present regularities with the ultimately possible, which governs and exceeds them all. "We find ourselves confronted with the task," Jean-Yves Lacoste writes perceptively, "of defending the possible against every possibility we can realize."[9] There is a possibility of its raining tomorrow, a possibility of living to be a hundred years old, a possibility of war breaking out in the Far East. In a typical list of such possibilities we would not normally include the lion eating straw like the ox, and the child playing safely on the hole of the cobra; experience of carnivorous lions and toxic snakes does not make that possibility appear a very present one. It represents a possibility that lies beyond and behind all present possibilities. But it is in relation to that more ultimate possibility that we may, and must, hope.

Are we entitled to describe it as a possibility at all? If not, it can have no practical bearing, for our purposes are strictly limited by possibility. "No one is moved to that which is impossible," says Saint Thomas, which means, simply, that "ought" implies "can," a truism that defines what deliberative reason is all about, which is *something to be done.*[10] Not everything that can be imagined can be done, not everything that can be imagined as done can be done by us, or done by us here and now. But this truism determines its concepts in both directions. Not only is "ought" restrained within the bounds of "can," but "can" is expanded to encompass the scope of "ought." When we teach a child the apparent untruth, "there is no such word as 'can't,'" we are teaching something morally true, namely, that a view of what is possible may be enlarged by awareness of what is given to us as an immediate duty. To an adult, more prosaically, we would say that "can" is predicated in different ways. It is not a straightforward matter of fact, and there is some sense in which whatever may be sensibly deliberated on, "can" be done. Some things are impossible to accomplish at first, but possible with persistent determination; otherwise we would never acquire difficult skills like playing the violin. Some things are impossible to accomplish *in toto* but worth failing at, since even failure may bring achievements in its train, as when a commander takes on a hopeless battle to win time for allied forces, or a logician undertakes to disprove the thesis that "'ought' implies 'can'" in order to reach new insights into the grammar of necessity. The benefits to allied forces and the insight into necessity are by no means clear in advance; there is no calculable military or research strategy on which a firm reliance can be built; it is a matter of being open to

9. *Être en Danger* (Paris: Cerf, 2011), p. 364.
10. *Summa Theologiae*, 1-2.13.5: *"Ad id quod est impossibile, nullus movetur."*

less perspicuous possibilities, not yet in view or only indistinctly outlined on the horizon of history.

Among the great unities articulated in Ephesians 4 — "one body," "one spirit," "one Lord," "one faith," "one baptism," "one God and Father of us all" — there is included "one hope" (Eph. 4:4). The idea that there is one hope, lying behind the many possible objects of anticipation on which we may reasonably fix our desires, is the idea of an end of history. An end of history, as has often been said, is an idea that only Christianity could give birth to, since only Christians have conceived of an ultimate validation of human action in a future appearance that is presently wholly imperspicuous. "It has not yet been shown what we shall be," they have said, "but we know that when he is shown to us, we shall be like him, for we shall see him as he is" (1 John 3:2). If the object of human striving is taken to be perfectly clear, then an end of history towards which all strive must be perfectly banal, identified with such common aspirations as we can count on finding in any striving whatever, the avoidance of pain, the maximization of pleasure, and so on. And with this not only the imperspicuous possibilities are hidden from us, but quite a few of the perspicuous ones, too, such as wisdom or virtue, and the horizon of anticipation, which, though restricted, was not without exciting possibilities, is now reduced to the commonplace.

The anticipatory regime, in which the present mood dictates the prospect of the future, does not afford a comprehensive view even of possibilities that may be quite apparent. It can tell of this possibility and of that, of this impossibility and of that, but even when it scans the horizon and sees hosts of contending possibilities, its point of view, founded on the present, excludes more than it includes. Hope may, and often must, look through a different window. It has its independent ground, not formed from anticipations, not even from the most probable or universally proven ones, let alone the most far-reaching and ambitious. The resurrection of Jesus from the dead authorizes hope, validates promise, points to the future of God's kingdom. That does not mean it sets a trend which history will always thereafter follow. Since the resurrection, we are told, "your life is hid with Christ in God" (Col. 3:3). The path that leads from the empty tomb to the parousia is no open highway. There are signs to be seen and wonders to strengthen hope: in the church, the Eucharist, faith in the Gospel, in a multitude of good works, some confessionally, some unconfessionally accomplished. We may catch sight of the hand of the God whose kingdom is promised on earth as it is in heaven. But future history is not a joined-up narrative, and the revelation of the kingdom is not the culmination of a process we can hustle along its way.

Hope stands out dramatically in its true colors when the possibilities for anticipation run out, leaving no prospect but death, so that nothing is left to hold onto but the promise. "When you were young, you girded yourself and walked where you would, but when you are old . . . another will gird you and carry you where you do not wish to go" (John 21:18). Jesus' famous words to Peter seem to echo a proverbial comparison of youth and age. When even to be washed and dressed is a task for others to perform, when we have lost the most elementary medium of our presence in the world, control of our bodies, the horizon of all undertakings is closed down. Then the light of eschatological promise shines across emptiness, like the sun radiating through outer space with no worldly atmosphere to interpose and catch its light, and it is the decisive moment for hope.[11] Because death refuses to be integrated into the shape of life, because at whatever point it meets us, it meets us as a rupture with anticipated time, dying is a service of God unlike all others, requiring a virtue that can subsist apart from all others. Faith and love die to us, as we die to their proper objects: the object of faith God's presence mediated through our agency, the object of love God's beauty mediated through a world irradiated with loveliness. "Suffer us not at our last hour for any pains of death to fall from thee" ran the medieval prayer, admired and translated by both Luther and Cranmer. Does this somehow forget that God is faithful and that he loves us? No, but it seeks to respond to a distinct challenge to obedience, one that is different from all moral challenges we have met so far within the spheres of faith and love. Hope must beg for its endurance at its hour of passing from this world in order that it may keep in view its destiny beyond this world. A Protestantism that imagines it has nothing to say in the face of death but to give thanks for the life of the deceased has come perilously close to accepting that the horizons of human existence are enclosed in this world. It is a short step from absolutizing the horizons of worldly life to treating God's presence in the world as a mere manner of speaking. There is a "methodological atheism" appropriate to philosophy, perhaps, but not to theology, and the virtue which bears witness against it is the virtue of hope.

All this should not conceal from us, however, the resources that hope, engaged outside the narrow focus on dying, may bring to anticipation. The horizon of imperspicuous possibility makes more possibilities perspicuous. We cannot describe hope as seeing further into the future than unaided

11. The remark of Gerhard Sauter is to the point: "Is not death the first tribunal before which every methodology, every attempt of thought to probe the future, must justify itself?" *Zukunft und Verheissung* (Theologischer Verlag Zurich, 1965), p. 60.

anticipation sees, or as seeing more clearly, or in any way achieving a quantitative increment on anticipation. But what it can discover within the immediate future is the possibility of a *witness* to ultimate promise, the power of an act which, whatever its objective and worldly possibilities, can articulate a clear message about the purposes of God. It is this possibility on which hope will focus deliberation, showing us ways of action that had apparently had no prospects but now seem to have them in the light shed by the promise. Even such apparently pointless acts as suffering martyrdom for the truth suddenly have a point, since they are aligned with a future known by promise, not by anticipation. The alignment of near and far is clearly not that of means to end, in an instrumental sense. No act of ours could be a condition for the ultimate future. On the contrary, it is the condition for our acting; it alone underwrites the intelligibility of our human purposes, rewarding them beyond our desert and judging them in mercy. But an action framed consistently with it and pointing towards it, underpinning its immediate purpose or purposelessness with hope in the eternal purpose, is given the possibility of "referring" to it.

Here we must pause, with gratitude if also with some consternation, over the corpus of literature on hope that our generation has been given by Jürgen Moltmann. The distinctiveness of hope based on God's promise, an eschatology which speaks of "the future of the risen Lord," a "contradiction to the reality which can at present be experienced," a resistance to the banal predictions of futurology, are all themes that owe their currency to his early writings.[12] He has warned against basing eschatology on extrapolation.[13] Yet

12. *A Theology of Hope,* trans. James W. Leitch (London: SCM, 1967), p. 18: "Hope's statements of promise . . . must stand in contradiction to the reality which can at present be experienced. They do not result from experiences, but are the condition for the possibility of new experiences. They do not seek to illuminate the reality which exists, but the reality which is coming. . . . Present and future, experience and hope, stand in contradiction to each other in Christian eschatology, with the result that man is not brought into harmony and agreement with the given situation but is drawn into the conflict between hope and experience." It would be difficult to find a better statement of the way hope makes action possible than that on p. 31: "The present of the coming parousia of God and of Christ in the promises of the gospel of the crucified does not translate us out of time, nor does it bring time to a standstill, but it opens the way for time and sets history in motion."

13. "Methods in Eschatology," in *The Future of Creation,* trans. Margaret Kohl (London: SCM, 1979), p. 42: "If we are clear about the scientific use of the word extrapolation, it immediately becomes clear how dangerous it is to build up theological eschatology on this method. It certainly then acquires an empirical basis, but it becomes more and more problematical the further it thrusts forward into the future." Or in "Hope and Development," also in *The*

from the beginning, too, and not only in later writings, his exposition of hope has been bipolar. In a puzzling relation to the promised future defying prediction there has been an insistence on intrinsic possibilities, from which he has developed his ethico-political program for the life of hope in the world. Only hope takes existing possibilities seriously, he thinks, because only hope sees the present as progressive, not static.[14]

We would not wish to pick a merely verbal quarrel with Moltmann's fondness for the word "anticipation." His understanding of "anticipated fulfillment" as an "earnest and pledge" of completed fulfillment, however, ought to raise more than an eyebrow.[15] Are those words, used in Scripture of the Holy Spirit and in contemporary sacramental theology of the Eucharist, now given substance in a political program? Moltmann does not conceal his attachment to the idea of a joined-up history of time leading always in one direction, and reserves his warnings for those who think that the direction lies on the surface of things rather than concealed in the crucifixion of God. Once the direction is assured, we need not pause over whether, or how, to press ahead.[16] His critique of prediction is directed against narrow statistical projections, not against the whole idea of anticipating the ultimate future. This uneasy synthesis of ideas is summed up in two startlingly juxtaposed sentences from his latest work: "An ethics of hope sees the future in the light of Christ's resurrection. The reasonableness it presupposes and employs is the knowledge of change."[17]

Moltmann illustrates the desire, too characteristic of systematic theo-

---

Future of Creation, p. 55: "We have two possible ways of talking about the future. We can talk about what is going to *be* and we can talk about what is going to *come.* This makes a profound difference. What is going to be can be calculated from the factors and trends of the present. Developments are analysed and possible rates of growth calculated. The possible future is extrapolated from past and present. This is the method of futurology and scientific prognosis. I would call this the calculable future. But the calculable future is not identical with the desirable and hoped-for future."

14. *Theology of Hope,* p. 25: "Hope alone is to be called "realistic" because it alone takes seriously the possibilities with which all reality is fraught. It does not take things as they happen to stand or to lie, but as progressing, moving things with possibilities of change." This opposition of fixity and change owes more to pre-Socratic philosophy than to Christianity, and is frankly incredible: *fear* is notoriously credulous of change, and to what do we owe the late-modern preoccupation with perennial change if not to nineteenth-century conservatism?

15. "Methods in Eschatology," p. 46.

16. "Methods in Eschatology," p. 47: "Just as anachronism limps after time, so prolepsis hurries ahead of it, already realizing today what is to be tomorrow."

17. *The Ethics of Hope,* trans. Margaret Kohl (Minneapolis: Fortress, 2012), p. 41.

logians, to make a fundamental theological concept serve as the immediate answer to every practical question, without giving space for deliberation to look around and understand the world and time it lives in. Hope cannot be the answer to any question of the form, "what shall we do next?" It is the *condition* on which that question can be raised and answered — answered on its own terms according to criteria of practical reasonableness. Hope does not and cannot ground the program Moltmann elicits from it: the struggle for economic justice, the struggle against political oppression, the struggle for solidarity against alienation, the struggle for hope against individual despair.[18] This program has roused a measure of exasperation on its own terms. Hans Frei exclaimed, "Reinhold Niebuhr, where are you when we need you?"[19] But it is neither Niebuhr nor any alternative politico-theological program that we need. Let us accept that the political clothes in which Moltmann has dressed his doctrine of hope offer nothing to object to; they are respectable, neatly cut, and fashionable; they have only the drawback that they appear to have been slept in. But political programs are historical, to be taken up, if at all, with the humility of any concrete task, in response to the practical demands of the context. No agenda for practical Christian witness can have universal and timeless validity. So we have to ask how the elements of this program, with its distinctive priorities, were come by. The suggestion that they were found on the straight road from the resurrection of Christ and the promise of the Kingdom is frankly unbelievable. What do those truths tell us of a corrective social norm such as economic justice? Insert them back into the narrative of salvation, of course, where they belong, speak of the redemption of created order, the revelation of divine rule in the advent of Christ, and the spoiling of political authorities by the cross and resurrection, and then, with this narrative for guidance, tackle the tasks of practical political reason *as they have arisen in our time,* and then economic justice, human dignity, solidarity, and so on will find their proper place, no doubt a prominent one, in a view of God's mandate to us. But this careful attention to the world and its redemption, to the needs confronting God's people in differing ages and circumstances, is precisely what Moltmann leaves out. That is the criticism made against him by the theologians of liberation: the program is too absolute, too dissociated from

18. *Ethics of Hope,* p. 37.

19. Hans W. Frei, "God's Patience and Our Work." Unpublished Pieces 1998-2004, transcripts from the Yale Divinity School archive, ed. Mike Higton. http://www.library.yale.edu/div/fa/Freiindex.htm.

a context, too much an axe-blow which pays no attention to the grain of the wood. Practical reasonableness is more than a knowledge of change; it is a habit of looking around one, taking the measure of the realities that shape the context of action before one embarks on it.

Endurance and Temptation

What, then, can be said about the working of hope *in action?* Supremely, that it involves endurance, *hupomonē,* a persistent confidence in the final vindication of goodness in the face of its recurrent denials. Moltmann was perfectly correct, of course, to turn from hope to "the crucified God." But what of the crucified disciple? When he might have encouraged us to take up our cross and follow after, he invites us, rather, to anticipate the triumph of the resurrection. We are to recognize those who bear Christ's cross in the poor, the oppressed and those who are economically exploited, but not, apparently, in ourselves. Talk of "solidarity" (which is, after all, political support *for* the suffering, not *co*-suffering) cannot conceal the assumption that Western Christians are permanently located on the site of vindication, always protesting and demanding change on behalf of others, not enduring together with Christ. There can, again, be no objection to the thought of protesting and demanding change — when and where that course of action arises in faithful deliberation as the practical requirement set before us in our moment. The point is simply that this conclusion is not reached immediately from eschatological hope, and is not a universal conclusion for every time and circumstance. Hope is our grasp of the promise that the God who rules the world we love will let his reign appear universally, and the only universal and unequivocal way we can and should describe hope is as courageous endurance in doing God's will, a refusal to be distracted or disheartened in pursuit of the end in which action can rest.

In common parlance we are speaking here of the virtue of courage, not in the classical sense of bold risk-taking *(andreia),* but as a readiness to face down pressing and anxious anticipations in the strength of a hope that supports us. The self-perfection of a Hercules needs *trial,* but it does not need *time.* Hercules displayed his virtues in his cradle, and patience was not among them. The proving of faith which a Christian faces has everything to do with waiting. The name of the virtue in the New Testament is *hupomonē,* which we render "patience" or "endurance," though with the annotation that it is not in any way a passive or resigned virtue, but is tied to that taut attentiveness which the parable of the waiting servants so remarkably conveys. If Shelley's Promethean version of this virtue seems grimly over-defiant —

> To suffer woes which hope thinks infinite . . .
> To defy Power which seems omnipotent;
> To love and bear, to hope till Hope creates
> From its own wreck the thing it contemplates;
> Neither to change, nor falter, nor repent;
> This, like thy glory, Titan, is to be
> Good, great and joyous, beautiful and free;
> This is alone Life, Joy, Empire and Victory.[20]

— the reason surely lies in the radical re-negotiation it undertakes with hope, which is no anchor within the veil holding fast to a promise, but a self-generating defiance of circumstances, conjuring up its own future reality from the imagination.

Endurance is better described, with Charles Mathewes, as acceptance — of "the gift that time most basically is."[21] But "most basically," because not everything that time presents us with is beneficent, and not every gift it presents us with is its real gift. Time is not self-evidently supportive of our selves and our agency. It compels the decay of our world; whatever we admired and whatever we have accomplished it takes away, and what it replaces them with is uninterpretable and ungovernable. The new is not the same as the good. The moral-theological question about time is this: how the new, uninterpretable, and ungovernable can be received as blessing rather than as curse. The answer is not to make up our minds to see it that way, to chatter banally about the need to "move on" and to "learn to adapt," which merely trifles with the problem, offering by a simple trick of redefinition to call evil good. Endurance needs a ground of hope, a purchase on God's ultimate purpose which it can lay hold on, and that, given the imperspicuity of the future, can only be a promise, not inherent in time but entrusted to it as a secret cargo. Endurance is not passivity, though it may defer decision and action until the moment is given, but a constantly receptive attention, resisting the threat of meaninglessness with a readiness to respond to meaning

---

20. Shelley, *Prometheus Unbound* 4.570ff.
21. Mathewes, *A Theology of Public Life* (Cambridge: Cambridge University Press, 2007). The passage entitled "During the World" (pp. 10-23) is illuminating throughout.

in meaningful action. Endurance confronts the emerging future in watchful expectancy, looking for the light of promise shining back on time and the moment of purposeful self-disposal it will show up before our feet. It watches for opportunity, and together with opportunity, temptation.

The New Testament term *peirasmos* speaks of whatever obscures God's promise from us. Saint James opens his Letter with the instruction to "count it all joy" when we fall into various forms of *peirasmos,* and declares that the man who endures it is blessed. He then warns us not to say that it is sent by God, for it comes from the collusion of our individual desires. This seemed to some English translators (the RSV initially, widely imitated by successors) to pose an intolerable paradox, which they resolved by employing two different English words, "temptation" and "trial," the first for a moral *peirasmos* of desire, the second for a circumstantial *peirasmos* of difficulty. James was thus left with no encouragement for the "tempted" and nothing but congratulation for the "tried." The voluntarist character of this translation is evident. It failed to understand how desire and circumstance collude within the context of world-time. Desire is precisely our emotional response to the sway of time over circumstance. There could be no temptation that did not have both an inward and an outward pole, weaving desire and circumstance together. If changing circumstance did not affect us, we would not desire; if we did not desire, changing circumstance would not affect us. We are, as a powerful scriptural metaphor from another source represents it, engaged in conflict, always active, always defensive. We are troops, armed piece by piece, who have to stand their ground when the battle presses hard (Eph. 6:11-18). The struggle means winning opportunities for action from the suffering of time, the transformation of passivity into "striving," refusing the passivity of despair by moral reflectiveness and prayer.

Can we take seriously Saint James's injunction to treat temptation as a matter of joy? The joy is, of course, joy at the *fact,* not the *prospect,* of being tempted. We are taught to pray, "Lead us not into temptation," and the martyr church of the early centuries knew very well the difference between accepting martyrdom and going out to seek it. Temptation confronts us as a *fait accompli,* a threat manifestly present and urgent. It should not take us by surprise, since we know it to be an inevitable feature of our pilgrimage in time.[22] We know, too, that God's purpose is to turn it to our good through our resistance. If we respond with joy, then, it is not that we do not appreciate the menace. Joy is the emotional register assumed by hope in the promise of the sovereign

22. Cf. 1 Thess. 3:3.

rule of God. It is the energy, drawn from the reserve of the future, by which temptation can be overcome. It is the taut resistance of the anchor to the fast-flowing tides of time. But joy is never objectless, but always *in* something. It is because the promise offers an understanding of our position among the goods of God's world and before the good of his ultimate time, that we can, in our endurance, discern the real reasons given us to be joyful and not despairing within our practical need. Joyful endurance is considerate. It weighs the unreal goods on which desire may fix itself against the actual goods with which God's purposes have framed our moment. It is, as we shall proceed to say, the key to patient *deliberation* on the acts we are given to perform.

Temptation is resisted at its inner pole of misplaced desire, the psychological attraction that impels a course of conduct other than we should wait for, a precipitate initiative, perhaps, or a refusal when opportunity lies open before us. What induces this desire, at the outer pole, is an event in time with power to distract and divert us. It may be the beckoning appearance of a good, or it may be the threatening appearance of an evil, perhaps death itself. We explore temptation under these two forms as "seduction" and "oppression" through the prism of the first and last temptations of Jesus.

He comes, led by the Spirit, into the wilderness of Judaea, equipped by the Spirit to fulfill his vocation. But he postpones setting out upon it, and devotes a significant period to waiting inactivity. It is a period of endurance, not only of time itself but of hunger, waiting for the moment to be given when he may say of the Spirit's mission, "This day is the Scripture fulfilled in your ears!" (Luke 4:21). But that waiting is full of intellectual and spiritual searching, not for the mission itself, which has been delivered to him, but for the manner in which it is to be pursued. The temptations of Jesus are a time of deliberation; the alternatives are posed, the necessary decisions made.

The struggle against seduction is understood by Saint Luke as a question of mastering impatience. His sequence of three temptations ascends from the goods of the body to the goods of the soul and then to the goods of the spirit: impatience for the sustaining of life, impatience for the political destiny of the world, and impatience for the public disclosure of God's glory. The supreme temptation of man, Luke suggests, is precisely to tempt God, to seek the fulfillment of God's purposes without having to endure God's time. We recall the question and answer which precedes the Ascension (Acts 1:6-7). So in the desert Moses was tempted and fell at Massah ("Temptation"), "when your fathers tempted me, tried me that they might see my works" (Ps. 95:8). So the decisive rebuke to Satan is, "You shall not tempt the Lord your God!" (Luke 4:12). Where Satan would have Jesus confront the future with imaginative anticipation, he will confront it with obedient patience. For Saint Matthew, with the second and third temptations inverted, the sequence follows a topographical order from the desert to the city and to the world. The range of Jesus' enterprise broadens, his influence grows wider, and at each stage the question is posed afresh: will it be exercised wholly under the sovereignty of God, in his time and way, or will the servant reach out for means to fulfill it that will alienate him from his service? It is the sovereignty of God that must shape man's engagement with his time for action.

For the struggle against oppression we turn from the beginning of Jesus' ministry to the end, to the suffering of the cross itself. The intention of his executioners is to reduce him to an object of contempt and pity. It is, perhaps, too easy for us in our meditation on the figure "woefully arrayed" to acquiesce in this; some recent interpretations of the "cry of godforsakenness" make the pathos of that utterance the limit of their reflection, finding only passivity and helplessness. The evangelists' narratives, on the other hand, show us in different ways how the ultimate condition of oppression is the greatest achievement of endurance, where passion is turned to active self-disposal. The devotional and dogmatic tradition of handling the cross, when it has known what it was doing, has seen not only an affliction but a supreme accomplishment.[23] We can observe this especially through what tradition has called the "seven last words from the cross," short utterances, as brief as can be imagined under the ultimate physical affliction, reaching out to God to convert the state of suffering into effective act. If instead of following the customary order we take the sayings from each Gospel in turn, highly contrasted in their manner though they are, the point becomes even clearer.

For Saint Luke the scene is framed by the ultimate oppression of mankind, the judgment of God which will cause the ordered world to collapse around man's head. So Jesus, on the road to Calvary, warns "the daughters of Jerusalem" that his death portends the great sorrows of that coming day (Luke 23:28-31). He dies as forerunner of the many righteous who will suffer as victims in the dénouement of man's sin. The centurion's words acknowledging him as "a righteous man" (23:47) interpret his death so, and the anxious mourning that falls upon the crowd is the first fulfillment of that proph-

---

23. Anselm of Canterbury, more insightful than later substitution-theorists, for whom Jesus was simply the passive object of God's judgment, makes of his death an *act of satisfaction* to the honor of the Father. And I cannot forbear to quote the beautiful Collect which forms the text of the opening chorus of Bach's *Johannespassion:* "O Lord our governor, how excellent is thy name in all the earth! Show us by thy passion that thou, the true Son of God, art even in thy deepest humiliation confirmed as Lord for ever!"

ecy. Luke's three words from the cross (23:34, 43, 46) place Jesus firmly in the place of the righteous Psalmist engulfed by his enemies. The third word, "Father, into thy hands I commend my spirit," is a quotation from Psalm 31, which has in view those who lay traps for the righteous and worship idols, the prayer of one who looks for vindication in his death, his life-project delivered from those who sought to render it impotent and ineffective. In the light of this we can appreciate the force of the first word, the prayer for forgiveness, which picks up the teaching of the Sermon on the Plain and of the Lord's Prayer (6:28; 11:4).[24] It is not meant to palliate the hostility to good in this act of cruel injustice; the ignorance of the tormentors, their failure to understand the difference between good and evil, is not pleaded as an excuse. Rather, it is the ground on which a plea for vindication must become a plea for divine forgiveness. No human forgiveness could overcome man's hatred of good. Only the gift of new creation will do. The vindication of the righteous requires a community of righteousness, but where is that to come from when the righteous one is the Son of God, and the offence against him incriminates all mankind? Only the forgiveness of God can create a world of vindicated righteousness. The second word, declaring God's mercy on the penitent thief, is a sign that their prayer has been answered. The suffering of the righteous one has been effective as a testimony; it has elicited faith and opened a way to God for the unrighteous.

By Saint John the emphasis is laid on two framing features, the words of the superscription and the pouring out of water and blood from the wound in Jesus' side, identifying him respectively as king and source of life (19:19-22, 34-37). Oppression from enemies is only marginally present; that question has been confronted in the lengthy trial scenes. The oppression is the sheer withdrawal of strength and life, and in face of it Jesus commands the situation, most notably in making provision for his mother, not implausibly understood as representing provision for the church, enfolding faithful humanity and faithful Israel (Mary) in the care of the apostolate. With the cry of thirst (19:28) physical want is placed in counterpoint to his conscious recognition and fulfillment of the purposes of God. Even here he takes the initiative.[25] It is a "fulfillment" of Scripture (referring to Ps. 69:21), but also

24. It may simply be noted, without drawing conclusions, that on the basis of a few but early witnesses the authenticity of 23:34 is doubted by some textual critics.

25. There may, as is sometimes suggested, be a double sense to the thirst, physical and spiritual. Cf. John Fenton, *Finding the Way through John* (London: Mowbray, 1988), p. 90: "The thirst of Jesus is not for drink of any kind, but for God and the completion of the work of drawing everyone to him."

a "fulfillment" of the purpose of love which brought the Word to his own, a love that must be carried through "to the full."[26] The drinking of the vinegar, not refused in this Gospel, is the gesture by which the incarnate Word accepts the fate of the flesh he took, which is rejection, since the vinegar was for the Psalmist the sign of enmity. Immediately upon this gesture the word "fulfillment" is confidently spoken as death overwhelms him (19:30).

Saint Mark's narrative, closely followed by Saint Matthew, could hardly feel more different. It knows of only one word from the cross (Mark 15:34; cf. Matt. 27:46), the cry of desolation taken from Psalm 22:1, "My God, my God, why hast thou forsaken me?" Otherwise the talking is done by others, and until the centurion's wondering exclamation at the circumstances of the death, it is all contemptuous. In the face of the solemn event, spoken commentary is idle mockery. Only the silent testimony of the written superscription identifies the paradox in the slaying of the King of Jews. Yet we should not mistake the scene for one of sheer obliteration of agency. The utterance itself, followed by the death-cry, situates Jesus in the place of the suffering Israelite whose persistent questioning of disaster is answered "from the horns of the wild oxen" (Ps. 22:21). Even in dying the sufferer reaches out for the purpose of God to be fulfilled in his existence, and the final cry is the moment of his answer, the tearing of the veil a sign that the purpose is achieved in the apparent purposelessness of death. The emptiness of speech up to this point is transformed by Jesus' cry and the death that follows it, drawing from the soldier, or soldiers, the confession that he is the Son of God.

In death, too, the righteous one makes his active response to the purposes of God and contributes to them. This is the boldest claim for hope imaginable, that purposeful action can persist in the "act" of dying. Much has been made in past tradition of the grace of dying well, and a good deal of it has suffered from the fault of trying to arrange death in some kind of aesthetic form that requires, apart from other things, certain conditions of emotional composure and intellectual focus that can by no means be counted on. The strength of Matthew and Mark's presentation of the crucifixion is that it defies such aesthetics, while still proclaiming the act of dying as the service acceptable to God. Here is the point where deliberation has no space left for a purpose, human resolution no strength left to endure further, and the completion of the act and the life depends on God's gracious acceptance. That, for these two evangelists, is the meaning of the signs that follow it, the rending of the curtain of the temple and (in

26. τετέλεσται . . . τελειώθη . . . Cf. 13:1, εἰς τέλος.

Matthew) the earthquake. Physical and mental resources are reduced to nothing, yet Jesus' death is accepted by God as the culmination of his life's service.

Sin against Time

The third elementary form of "possible sin" is that of *anxiety*, sin in respect of time, a failure to allow the promise of God's good future to illuminate the time given us now for action. Anxiety is a passion, a species of fear. Fear at its most general extends to all futures, and therefore to everything that will or may transpire, or may be anticipated as transpiring, within and beyond the scope of our capacity to act, but anxiety is the fear we experience specifically in the face of action and its perilous opportunities. It is not to be denied a useful function in focusing our deliberations upon a purpose. An anxiety-free existence could mean only that we were inattentive to the peril of opportunity, either inertly forgetful of our agency or failing to appreciate how our fate must hang on it. We are summoned to display confidence, but confidence must be won *by* deliberation *out of* anxiety; we are not endowed with it as a birthright. Passions have their proper place in practical reason, fear and anxiety among them. But passions are not to be indulged in. They are the emotional springboards which we must press down upon if they are to launch us into action. So when Jesus declares, "Do not be anxious!" (Matt. 6:31), he means, "Cease to be anxious!"[27] It is a call to set the unknown future of life and action in the light of God's promise. That is to say, it is a call to hope. Anxiety prepares us for our moment of response when the Spirit repeats this call to us, ordering us, as Jesus ordered Peter, to step out of the boat of our anxiety and to walk the waves.

This possible sin is situated, then, on the border between anticipation and purpose. Pure anticipation may fill us with fear or optimism, but it cannot make us anxious. Anxiety occurs only when our happy or unhappy anticipations are brought to bear upon the question, "And what shall we do?" The realm of anxiety lies where that question has been put but not yet answered. When the purpose is fully formed, our anticipations can be set

27. So Hans Urs von Balthasar, helpfully, in *Der Christ und die Angst* (Einsiedeln: Johannes Verlag, 1951), p. 57, positing two kinds of anxiety, a sinful anxiety and the anxiety of the cross, and adding that the relation between the two can be defined only by the *movement* from one to the other: "A real movement, a firm step! Faith in the New Testament is described as something palpably secure, reassuring, confirming."

aside. We know what is to be done, and all our attention is bent on doing it, leaving no room to worry about what will happen. Up to that point, however, anticipation accompanies our deliberations with a sequence of alternative possible futures of oscillating emotional tone, now encouraging, now discouraging, now clear and now obscure, like light reflected off troubled water. In these swirling eddies the current of responsibility spends its emotional pressure. The passage of time from future through present to past then ceases to communicate God's goodness. It suggests nothing but loss and decay; we are fearful of its passage, and we want to hold it back.

Refusing to let time be time and God the Lord of time, anxiety generates its various sins against time. As before, we take four progressive soundings from the more immediate to the more deliberative forms of this sin, two of them here, and the other two in chapters 8 and 9, respectively. Anxiety can prompt a close-drawn, myopic imagination, looking no further than the end of its nose; it can also prompt a nervously far-seeking one, that scans the horizon and is crushed by responsibility for what it cannot yet see. And, of course, there is much in between.

(a) Anxiety's most immediate manifestation is in *greed*. As Jesus teaches, it easily wraps itself up in care for material resources: "What shall we eat? What shall we drink? What shall we put on?" Anxiety as such is a spiritual state, fearful for our future competence as agents, but in this form it is constituted precisely as unawareness of the self as spirit traversing time, seeing self as a creature of material forces. Worry about material goods is the surest proof that we are spiritual beings, for it is a fortress set up to exclude the demand that time makes on us as spirit, a fortress constructed of immediate objects of sense that can be held onto. The goods of food and clothing are imaginative surrogates for the spiritual courage of endurance. Lacking a sense of God's provision for the future, we cannot think of what is permanent and enduring about ourselves, so that in the passage of time we see only transitoriness and loss. The tempter says,

If you let slip time, like a neglected rose
It withers on the stalk with languished head.[28]

Yet time must slip; it is the form in which time is given. If we will not let it slip, we will not have it, and then we shall debar ourselves from living and acting.

28. John Milton, *Comus* 743-44.

Simple consumption, let us be clear, is not in itself greedy. If someone wants a meal and has the price in his pocket, he had better eat and drink; the better the food, the better for him. If someone can afford clothes to hang on her limbs, she had better dress herself, and an eye for a good cut and a nice color does no harm. Greed begins when the gratification of consumption leads us to eat and drink too much. Yet the belly is of finite dimensions, and so, too, are our sins against it, liable to be punished in the course of nature, sometimes cruelly. The regime of anxiety takes a firmer hold when it comes to what we cannot consume, but merely accumulate: the clothes in our wardrobe we do not wear, the paintings in storage we do not hang on the walls, the books on the shelves we do not consult. Accumulation serves no purpose other than to possess. And of all forms of avarice the accumulation of abstract wealth bears on its face most plainly our anxious quarrel with time. Money, especially in its virtual form as a balance recorded on some bank's webpage, offering no gratification to the eye, no present sensation to engulf our anticipations of the future, is simply dissociated power, devoid of definite purpose. It can, of course, be *given* a purpose, if we will only form definite projects for expending it constructively, turning accumulation into prudent provision. We may save up to found a business, to buy a home, to provide for retirement, to insure against illness, any one of a number of perfectly sensible things, the doing of which will involve us in building up financial reserves. But without such purposes we have no more than a vague idea of being armed against anything and everything, providing ourselves with a power to master the future, a talisman to help us ride time's waves. The problem is not that we are saving up, but that we have not found an endeavor worth saving up for. Our practical posture is defensive, the product of moral and imaginative exhaustion, which is why, of course, it is also addictive.

(b) At a spiritual level, but still passionate, anxiety is revealed in *impatience*. Impatience refuses to wait on God's time for the opportunity. In the days before the adjective "passionate" became common advertisers' copy, applicable to milk-production, kitchen cleaners, and numerous other strange things, it had a valuable use in signaling the ambiguities of a stormy urgency which cannot abide God's time in patience. Passionate impatience has a sense of the present that blocks out the future; it draws all the meaning-giving of God's promise forward, insisting on a self-evidently effective present, which has taken an advance on the future, already resplendent with the glow of completion. Such a present is simply stolen from time; it cannot contain the promise. The story is told of a theologian who convened a world conference of distinguished persons to agree to a collective statement to be published the

next year to mark an important anniversary. When the conferees gathered, they found set in front of them a complete text of the statement they were supposed to pass the coming hours and days preparing. The anniversary was celebrated a year early. Impatience likes to be ahead of the game, and although it seems to suggest an admirable attention to the promise of the future, it is, in fact, unsure of it. It has to get in first and wrench the future out of its futurity. "Then come kiss me, sweet and twenty, Youth's a stuff will not endure."[29] Behind the importunate kiss that will not be put off and the text officiously prepared in advance of the meeting there lies a consuming anxiety that the future will not deliver what we expect from it.

A tradition of Protestant exhortation, taking its cue from the story of Jacob's wrestling by the Jabbok in the night (Gen. 32:22-32) and Jesus' parable of the importunate widow (Luke 18:1-8), has attempted to make a virtue of impatience in the struggle of prayer to wrest fulfillment of the promise out of God's hold. "Lose the habit of wrestling and the hope of prevailing with God," wrote P. T. Forsyth, "make it mere walking with God and friendly-talk, . . . you lose the food of character, the renewal of will. . . . Redemption turns into mere revelation."[30] The expression "mere revelation" betrays the alien provenance of this idea. How could a disclosure of God's purposes be "merely" a revelation? The conception is of Kantian autonomy, strengthened by hand-to-hand wrestling with a divine adversary, and in promising a reserve of "character" and "will" built up by "overcoming" God, it points to a different notion of prayer from anything to be learned from Jesus of Nazareth. For him prayer may be altogether too drawn out, too histrionic and stormy, to evince faith in a generous Father. Even the widow of the parable is not meant to encourage dramatics, for God is not like the unjust judge she has to deal with. He needs no bribing or bullying, but gives out justice speedily and readily. We are urged to persistence and consistency. Our prayers may gain intensity from their circumstances, of course. When someone we love is in peril, it is natural that we pray with tears and terror. But when we find ourselves at our last breath, passionless prayer will have to suffice, for the energy of passion will not be at our command. Wrestling in prayer is wrestling with ourselves, not with God.[31] Either way, impassioned

29. William Shakespeare, *Twelfth Night* 2.3.
30. *The Soul of Prayer* (London: Independent Press, 1949²), p. 94.
31. I am grateful to have learned these lessons half a century ago from a book by the Norwegian pietist O. Hallesby, *Prayer*, trans. C. J. Carlsen (London: Inter-Varsity Press, 1948), pp. 85, 122. Not many of the humble books of devotion I read in youth stand up to rereading now, but this one has shown itself remarkably well-focused.

or unimpassioned, we must set our minds to ask for what God has in store for us, and so deploy our grains of mustard seed. When prayer is answered as we have made it, we may be surprised at the matter-of-factness of it all, so solid and evident is the new reality, so evanescent the terrors with which we seem to have struggled.

Impatience on its reverse side becomes procrastination, putting off unpleasant tasks. Proverbially "the thief of time," stealing our future from us, it is, perhaps, more truly the *theft* of time, stealing from the future what belongs to it, expropriating gratifications that are not yet due. Anxiety, again, makes the tasks we have been given seem too burdensome to set our hand to. It makes us inconsistent with ourselves, avoiding the very undertakings we have planned for and so evading the fruit of our own deliberations. A man seeks reconciliation with an estranged wife, whom he loves and misses badly; having established through intermediaries that on her side, too, there is openness to reconciliation, he must try how far an honest exploratory meeting can get. But how will he conduct himself at it? How will he cope with his own emotions if he meets with more coolness than he would like, or feels he has expressed his own feelings badly? The whole endeavor is put in a threatening light. So he seizes on an excuse not to keep the appointment, which he has taken such pains, and put others to such pains, to set up.

To counter greed and impatience we are summoned to "deny ourselves," putting aside material things at which we clutch in order to clear our sightlines for the promise. Deferring gratification familiarizes us with the tension always necessary in relation to the future. It teaches us to endure the frustration of the appetite to possess, the urge to be up and doing; it teaches us to accept what we may feel as the shame of patience, the appearance of ineffective tarrying, all in order to be ready for the moment of action when it is given us. Keble, with forceful rhythmic emphasis, states it so:

> The trivial round, the common task,
> Would furnish all we need to ask:
> Room to deny ourselves, a road
> To bring us daily nearer God.[32]

"All we need to ask" is the path before our feet. Banal and routine tasks of life, devoid of interest if we are looking for spectacular possibilities, provide the access, narrow but direct, to the promise that will "fit us for perfect rest."

---

32. John Keble, "Morning," *The Christian Year,* p. 12.

Keble's point is not that the banal and routine, though small, are *large enough* for a great movement of self-denial; it is that they are *small enough* to keep us patient, and so to keep our line of vision to the future upon the promise. Those who have great things asked of them have need of their small tasks, too: besides writing their masterpieces they should remember to put the recycling bins out, and then, perhaps, they will be more patient with the work of composition. And when what seem great things are asked of us, we must pray for the vision to see that they, too, are small enough.

CHAPTER 8

Deliberation

Purpose and Deliberation

Practical reason terminates in concrete purposes, from which action flows seamlessly. Purposes miscarry, of course; they may be faultily conceived, so that exertion does not follow the line of thought, as when I reach to offer someone a cup of tea and knock a plate of biscuits off the table; they may be defeated by accident, as when I stand up to greet a visitor and collapse on the floor in a faint. But if no exertion occurs, no purpose was formed. A purpose is the ripe bud of thought that opens into execution; it is the idea of doing what we immediately proceed to do.[1] But purposes are customarily said to be "formed," and that is not an accident of speech. They require a train of thought to incubate and mature them, to be their womb until they are ready for execution. If purpose is prepared for in faith, its formation involves an endurance of time, and all endurance of time, even that of death on a cross, forms a purpose. Projected upon the ordinary exercises of practical reason, we call the endurance that forms purpose "deliberation."

Practical reasoning does not begin with deliberation. It begins with *finding*: we awake to our responsible agency; we appreciate the vast array of goods that the created world presents to our admiration. But then it must narrow its scope, focus on what is to be done, and engage with its time. Time

---

1. In 1916 Max Scheler identified a "purpose" *(Absicht)*, as distinct from a "goal" *(Ziel)* but prior to a "conation" or "striving" *(Streben)*, as a *Zu-verwirklichen*, a "to-be-realized." *Formalism in Ethics and Non-formal Ethics of Values*, trans. Manfred S. Frings and Roger Funk (Evanston: Northwestern University Press, 1973), pp. 30-44.

passes, ordering the goods of the world in their sequence, commanding their coming-to-be and ceasing-to-be, and about this passing world-time we may reflect, and perhaps even become wise. But time does not merely pass; it comes to us, opens before us, and demands that we step into the future to meet it. Deliberation is the response of thought to this opening, thought reaching forward to the immediate future.

To see how it differs from reflection, we need only consider the habit which comes to us quite spontaneously of trying to reach judgments on past and hypothetical decisions: *whether it was right* for Churchill to authorize the bombing of Dresden, *whether it would be wrong* for a couple that failed to conceive a child to employ methods of artificial fertilization, and so on. There is nothing unusual about such questions; they play a large part in informal moral education, and can almost qualify as the most common form of moral reasoning we ever engage in. But they are not deliberative questions; they do not address the future that is given to us. No concrete purpose is formed in answering them. They are questions of moral reflection, oriented to past and hypothetical narratives, seeking the generic wisdom narratives can yield. Churchill stands for all who have to make decisions in war with terrible implications, the couple for all couples facing the dangerous opportunities a technological age has devised. It is good to ask such questions in such a way. They fix paradigms in our minds, to which we may turn when we face a difficult decision of our own. Yet they are like practice-exercises; there is nothing that they resolve. Deliberation comes to the moral question with live ammunition. It pursues the practical question in the actual future-present (how shall I purpose, here and now?), not as in some other thinkable time and place (what *might* I purpose if I were differently circumstanced?). It brings the moment of time into focus and scans its possibilities for indications of the direction God has given. Its aim is to form a purpose, not an opinion or a judgment. A purpose can never be formed in advance of the opportune moment, but must be received as a gift of providence at the moment. Yet without the work of deliberation leading up to it we are not in a position to receive the gift; it must first be searched for and recognized.

If deliberation reaches forward, it also waits. It is the ratiocinative content of that endurance of time which the hope of the final promise imposes upon us. Its function as thought is to prevent our rushing headlong upon our opportunity. Behind the Latinate name there lies a metaphor: *deliberare* is "to weigh." The corresponding word in Greek, *bouleusis,* contains a different metaphor, that of political argument and debate. Both metaphors present this type of thinking as a work of examination and judgment, and we should accept their suggestion. They also imply that this judgment takes the form of a comparison of alternative possibilities, but here we should not accept it. The essential element in deliberation, as Christians have understood it, is not a comparison but a *search*.[2] Weighing or debating alternatives is a matter of reducing two possibilities to one, but search has the task of finding one possibility where there was none. Deliberation hunts for a lost coin, lights the lamp, sweeps out the house, peers in every corner, until it lights on the precise shape and form of the piece it has been looking for. Without searching there can be no finding, but finding is by no means an inevitable result of searching. For deliberation is not an *inferential* train of reasoning, carrying a conclusion wrapped up in its premises, only waiting to be teased out. The search is concluded only when the various determinants of the situation in which we find ourselves, constraints, obligations, expectations, desires, and hopes, moral laws that lay claim on us, and the mission we are embarked upon, all line up with a possible action that lies open before us.

It is important to be modest enough in speaking of what it is that the deliberator seeks. One may deliberate on matters of no great moral weight — which screwdriver to apply to a 2mm screw, what to serve guests at dinner, and so on. If we too quickly assimilate the deliberative "ought" to a direct command of God or a life-shaping obligation, we risk making most commonplace deliberation simply disappear from view. However true it may be that any and every true path of action is a response to a leading of God, we must not skate over a range of relatively self-standing intermediate objects of search. Among the goods that we appreciate, we seek just *one* good which will provide what is lacking in our general appreciation, one which will allow a precise determination of a practical purpose. It is a good of a specific kind, *an action* (which not all, or even most goods are), an action that is *possible to perform* (not already performed and so actual), and that is possible to perform *at the moment of time* defined by the immediate future-present horizon (not possible only at some other time or by some other agent; this does not, of course, rule out the pursuit of goals that are not susceptible of immediate fulfillment, where a credible path of possibility connects what is done now to what may be accomplished in future). To light upon this one good, we need to appreciate many goods; possible goods are

---

2. Cf. Maximus Confessor, *Ad Merinum* (PG 90.16): "They say that deliberation is exercised in a search for something within the field of what is open to us to do; the object of deliberation is the object of a search, while the object of choice (προαίρεσις) is something on which we have already reached a judgment." The idea of deliberation as a ζήτησις was drawn from a hint in Aristotle.

known by their coherence with actual goods, good actions by their context in good relations of time and proximity, and so on. If I wonder whether it would be good to sing a loud high C at this moment, I must first appreciate the music that is being played. Unrealized states of affairs, realized states of affairs, existing relations, occurring events, all may be determinants of the action I seek to make a purpose of. Yet to seek it is to narrow the focus of attention very considerably. The question, "Who will show us any good?" must be sharpened to become, "Master, what good thing shall I do?" (Ps. 4:6; Matt. 19:16).

In speaking of forming "a" purpose, we use the word "purpose" concretely. The word is used also in a general sense, without an article. In this sense it is already implicit in the self-awareness of faith. But in the course of a purposeful life, and even in the course of an unpurposeful one, we form many definite "purposes," proposing courses of action to ourselves from one moment to another. All practical undertakings, large-scale and small, flow directly from a purpose: courses of action, practical schemes to be carried through in a series of acts, policies for kinds of action and avoiding kinds of action which are to govern future decisions not yet envisaged, visions of how our lives should be conducted as a whole. This does not mean that all purposes are formed for execution in an instant. The launching of thought into action is not always a single moment at which we come down to earth, cry "Well, then!" and jump up from the armchair. There are some things to be done before lunch, some things to be done before death. Yet they all, short-term and long-term, answer the question of what is to be done *today*. A policy is not an imaginative projection about what the future holds; it is a path we follow from now on, even if it does not involve us in doing anything definite for some time. We may pull out a gun and fire; we may vow never to carry a weapon. Either way, it is a purpose we have formed. Far-reaching purposes of policy enfold more immediate purposes like files containing documents which help us to find them quickly without having to go through deliberative suspension every time. The reason we do not constantly lurch from one life-shaping decision to the next is that there are paths on which we have already set out, which make the next step clear.

That is the importance of baptism. In adopting an ultimate moral purpose that is to form our whole lives morally, we are not faced with re-forming ultimate purposes over and again. That does not mean there are no purposes left for us to form. A multitude of possible proximate purposes may suggest themselves, not all of them suitable expressions of our ultimate purpose. Our purposes have to fit into one another like Chinese boxes; what we purpose to do before lunch must not be incompatible with what we purpose to do before death.

At this point it may help to introduce the term "decision." If "purpose" refers to the thought from which the action flows directly, "decision" refers to that "cutting off" *(de-cidere)* which the forming of a purpose imposes upon the train of thought leading up to it. Not all purposes are made decisively, that is to say, with a conscious imposition of closure on deliberation. Sometimes a purpose may be formed without our being aware of it; we simply realize that we *have* formed it; somewhere and somehow the deliberation has reached its term. "Decision" passed from being a watchword of existentialist ethics to being dismissed by neo-Aristotelians who scorned to believe, in James McClendon's delectable words, that "being divided against itself were the soul's main business."[3] Two passing remarks need to be made about this dismissal. In "cutting-off" deliberation, first of all, the soul does not cut *itself* off, nor indeed any other soul. Decision is not an act of "judgment," finding for one claimant and against another. It cuts off only the potentially indefinite play of imagined future possibilities, and does so for the sake of realizing itself in one actual future. Secondly, the whole function of deliberative thought, which imagination of possibility serves, is to bring us to a formed purpose. To linger forever over imagined possibilities is to frustrate that goal. If there may sometimes be an anxious suspension of possibility that causes pain, even psychological crisis, nothing different in principle is happening from when the purpose forms easily and smoothly. Life lived as a sail across a calm sea, purposes flowing in order and without stress from wise counsels taken long before, is something to thank God for, but it cannot be a moral ideal. No theory can give us the right to expect that discipleship will be a morally perspicuous existence in morally unruffled times.

More problematic than "decision" is "choice," a highly popular term in some intellectual quarters, as well as in common speech. "Ethics is about choices!" is a slogan worn so smooth that it seems cantankerous to hold it up to the light. Once we do so, however, we find it difficult to free "choice" of the implication that it is *between* or *among* possible objects. But a purpose is not "between" this and that, it is simply "for" a given course of action, and there is no reason why our purposes should always be formed by choice. Often they are clearest and firmest when just one course of action stands out as supremely fitting. An appointment committee, faced with a field of candidates in which one is preeminent, may, perhaps, have no choice, but that does not

3. James W. McClendon, *Systematic Theology: Ethics* (Nashville: Abingdon, 1986), p. 58.

mean it does not act freely or form a settled purpose. All choices are purposes, but not all purposes are choices, and the more weighty a purpose is, the less likely it is to be a choice between competing alternatives. Choice between apples and pears we understand. But choice between champagne and cyanide? Choice between right and wrong? Those are perplexing notions.[4]

It is true that deliberation moves in the sphere of possibility, and possibilities may often be distributed alternately: either A is possible, or B, but not both. Where the field of possibility is wide, it must be narrowed. But choosing is not a rational or responsible method of doing that. Among things that are possible to do we may identify things *not given us* to do. We may narrow the field of possibilities by eliminating what may be thought as "moral impossibilities." Kant made a great point of the moral incoherence of acts which, though possible to perform, subvert the logic of the commitments implied in them, and are, in a sense, self-contradictory — making promises one does not intend to keep, for example, the logic of which is "that there would be no promises at all."[5] The category may be extended to include things, not self-contradictory in principle, which contradict the reality of the moment as we have reached it. Faced with the opportunity to make a worthwhile purchase, I may exclude paying with a forged check, the simplest form of moral impossibility ("there would be no checks at all"), but shall also exclude paying with cash from my wallet with which I meant to settle an outstanding debt. That, too, would be a "moral impossibility" for me at this juncture, given the commitments I actually have.

Yet the goal of deliberation is not simply to eliminate impossibilities, leaving every moral possibility in play. What it seeks is an *objective determination,* one possibility which (for me, at this juncture) is the right one. The right purpose is a purpose obedient to God's purpose, but it can be so only if it is sufficiently determined objectively, by such indications of God's purpose as are given us. "Choice" is a subjective resolution of practical alternatives where no objective resolution is conclusive. But discerning objective grounds is what deliberation is about; choice is appended to deliberation where deliberation runs out. There are, indeed, choices to be made: do I serve my guests apples or pears at lunch? if I am walking to a destination southeast of me, do I take the eastbound street first and turn right, or the

---

4. On this theme Karl Barth's early critique of "Hercules at the crossroads" as "a pagan image for a pagan thing" continues to be worth revisiting. *Ethics,* trans. Geoffrey W. Bromiley (Edinburgh: T & T Clark, 1981), pp. 73-76.

5. *Grundlegung,* 4.403.

southbound street and turn left? But such residual alternatives, supervening on deliberation, tend to be morally "indifferent," trivial and inconsequential. The medieval scholastic joke about "Buridan's ass" which starves to death between two equal and equidistant bundles of hay is a joke about the concept of indifferent liberty as a rational power to resolve indeterminacy of purpose. Any relevant difference between the bundles would be enough to determine the inclination, but since a creature of instinct is powerless to act with no external determination, it must be powerless if it finds no objective difference. Human beings, of course, can resolve such dilemmas; they can impose subjective determinations by choice, and can devise techniques, like tossing a coin, to supply the want of either subjective or objective determinations. They do not starve to death in the aisles of supermarkets. But as a matter of fact, when did we ever hear of an ass starving to death before two bundles of hay? Buridan's ass is a joke, pointing out that something has gone wrong with the premises. Perhaps such occasions of indeterminacy never arise, so that the wonderful human power of resolving indifferent alternatives has only trivial uses like picking which side will bat first or deciding whether to offer guests apples or pears. This, at least, we may say: pure choice is an abstraction, and for this reason no model for practical resolutions, which, if they are not trivial, turn on objective differences.

The prominence given to choice in popular moral theory owes something, it must be admitted, to the greatest of the scholastic theologians. Aquinas thought that reason created and supported freedom by making comparisons among things; freedom, in turn, consisted in the openness of judgment to alternatives.[6] Practical reason, then, was a double movement: first an "inquiry" called "counsel" *(consilium),* which reached a "judgment" that one thing was preferable to another, then a "choice" *(electio),* which supplied the moment of *appetitive* preference.[7] The act of choice occurred at the point where judgment and appetite converged. If the choice was a right one, it was not by obedience to an objective determination, but by agreement with the mind's own prior judgment. That meant that deliberation terminated in the judgment, which lost sight of the very way in which deliberation differs from reflection, namely, by terminating in a purpose, not an opinion. A purpose is an answer to the deliberative question, "What is to be done?" A determinate answer to that question is *already* practical; it is not

---

6. *Summa Theologiae* 1.83.1: *"Quia judicium istud non est ex naturali instinctu in particulari operabili, sed ex collatione quadam rationis, ideo agit libero judicio, potens in diversa ferri."*

7. See principally *ST* 1.83.3; *ST* 2-1.13.1-5; 14.1-4.

a proposition, "this sort of action is better than that," which still needs to be set alight by putting a match to the fuse. Thomas, we might think, has given the name "counsel" to what is simply a reflective act of comparative evaluation, not a deliberative train of reason, and the name "choice" to an act of affective propulsion, rather than to a real selection among alternatives. But if he has done so, it is because the pervasive scholastic division between reason and will has presented practical reason as theoretical reason reinforced by affection. In this analysis we are reasonable beings who *also* act, not beings who *act reasonably*.

A purpose is not a choice, but the last term in a train of deliberative thought. Nor is it an end-of-action. A purpose is a mental representation of the action about to be executed; an end-of-action is a mental representation of a state-of-affairs, an anticipation of how the world will be when the act is performed. From among various anticipations, fearful and hopeful, accompanying deliberation, one is selected, which represents the effect of the act in a positive light. If we speak of the end-of-action as the "intended effect," we stretch the language of intention a little, but not too far. Strictly, the effect is imagined; only the act is intended. But as this imagination serves to resolve the purpose, we may think of the intention as embracing it. The imagined *effect* of an action, we must now add, is not the same as an imagined *consequence*. Consequences follow *after* the act, the effect is realized *by* it. The end-of-action is simply the world conceived imaginatively as it may be when the purpose has been executed. From the other side, the end-of-action is the act anticipated as "effected," situated in the world as an achieved performance. The end-of-action is an *anticipation*. The difference between what is anticipated and what is actually effected can, of course, be very great, and may mark the difference between the success and failure.

The end-of-action may be imagined clearly, or only vaguely. A purpose needs to be clear, clear enough to channel the exertion of effort with sufficient precision to perform the action successfully. An imagined end, on the other hand, need not be very clear. We often suppose that the clearer the imagination, the more effective the action will be. "If you aim at nothing in particular," we are told, "you are sure to hit it!" Actually, the most precisely imagined ends-of-action may often be the most delusive ones. They are, after all, imaginations *of the future world,* and the future world, even as it touches directly upon ourselves, will be formed by many other factors than our action. As I invest my savings in a deposit account, I form an attractive picture of the "security" I shall enjoy as the interest accumulates, and perhaps spice the picture up with some possible further consequences: myself retired, getting up late and settling down in the armchair to read a novel instead of rushing for the train, and so on. Not only may the armchair and the novel be defeated by any number of contingencies; so may the security. A rumor about the banks or a curve in the inflation rate can melt it like snow in sunshine, or it may simply be much more difficult to *feel* secure than I imagined it would be. Better, altogether, not to be too clear what the effect of this investment is to be. It commends itself as a sensible thing to do, given my circumstances and the extent of my knowledge, without an elaborate scenario. A great many of our actions are like that.

It is a recurrent mistake in the theory of deliberation to suppose that the end shapes the action backwards, as it were, pulling it towards itself, so that every well-formed purpose is conceived as a "means" to a well-chosen "end." There is, to be sure, a good use of the language of means and ends. But it is abused when it is taken to suggest that every act should be *devised* as a means-to something, a practical instrument to achieve an imagined state of affairs. This narrows the function of prudence to mere administration. Some of the best acts, most productive of good effects, are those done, as we say, "on principle," i.e., determined largely by a range of factors other than the imagined future. It does the child good, Dr. Spock advises me, to be told that he can't always have what he wants when he wants it. When the hard word must be spoken and the tantrum is imminent, it is far from obvious what that good will look like; I have simply to act on a sensible principle and wait for years to pass before the benefits show themselves.

Once all this is said, however, even the most straightforwardly principled purpose cannot be formed *without* an imagined end. One may imagine it perceptively or self-deceivingly, one may imagine it precisely or vaguely, but one cannot just *intend* the act without imagining what it might look like as an accomplished fact. To take an extreme case, the action proposed may be to die courageously as a martyr. In the shifting emotions that accompany the approach to death, the martyr is bound to anticipate alternative possibilities: that his end may in some way "do something," or that it may serve no purpose at all. In resolving to maintain his course to the last, not pleading for mercy, not renouncing his cause, not betraying his associates, he must somehow adopt the more positive anticipation to support his purpose. Though he cannot make it come true, he can stake his actions on its being true. "Power shall have another day!" as Edmund Power, early champion of Irish nationhood, cried from the scaffold in 1798. What kind of day? Recognition of his sincerity? A change of political wind? Others to take up the struggle? A descendant to bear his name with pride? Victory? He could hardly have said. But the simple idea of that "other day," however vague, was needed to fix his resolution on that last and most difficult act.

Against Deliberation

Theologians have sometimes been uncomfortable with deliberation. A notable instance is afforded by Karl Barth's most considered statement on the nature of Christian moral thought, that section of the *Dogmatics* which he headed "God's Command."[8] What Barth hoped to achieve in this statement was a sharpened focus on the immediacy of the moral response to God's summons to practical decision; what he feared and deprecated was a prevarication before the command of God which might take refuge behind the claims of practical thought or reason. In the section entitled "The Sovereignty of the Divine Decision" (§38.1) he invited us to think of our lives as a series of decisions in response to God's decision "about our whole being," a phrase which is paraphrased, "what we do and do not do." A memorable exploration of the question, "what are we to do?" treats each word in turn: "what" because a new answer to this question is continually needed; "ought" because it is never the answer we naturally incline to; "we" because the question cannot be put impersonally; "to do," since it has to do not with observational knowledge, but with existence. As good an introduction as could be devised, one might suppose, to the task of deliberation, admirably sharpening a focus on the moment when a purpose is formed and an active response to God's demand is made.

Yet in the account that follows decision is left isolated and absolute, answerable only to the immediacy of the divine, unapproachable by thought, and refusing every attempt to give it form. "The Definiteness of the Divine Decision" (§38.2) presents divine decision as a judgment, which at the same time is "a unique and concrete command bearing specifically upon each situation."[9] Unlike human commands, Barth thinks, divine commands function not only as generic laws but as definite prescriptions for the individual case.

8. *Kirchliche Dogmatik* II/2, §36-§39 (EvangelischerVerlag Zurich, 1942). [= *Church Dogmatics,* Vol. 2, Part 2, trans. G. W. Bromiley, T. R. Torrance (Edinburgh: T & T Clark, 1957).]

9. *KD* p. 738 [= *CD* p. 662]: *"je in dieser Situation speziell betreffendes konkretes Einzelgebot."* We may add that the scope of the critique is greatly enlarged by the equivocal use of the German adjective *allgemein,* which sometimes means "general" in the sense of commonplace, sometimes "universal" with reference to everything and everybody, sometimes "generic," referring to classes as distinct from particulars.

Only divine commands perform both these functions simultaneously; human commands will be one or the other, either an "empty form," "universal" yet by the same token "formal and abstract," or concrete and particular, but lacking authority. The objection that God *has not* in fact given his command with such particular definiteness is dismissed with a striking conversion of past tense into present: "God . . . *is present* to . . . each individual . . . in the smallest of his steps and thoughts."[10] So it is not a question of what God "has" or "has not" given (for the command of God is not to be found in Scripture or salvation history), but of his always immediate presence, which might be named as that of the Holy Spirit, but is not. The commands recorded in the Bible are simply historical events, concrete commands given to particular people at particular times in the past, and apparent exceptions (the Decalogue, the Sermon on the Mount, etc.) are summary compendia of a multitude of such particular commands, disclosing the background against which the present dealings of God with man are now transacted unconditionally. The negative form of the Ten Commands is designed to express not what God commands, but only what "must not in any circumstances take place."[11] Yet all these historical commands of Scripture are relevant to us. We "should be" contemporaneous with and of the same mind as those who rightly heard them as their own.[12]

It is a difficult but important discussion, about which more deserves to be said than can be said here.[13] But this brief comment at least is required: Barth's preoccupation at this point lies with achieving the sharpest possible

10. *KD* p. 746 [= *CD* p. 669]: "*Der Einwand wäre darum ohnmächtig, weil der an der objektiven Tatsache zu rütteln unternimmt, daß Gott . . . der Welt und so auch einem jeden Menschen gegenwärtig und nahe ist und so als Gebieter und Richter auch der kleinsten seiner Schritte und Gedanken ihm gegenübersteht.*"

11. *KD* p. 764 [= *CD* p. 684]: "*Es wird ein bestimmter Bereich abgegrenzt, aber nicht nach innen, sodaß es zu einer Bezeichnung und Beschreibung dessen käme, was innerhalb dieses Bereichs zu geschehen hat . . . sondern was daselbst nicht, was daselbst auf keinen Fall und unter keinen Umständen geschehen darf.*"

12. *KD* p. 783 [= *CD* p. 701]: "*Die Bibel will, daß wir jenen anderen Menschen hinsichtlich des Gebotes Gottes . . . gleichzeitig und gleichartig, daß wir ihm gegenüber ganz und gar die Genossen jener anderen Menschen werden.*"

13. A question that would merit fuller discussion is the consistency of this with other approaches to Ethics in the *Church Dogmatics*. Some interpreters such as Nigel Biggar, *The Hastening That Waits* (Oxford: Oxford University Press, 1993), have found him more open to casuistical practice than is evident here. With any great thinker it is an open question how much overall coherence should be assumed and how much freedom to pick up new threads should be allowed for. Our discussion of §§36-39, then, takes the section as it presents itself, a formal programmatic statement to be judged on its own terms.

opposition between "the way of theological ethics" and what he calls the "general concept" of ethics. The famous simile comparing the theological annexation of ethics to Israel's conquest of the promised land gives this a colorful appearance, though Barth's more detailed policy ("we may get our concepts where we find them") suggests war for booty rather than under the ban.[14] While conceding that the "general concept" is a varied one, he seems to have in mind some version of idealism, Platonic ("the idea of the good") or Kantian (the categorical imperative) or some Christian alternative ("the Kingdom"). Whatever concessions may seem to be offered from time to time, Barth refuses the thought that Christian moral thinking can take form in generic rules, even those which he apparently concedes to have been given at some point by God himself. His presentation of moral thought (never clearly distinguished from moral theory) is thus dictated, and, in the end we must say, distorted by the strife of the faculties. For fear of compromising theological distinctiveness he denies human decision the deliberative space required to understand God's generic commands, and attempts to put it on the spot before a definite prescription "self-interpreting to the smallest details."[15] This last phrase focuses the problem exactly. We need raise no difficulty over a concrete, particular will of God that demands our obedience, which can reasonably be referred to as a "definite command." The difficulty arises with the refusal of a role to intelligence. Barth claims so much for the definite command that no work is left to the generic, and so no work for our thoughtful interpretation. This has the troubling effect of representing human decision as an exact mirror-image of the sovereign decision of God. It fails to notice how our decision must be different from God's with respect to time, relying on retention and protention, a work of deliberation in forming a purpose.

Barth's reasons are not the only ones that have caused deliberation to be excluded from theological accounts of decision. Idealist theologians may be attracted by the thought of a quantum leap from idea to act without intermediate thought: at one moment we contemplate the good, at the next we "embody" it.[16] The miracle of thought concretely incarnate in history reminds them of the incarnation of the Word made flesh. (How many theo-

14. *KD* p. 568 [= *CD* p. 513].

15. *KD* p. 741 [= *CD* p. 665]: *"Es bedarf keiner Interpretation . . . es durch sich selbst bis aufs Kleinste und Letzte interpretiert ist."*

16. Though with a concrete example in mind, I have special reasons at this point for departing from the usual good practice of naming and quoting. No reader of twentieth-century theology will be at a loss to recognize a familiar pattern here.

logians can resist following that analogy, whenever and wherever?) This conception, no less "idealist" for its wish to see the idea materialized (do not even the gentiles do the same?), has been tripped up by confusions over time. It thinks of an unbroken continuum, a "history," in which past and future are homogeneous and neighboring segments. Into the continuity of history action inserts an idea which has pre-existed in an ideal sphere. But that is not possible. The power to act is the power to *initiate,* to bring to pass what has not been. It is true, of course, that action results in fact, leaving concrete additions to the tale of events behind it, and in imagining an end-of-action we anticipate that fact. But it is true of any occurrence whatever, an earthquake, a lover's indecision, the slumber of the unconscious, that it results in fact. We do not need ideas and actions to produce facts. When we have to speak of *acting,* it is not with ideas inserted into the flow of history that we have to do, but with the future-present moment, the time given us in the "next" of open freedom, and with the purpose that reaches forward to grasp it. From which we must proceed to the conclusion that action does not in any useful sense "embody" or "materialize" idea. Thought *acts on* matter and time, it does not *become* matter and time. And the thought which acts directly on the material world is not idea, but purpose. Purpose depends on idea, and without idea no purpose can be intelligible, but purpose is not idea. In forming itself as purpose, thought has stripped away the ideal contents of the mind and narrowed its focus to a course of action fit for the next moment. That is what we understand by deliberation.

A third case, that of Schleiermacher, is of special interest, as illustrating a tendency to keep deliberation in reserve as a fallback, to be resorted to when ordinary moral experience, which proceeds without it, finds itself interrupted or disturbed.[17] Schleiermacher conceived Christian Ethics, which he did not distinguish from Christian moral thought, as a descriptive science; the Christian moral "ethos" which it described was a calm and untroubled one, requiring no discursive thought to sustain it. But moments of perplexity could arise, when a purpose could not be formed without difficulty. In these disrupted moments, "where something is in dispute and the morality of an individual cannot determine itself," moral thought, though not "bringing forth" action, comes to our aid by "eliminating" conflicts of duty. These are of two kinds, one at the level of theory, the other "in relation to the moment."

---

17. Friedrich Schleiermacher, *Introduction to Christian Ethics,* trans. John C. Shelley (Nashville: Abingdon, 1989), pp. 96-99. Elements in the argument, the record of which we owe to students' lecture notes, are elusive, but the outline is clear enough.

The first springs from contradictory ideas, the second from complications of circumstance. In the first case the conflict is unreal and requires only clearer thinking. The second kind may be real; an example might be owing money to creditors while one has urgent claims on one's charity. For such a dilemma as that there could be no universal resolution, since no moral rule instructs us to discharge the last penny of debt before giving the first penny of charity. What, then, can thought do? It can clarify the contingent circumstances that give rise to the problem, so that the agent can discern possible compromises that involve no loss of integrity, and that should be sufficient.

Schleiermacher thus assigns moral thought the limited role of smoothing out the ruffled surface of moral experience, restoring continuity to the ordered harmony of our lives. In this he owed something to the casuistic tradition, which saw it as the task of deliberation to bring all cases under a unifying framework of moral law, eliminating radical exceptions or irresoluble dilemmas. The distinctive feature of his treatment is that the role of moral thought is so strictly limited, confined to sorting out an occasional dilemma and to clearing up conceptual misunderstandings, as to allow the principle that thought does not bring forth action. But the association of deliberation with dilemma is too easily assumed. A dilemma is an *affective* experience, a state of painful perplexity that may or may not accompany the forming of a purpose; deliberation is a *train of thought,* which may unfold anywhere on the spectrum of affective tonalities, so anxiously that the question may seem insoluble or so calmly that one is hardly conscious of having to think about it. That a train of thought may arouse, or dissolve, perplexity, says nothing for or against it *as* a train of thought. And why should not the same train of thought that may dissolve perplexity equally well anticipate it, avoiding the moment of painful irresolution by thinking it through in advance? Deliberation that can heighten or lessen our dilemmas may surely prevent them, too.

Laying these three ways of dispensing with deliberation side by side, we may align them with different emphases on the persons of the Trinity, on the sovereign Father in Barth, on the Incarnate Word in the idealist construction, on the Spirit in the church in Schleiermacher, in each case carried through at the expense of a rounded Trinitarianism. In that section of Barth, especially, it is notable that the commanding God of II/2 looks like a solitary First Person, not at all meeting the challenge Barth boldly issued to himself at the outset of the *Dogmatics* that theology should be framed from beginning to end by God's threefold way of being. A Trinitarian theological ethics must have room for creation and saving history, for the vis-à-vis of human rationality and divine determination, for the mutual inherence of individual and communal thought. In all these three theological prolegomena to Ethics we listen in vain for talk of the indwelling Spirit quickening our thoughts to correspond to the objective gift and historical command of God. We listen in vain, therefore, for the *prayer* for the Holy Spirit, which is the act of thought from which all moral reflection and deliberation springs.

Prudence

Together with deliberation we name prudence as the common term for the virtue of excellent deliberation. As used in the Western moral tradition, prudence is a special virtue, focused upon the deliberative step in moral thinking and the formation of concrete purposes, not a general virtue covering awareness of responsibility and appreciation of moral value. This has occasionally given it a slightly shady reputation for expediency or compromise. Its philological origins point to its future-looking orientation: the prefix *pro-* ("forward") combined with the stem *vid-* ("to see" or "to know.")[18]

If the idea of deliberation required some refocusing in Christian moral theory, so did the idea of prudence. Given the confidence with which it was taken over into the moral theology of the high scholastic theologians to translate Aristotle's *phronēsis,* it may surprise us to find a definite caution towards it in patristic sources. We may take as typical Augustine's critique of the account of prudence he found in Cicero's rhetorical treatise *De inventione.*[19] Cicero described *prudentia* as "the knowledge of all that is good, evil, and indifferent," i.e., a comprehensive view of moral values, and *providentia* he thought of as a subordinate part of prudence, that which had to do with future good and evil. Providence was ranged alongside two other subordinate parts, *memoria,* the recollection of the past, and *intelligentia,* the understanding of the present. Augustine made three distinct objections:

---

18. Its Latin original, *prudentia,* was closely cognate with *providentia,* though already in the classical period the two had become differentiated, one representing a moral virtue, the other the capacity for forethought or anticipation. Its later Western use was strongly affected by its employment in the scholastic period to translate Aristotle's *phronēsis,* practical thinking.

19. At an early period of his career Augustine copied out the passage of Cicero's *De inventione* 2.53.159 for the convenience of his monks, presumably because he was using it for teaching purposes (*De diversis quaestionibus* 83.31). His direct criticisms of it come later, in *De Trinitate* 14.11.14. In the interim he can also be seen correcting it in the course of developing his theory of time at *Confessiones* 11.

(i) we cannot make a virtue out of foresight, or "providence," for that belongs exclusively to God; (ii) we cannot attribute a comprehensive view of the moral universe to a virtue called "prudence," for that place belongs to love; (iii) an intelligence which understands all things as present is not accessible to human beings in the flux of time, but only to God.

Substituting "love" for Cicero's overarching "prudence," Augustine replaces the forward-looking "providence" with a practical attitude to the future fit for human beings, named variously "will," "intention," "desire." And in both cases he does what he is commonly reputed to do, replace a cognitive category in classical philosophy with an affective one. Yet there remains a role for the virtue of prudence, "the discrimination of what should be sought and what avoided," an intellectual service of love in vigilant attention to the perils and promises lying hidden about our paths.[20] If the temporal directions in which our minds may turn are only two, past and future, and we are like salmon leaping upstream, there is a task of coordinating memory and intention, of negotiating a successful passage from past to future. It is a task to be performed in relation to temporal things, not, like Cicero's *intelligentia,* in relation to eternal things, which are the province of love alone. "A forward-looking intention," Augustine writes elsewhere, "must be linked to a backward-looking memory."[21] That I take as a summary of his conception of prudence, a virtue that serves love in relating experience to new challenges.

Action is initiative, beginning; but new beginnings are never new creations. We approach them with a legacy of decisions already made by ourselves and others. Whatever is truly possible on the future horizon is possible for *this* state of affairs that has taken shape on the past horizon. Rational action answers to what is the case — not merely affirming and perpetuating whatever state of affairs has come to pass (for it may denounce it, and try to overthrow it), but *referring truthfully to it,* at least, and framing itself as a response to it. To be either radical or conservative one must be connected. To plot a revolution against the King of France these days would neither be radical nor conservative, merely dissociated from reality. Our actions must bear an intelligent relation to reality — "intelligent," not merely "intelligible," since the intelligence of action is present in the agent's purpose, not only observable from outside. But reality is not simply an *ensemble* of bare facts

---

20. *De Civitate Dei* 19.4. Cf. *De moribus* 1.24.45.

21. Augustine, *City of God* 7.7: "*Necesse est a memoria respiciente prospiciens conectatur intention,*" an aside in the course of a rough demolition of the Roman pantheon, prompted by mention of the gods of beginning and ending, Ianus and Terminus. The same principle is affirmed by St. Thomas (*ST* 2-2. 49.1).

about the world but an order perceived in love. It is a work of prudence to bring this order to bear on the future horizon of action.

How does it perform this work? Saint Thomas suggests that it performs it by "commanding," a profound insight. Practical reason includes a loving admiration of the ordered good irrespective of any demand it may or may not make; the specific role of prudence is to conceive that ordered good as *directive*, as a *normative* order that lays claim on our freedom to act. Moral reflection as such knows no "laws"; it discovers ordered goods, but not imperatives. This does not mean what we might be tempted, under the influence of modern voluntarism, to make of it: the goods are present in the order of the world, but an imperative must be supplied by the agent's will. The moral laws that direct us are not something *over and above* the good order of the world; prudence does not confer normativity on value, but recognizes the normative implications of value. We admire the goods of the created order affectively; in prudence we discern the system of moral law that they imply — "law" meant in a general sense of *directive* proposi-tions *generically* framed, not laws in a political context, promulgated and sanctioned for the use of a political community. Moral laws are historical formulations, belonging to memory, as moral order belongs to understand-ing. They gather up and recollect realities glimpsed and partly understood through practices and traditions, but their authority depends on their foun-dation in the realities of creation and redemption; they claim obedience because, in a historical form, they represent the truth of things. Laws are not "invented," as the iPod was invented, but neither are they "discovered," as the solar system was discovered. It is harmless enough to say that they are "constructed," as diagrams, arguments, and formulae are constructed, unless we unwarrantably conclude from that that they must in some sense be artificial, or merely heuristic. The Scriptures speak of law as "written in the heart"; to think in a law-governed way is the endowment of the human mind with which it can encounter the regularities of the universe. It is so in practical reason as it is in theoretical. We might say that what theories are for reflection, laws are for deliberation: capturing the changelessness of changeable realities, open to refutation and disproof, securing for thought the wisdom attained by reflection.

There is therefore a *critique of retrospection* required of prudence as well as the critique of anticipation on which we have already expanded. If on looking back we fail to see the order and history of the world presented to us normatively, we shall fall into a historicist despair of world-time. "Say not, 'Why were the former days better than these?' For it is not from wisdom that you ask this" (Eccles. 7:10). We cannot *not* see goods in the past, for the world God has made is good as a whole, and it is full of goods. But we may see these goods from a distorted angle, as doomed to be swept away by time, constantly succumbing to entropy, by their impermanence attesting the triumph of de-creation over the good hand of the Creator. We must look on the past not only as *history* but as *the history of God's world,* a goodness sustained and upheld to the end. Thus in framing normative laws prudence becomes a way in which we can remain constant to the vision of God's goodness that has been given us. Jesus connects "remaining in my love" with "keeping my commands" (John 15:10). In the goods of earth and heaven we find provision for our present agency, affording resources for the moment in which we are given to act. The unwisdom which asks why past times were better than these has assumed a false position, that of an aesthetic observer valuing goods of different ages from some supposed time-transcending viewpoint. Our position in time is not capable of judging the present against the past, any more than it can judge the present against the future. It is a moment of deliberation, of making up our mind to act. Many detailed cultural comparisons between different times are, no doubt, not illusory: if it is said, for example, that the examinations routinely passed by eighteen-year-olds in Britain half a century ago are too difficult for university graduates today, the claim may be put to the proof. But even if we validate it, we cannot extrapolate from one moment of proven decline to universal entropy. It is not wisdom to pretend to do so. Luxuriating with morose aestheticism in the decadence of our times, we rob ourselves of the normative significance of our knowledge *as law,* showing us the ends and modes of action we may presently conceive: to teach the young, and teach them carefully!

Should we prefer to speak of "principles" rather than "law"? This would have the rhetorical advantage of avoiding irrelevant overtones of alienation that may cling to the term "law" from its other uses. The "principled" agent, as we commonly use that epithet, approaches decisions consistently on the basis of generic truths which he or she has learned. The metaphor of "first" things *(principia)* suggests the polarity with "last things," and supports the dynamic understanding of moral thought as proceeding *from* a truth grasped *to* a conclusion for action. It has, however, two weaknesses: (i) It may suggest a misleading primacy for formal and structural elements of a worldview, principles abstracted from the variety of lived experiences, so encouraging a doctrinaire perspective. It may seem that a rule like "Never embark on a course of action you cannot go through with!" is somehow more of a "principle" than "Never betray a friend!" We need a term that can function at every level of specificity. (ii) It may suggest that deliberation from first things to last is a deductive inference, flowing with logical elegance from axiomatic foundations to practical conclusions. This fails to convey the *complexity* of deliberation, its role of correlating many kinds of information and interpreting situations, a point on which we shall have more to say shortly. We shall stick, then, to the word "law," with all its asperous overtones, and these may not entirely be a disadvantage. We are not at this point dealing with the alienation of the agent from the moral order which makes law "the knowledge of sin"; yet even apart from this there is a challenge which may have its own sharpness, the confrontation of a task which requires to be taken up seriously and intentionally.

For law-governed action is by no means a matter of course. Despite the natural tendency of our mind to think in an argued way about what we do, reaching out for analogies and entertaining hypotheses, it is perfectly possible, and often more comfortable, to make decisions on a moment-by-moment basis. If we value action on principle more than we value action on impulse, that is because we are jealous for the place of prudence in our decisions. Every decision between right and wrong is also a decision between considerate and inconsiderate action. Respect for moral laws is respect for the virtue of prudence, and one of the recurrent themes in the Wisdom literature is the interdependence of law, prudence, and the quest for wisdom (e.g., Ecclus. 15:1-8). Correspondingly, prudence is itself a moral law, since rational deliberation is itself a duty. We may, of course, act prudently without spelling out, to ourselves or others, the laws we conform to. Habitual and intuitive prudence is as possible as the habitual practice of any other virtue, and for many purposes we may think it preferable. We can express a law-governed purpose as a simple judgment of particular obligation: "it would be wrong for me to sign off this expense claim!" But decisions are sometimes too weighty and too much in need of careful thought, to be resolved assertorically. When an act is put in question, reiteration of the bare particular does nothing to answer the question. That is why even those who act most intuitively, and are most proud of doing so, are liable to be found appealing to laws to justify themselves later on.

The Ordering of Law

Prudent deliberation conceives moral laws within an ordered system. Laws come in many forms and stand at variable distances from reality. Typically, if loosely, we distinguish "moral law," articulating the moral order as a whole in its demand upon us, from "working rules" hypothecated upon a given task. There are other variants: laws which we formulate for ourselves and laws formulated for us by others, laws enjoined on us and laws taught us for our instruction but not imposed, and so on. For pedagogical purposes we assemble moral laws in codes: ten in the Decalogue, six hundred and thirteen in the Torah, etc., but they are in principle innumerable, depending on the aspects of reality that need directive formulation at any moment. In principle, too, many may always be reduced to one. That was the critical discovery made by the rabbis in their attempt to provide a comprehensive exposition of the law of Moses. There were "greater" commands and "lesser" commands, and obedience to "the law" as a whole depended on getting the relations among them right. The discovery was, the synoptic evangelists report, taken up by Jesus, who identified two commands of love, love of God and love of neighbor, as the first and second commands of the law. "There is no other commandment greater than these," said Jesus, and in Saint Mark the "scribe" who asked the question, speaking on behalf of the rabbinic tradition, was enthusiastic about the answer: "You are right, teacher. . . . To love him is more than all whole burnt offerings" (Mark 12:31, 33). Saint Matthew, on the other hand, shows Jesus making neglect of this distinction a matter of criticism against the Pharisees: "You tithe mint and dill and cummin, and have neglected the weightier matters of the law, justice and mercy and faith" (23:23).

How is the distinction of "greater" and "lesser" to be understood? Is it simply a matter of priorities: if we cannot keep them all, let us be sure at least to keep the greater ones? This suggestion ignores the *interconnectedness* of the commands, proposing that we may persist in loving God and neighbor even when circumstances force us to dishonor our father and mother, to kill, to commit adultery, to steal, and so on. How would we, or anyone else, *know* that we loved our neighbor while dishonoring our parents, murdering our enemies, making secret assignations with our friends' partners, or stealing our neighbor's banking details? Not every kind of act is consistent with loving the neighbor. The late Basil Mitchell illustrated the point pleasantly by devising a party game which he called "Adverbs," in which one team goes out of the room and has to think of an adverb. Its members are then readmitted one by one, each member being given a specified action to perform "in the manner of the adverb," so that the other team can guess what the adverb is. "The unsophisticated choose a word that is easy to act and an action that is easy to perform in the manner indicated by the word, e.g., the word is 'angrily' and the action is shutting the door. But with more experienced players the fun consists in the one team choosing a word which will test the ability of the actors and the other team, thinking of actions in the performance of which it is hard to evince emotion at all or which are normally associated with one very specific emotion. For example the word is 'lovingly', and the action is putting on the kettle or strangling your wife."[22]

Saint Paul apparently speaks of the love of neighbor as a "summary," a wide-ranging category which includes all the more limited ones: "The commandments, 'You shall not commit adultery, You shall not kill, You shall not steal, You shall not covet,' and any other commandment are summed up in this sentence" (Rom. 13:9). This inclusive relation invites us to deploy an analogy with biological genera and species, which underlies the termino-logical convention of contrasting the "general" with the "specific." We may think of love of neighbor as a "moral genus-term" and honoring our par-ents as a "moral species-term." This analogy illuminates two features clearly: (i) Despite the fact that traditionally we use only the two words, "genus" and "species" (the botanists' "variety" is not admitted to the metaphor), the phyletic tree in principle allows for infinite levels of division, presenting a spectrum from extreme generality to extreme specificity. (ii) At every point on the tree we are concerned with *kinds,* not with particular instances of the kind. So it is with moral laws; if the law of greatest generality is love of neighbor as self, there are other laws which govern more specific kinds of situations. We can amuse ourselves, if we have a precisionist turn of mind, by inventing highly specific rules to govern occasional situations generically. It is an art bureaucracy depends on.

The analogy is useful but not exact. The zoo may show us a weasel, a wal-laby, and a whale, but there is no cage devoted simply to mammals. Weasels, wallabies, and whales are mammals, but we recognize them by their species, not their genus. It is theoretically enlightening to know that a close bond between a mother and her young is a consistent mammalian trait, but what we need to be told for practical purposes is not to come between a *weasel* and her young, not to take a *human* mother's baby away from her, and so on. The species determine the genus, not the genus the species; the cetacean preference for the ocean determines how we do not define a mammal; the mammalian preference for dry land does not determine how we do define a whale. But in the case of moral laws the lesser "depend on" or "derive from" the greater. If there is no such derivation, teaching about love has no practical

22. "Ideals, Roles and Rules," in *Norm and Context in Christian Ethics,* ed. Paul Ramsey and Gene Outka (London: SCM, 1969), p. 351.

importance, since the general law will be wholly accounted for by a list of its species: "Do not murder, do not commit adultery, do not bear false witness." Is it solely for pedagogical reasons that we would classify the ten commands of the Decalogue into two groups, love of God and love of neighbor? What force, then, could there be in Jesus' teaching of the "new law"? At the very least it must serve as a hermeneutic key to control our understanding.

If the summary *enfolds* the moral laws, and so is determined by them, and at the same time *informs our understanding* of them, we may speak of a two-way control between the law of love and the detailed moral laws. Paul's description of the love command as a "summary" is an arithmetical metaphor; it refers to a "sum total," which is what the laws "add up to." Elsewhere he speaks of love as "fulfilling" the whole law (Gal. 5:14) — a verb which characteristically evokes salvation history. These two analogies come together: love is both the "sum" and the "fulfillment" of laws; it is the culmination and final outcome. The sum is not totaled without its constitutive elements; the fulfillment completes, without superseding, what has gone before it. The higher morality of love, distinctly evangelical, reached in the course of moral history, is characterized by Saint John as a "new command," and yet, he insists, the "new command" was also an "old command," not simply different from what went before (1 John 2:7-8).

The priority assigned to the "great commands" was due to their being comprehensive. They encompassed all the more specific kinds of actions that may be required of us. Jesus teaches, in Saint Matthew, that the love command is greatest because the other commands "depend" on it (Matt. 22:40). Wide-ranging categories enfold more limited ones, and they interpret one another, the greater ordering the lesser in terms of scope and mutual relations, the lesser embodying the greater in concrete forms. The greater laws alone do not tell us enough about the ordered reality of the world: if we relate to others as family members, strangers, and even enemies, the greater law of neighbor love requires exposition as family love, as love of strangers, and as love of enemies. But the relations in which we stand to others are not self-explanatory or self-authorizing. We may doubt whether we ought to treat our own child differently from any other child, whether we owe anything to our own nation that we don't owe to every nation, whether a starving farmer in Africa makes any claim on us at all. Unless these various claims are accounted for and re-authorized within a comprehensive order, we are left uncertain of their moral authority. That is the fate of the inhabitant of the polytheistic universe, owing one thing to the god of the hearth, another to the god of the city, a third to the god of the stranger, stumbling from one field of authority to another, never knowing whether their different demands can be harmonized. The teaching of a unified moral law is the vindication of monotheism.

But if the coherence of our obligations attests the will of one creator, it also conveys the gift of coherent agency. It promises a path through the complexities of life, a way of negotiating the plurality of demands that are made on me. This was in the mind of the Deuteronomic legislators when they published their consolidated law code, in which the detailed requirements were summed up under the command of loving YHWH with heart and soul and mind. The commandment, they urged, "is not in heaven, that you should say, 'Who will go up for us to heaven, and bring it to us, that we may hear it and do it?' Neither is it beyond the sea, that you should say, 'Who will go over the sea for us, and bring it to us, that we may hear it and do it?' But the word is very near you; it is in your mouth and in your heart, so that you can do it" (Deut. 30:12-14). This is a deeply philosophical reflection on the power of a coordinated moral field to elicit competent moral agency. But from where does such coherence come, if not from a "second law-giving," a self-disclosure on the part of God himself with a law that interprets the plurality of laws, and is therefore at the same time a Gospel? It was not for no reason that Saint Paul read that passage of Deuteronomy as a prophecy of Christ.

Consequentialism

We make at this point a third sounding in the sin of anxiety, which is the sin against time. It is not, like our first two soundings, passionate. It is a sin of deliberative thought, masquerading as prudence. The only foresight available to prudence, as we have said, is the anticipation afforded by immediate practical possibilities. But by attributing false visibility to remote or ultimate futures, sin corrupts prudence, diverting it to the devising of intermediate steps to a goal that is taken as given. (I use the term "intermediate steps" to refer to what we often call "means," i.e., instrumental measures designed to achieve a proposed state of affairs. But the word "means" is ambiguous, and not every use of it has this instrumentalizing of prudence in view.)[23]

We are dealing here with what philosophy has christened "utilitarianism," and is more properly named "consequentialism": the positing in

23. St. Thomas, indeed, in taking up Aristotle's claim that prudence has to do with *"quae sunt ad finem,"* guards carefully against that instrumental understanding of it (*ST* 2-1.8).

thought of a future best possible outcome, working backwards from which each decision may be made securely and transparently in the light of it. The critique that Ethics must mount against every attempt to expand or totalize anticipation tells eminently against the ancestor of all such attempts, "the creed which accepts as the foundation of morals utility" of John Stuart Mill.[24] Mill's focus on happiness is no radical innovation in ethical theory; it merely de-theologizes the eschatological eudaemonism of Augustine and Thomas, robbing it of its dependence on promise. His real departure from tradition lies in assuming that the "foundation" of any moral program for action lies in what it "tends to promote," i.e., that its justification lies in the anticipations that it reasonably creates. Elizabeth Anscombe identified the issue with utilitarianism half a century ago in saying that it treated the object of all human striving — "happiness" in the classical formulations — as unproblematically perspicuous, when in fact it was obscure.[25]

Yet it is not as a *theory* that consequentialism is a sin. In extending the name beyond theory to habits of mind and practice which narrow prudence down to anticipated consequences, we are hardly departing from common speech. The steps by which this distortion is reached should be marked with some care. The first step is to extend the view from the consequential *tendency* of an act, which prudence must certainly take note of, to the idea of a *final and decisive outcome,* an ultimate point which reveals conclusively the nature of what was done. There are contexts in which this extended view is innocuous, especially those which call attention to the shape of a human life. The proverbial wisdom of antiquity remarked that the measure of a life lay in its end: "Call no one happy before the end, and a man is known by his children" (Ecclus. 11:28, echoed at Matt. 11:19; Luke 7:35). But this final and revelatory state, once cast loose from its point of reference in the judgment of God, is then, in two parallel steps, both instrumentalized and universalized. Instrumentalized, by reducing each act to a work of production, a *bringing-about* of a presumed last state, which then becomes the exclusive normative criterion for it, the "product" which is the success or failure of an act of "making." The projected last state of affairs is thus treated as an object, the value of which can be substituted as a norm for the quality of

24. *Utilitarianism* 2: "The creed which accepts as the foundation of morals, Utility, or the Greatest Happiness Principle, holds that actions are right in proportion as they tend to promote happiness, wrong as they tend to produce the reverse of happiness." In *Utilitarianism; Liberty; Representative Government* (London: Dent, 1910), p. 6.

25. G. E. M. Anscombe, *Intention* (Cambridge, MA: Harvard University Press, 2000[2]), p. 77.

action that produced it. Universalized, by substituting an idea of *welfare in general* for the ultimate welfare *of the agent,* so severing the evaluative norm from the agent who produces it: how *I* have performed is judged solely by *what* turns out in the world, not by how *I* turn out. The fourth step is to measure all such posited universal outcomes on a single and simple scale; "happiness" was what Mill called it, but it can be called anything at all. The term "happiness," used in a more traditional way, has its proper place in the discussion of our final good; the problem here lies in the thought of a homogenizing measure that will serve to make every different value quantifiable and computable.

There is also a fifth step, often overlooked but important to draw out, since it helps explain the appeal of consequentialism to ideologies of history and its connection with anxious representations of the future. As the known goal of each and every action is now one and the same, the whole history of human action can be represented as striving for this single end. Without actually writing a "history of the future," consequentialism posits an ideal future which, whether it will transpire or not, is the necessary and sole validating point of reference for anything done in the meantime. Here we encounter the notion of history as a theater of "progress," a notion which, as has often been said, only Christianity could have given birth to, since only Christianity finds an ultimate validation of all human action in a final state of all affairs which is also a state of happiness, yet in its modern form relating to Christianity as a heresy, taking as perspicuous what Christians know only as an object of promise.

With the skeptical withering away of eschatological faith the habit of looking to an ultimate future to justify the course of the present persists, as formerly in totalitarian socialist ideology, so now in the increasingly totalitarian democratic one. The difference now is that only our own actions can bring it about. In place of a *promised* future there is a *total* future, an overall utility or happiness which justifies both in the long term and the short, all history on the one hand and whichever of our actions, on the other, is conceived as a means to it. But here is the true occasion for skepticism. Future time is not susceptible of justificatory calculations that embrace both near and far at once, for the future is not, like the past, a joined-up narrative. The consequences of acts can only be anticipated and evaluated from the state of affairs *into which* we act — illumined and interpreted by God's promise, to be sure, but not identical with the promised world. That is why one careful Christian reader of Cicero rejected his doctrine that since some duties were derived from "the fitting" and others from "the useful," the task of deliberation was to negotiate a *modus vivendi* between those two rival principles. Ambrose replied that the fitting and the useful were not equipollent categories. Immediate utility was relative to, and so derived from, what was fitting, while ultimate utility could only be understood in relation to the Kingdom of Heaven, and as such was not a transparent criterion for concrete actions. The final end could not be drawn into our practical reasoning, but only received as a divine complement to "the fitting" act, the paradigm of which, he argued, was the act of worship.[26]

Taken as a general account of what makes human action right and wrong, consequentialism does not correspond to the experience of prudential deliberation, but does it the crudest theoretical violence. Projected actions offer themselves to deliberation accompanied by anticipations (sometimes clearer, sometimes less clear) of what may follow from them. In some contexts these anticipations assume greater weight than in others; in some technically defined actions, the essence of which is skillful practice of some art — initiating medical procedures, devising government policies, etc. — the proximate utility may assume such great weight as to create the impression that no other feature is important. But even in such contexts that is a false impression, for the other features have been looked after by the routine disciplines of the art — securing the patient's consent to surgery, for example, or clearing a proposed military operation against international law — leaving the surgeon or general free to think only of what will make the intervention a success on its own terms. Prudence involves taking note of proximate anticipations and giving them their due weight. Such judgments of proximate tendencies are one thing; quite different is the idea that every act is judged, and judged solely, by its *overall* outcome. There *is no* overall outcome; there are only "outcomes" of varying proximity. Viewing these in prospect, which is how we must view them, the one certainty is that we shall not anticipate them all, so that they are not a fit measure of our acts.

To represent action as a calculation within a known set of regularities, or as the fashioning of future states of affairs according to certain rules of art, is to misrepresent it entirely. Action is adventure, the injection of new initiative into the stream of future events, the product of which cannot be controlled or foreseen. The only criteria available to us, therefore, are

---

26. Ambrose, *De officiis* 1.9.28: *"Nos autem nihil omnino nisi quod deceat et honestum sit, futurorum magis quam praesentium metimur formula, nihilque utile nisi quod ad vitae illius aeternae prosit gratiam definimus, non quod ad delectationem praesentis."*

derived from past experience, which includes our experience of successful and unsuccessful anticipations, as well as our rules and our interpretations of situations, and these cannot be guaranteed success in predicting the achievement of any goal, let alone a final one. What is to be said of the *ultimate* "success" of faithful and true action must be said in terms of hope for God's Kingdom.

The Particular

That the moral life is "more than just keeping laws" is one of those truisms from which it is hard to dissent; even confining ourselves to the exploration of prudence, we shall see many ways in which it is true. But "more than" is not "less than." The bugbear of a pedantic adherence to rule as opposed to alert intelligence risks sending us off on a false trail. There is no intelligence of the pure particular, because the particular is always a particular *something*. Laws have justificatory force precisely because they are intelligible categorizations. How would we ever keep a law, other than by grasping the meaning of the law together with its particular relevance to the situation we face?

These are two things we grasp simultaneously, and in different ways. An example from the nineteenth-century moralist Antonio Rosmini illustrates the only alternative to this account, which is that the particular is reached *by deduction*. I deduce my obligation to care for my sick mother from the most general principle. The ultimate general moral principle ("the good is to be pursued"), when applied to human beings, yields the more precise principle, "I must respect this intelligent nature," and that in turn, applied first to relations between parents and children and then to children with *sick* parents, yields further principles of specific duty, and these, finally, can be made to yield the "most particular laws, which would tell us how this person is obliged to act *here and now*."[27] Rosmini would not be embarrassed, of course, if we pointed out that such a progress required special knowledge, about what a parent is, what it is to be sick, and so on. He knows well enough that his train of thought needs good solid syllogisms with informative minor premises. The objection, rather, is that the information in the *last* minor premise, which he (or his

27. Antonio Rosmini, *Conscience* (1839), trans. D. Cleary and T. Watson (Durham: Rosmini House, 1989), pp. 2-3.

translator) calls the "most particular," could not be learned from any study of human relations. It concerns the way things *actually are* between me and my mother, and that is something I can only *recognize*. There can be no "particular" laws, since moral principles and laws are always generic, concerned with kinds of case, whether more or less specific. Particularity, moreover, admits of no "more" or "most," or "less" or "least," for the particular cuts across the spectrum of more or less specific principles with a unique application.

Deliberative inquiry has no "conclusions"; it does not flow deductively to a logical resting place. At a certain point, a potentially indeterminate inquiry is cut off; the purpose must be formed and acted on. When prudence "applies" a moral rule — say, about how to treat an elderly parent who has episodes of confusion — in a particular judgment, "This is what my mother needs of me now," there is a leap of thought from the generic to the particular. It involves a simple recognition of the relevance of the rule to the case and the case to the rule: "But *my* mother is elderly and sometimes confused!" Theoretically, recognition is a mysterious act, learned only by practice though usually performed without thinking. There is no general rule for recognizing. No logic, as Lewis Carroll understood, could prevent someone from mistaking one kind of thing for something different:

> He thought he saw an elephant
> > That practiced on a fife.
> He looked again and found it was
> > A letter from his wife.[28]

No imaginable generic instruction could correct errors of this kind. No rational law, however specialized, tells me what I confront at this moment. My immediate duties may be determined wholly by laws governing the relation of children to parents, but until I look carefully where I stand, I cannot know they are. There is no "here and now" so utterly transparent that I can say that my duty is obvious without a moment to look around me. Even where it *appears* that the situation is governed by one recognizable moral

28. "The Mad Gardener's Song," in *The Complete Works of Lewis Carroll* (London: Nonesuch, 1939), p. 320. The distinctiveness of recognition and its failure, "agnosia," is highlighted in Oliver Sacks, *The Man Who Mistook His Wife for a Hat* (London: Picador, 2011²), pp. 9-24, which describes a "right-hemisphere" syndrome in which a patient "saw nothing as familiar . . . [but was] lost in a world of lifeless abstractions." "He could not make a cognitive judgment, though he was prolific in the production of cognitive hypotheses."

law which everyone agrees must be followed at all costs, that appearance is not reached by inference alone, but depends on inspection. Laws engage us multiply, not singly, one at a time. "Which law applies *here?*" is always a relevant question.

Prudence has, then, the task of interpreting the present situation morally. The two sides of its interpretation are correlated: the grasp of the particular is not an inference, not a conclusion derived from premises. The traditional term "subsumption" may suggest misleadingly that the whole difficulty lies in discovering which law a case fits under — the meaning of the laws themselves being clear. But the very act of recognition involves some re-learning of the law. As when we first see a black swan, we have to stretch our idea of the swan beyond the idea of a white bird with a long neck, so, too, we may have to stretch our idea of what any moral law demands of us. Laws, we repeat, are constructs, mediating the order of reality. New experience may prove too much for them, as an experiment can prove too much for the current scientific theories. We have a law that we should not lie. As we seek to live by it, experience presents us with complications: untruths that are not lies, truths that are not to be told, truths which could carry false suggestions, untruths employed as means to communicate truths, and so on. And so we need to understand this law more precisely in order to relate it to other laws such as those requiring kindness to the vulnerable, resistance to injustice and cruelty, and whatever else may happen to intersect with the demand of truth-telling in a given situation. All of which involves exploratory hermeneutic engagement.[29]

How, then, do we distinguish responsible exercise of prudence from what we call "rationalization," which is to say, the *post hoc* fabrication of excuses? The idea that moral reasoning should be deductive appeals to us precisely because it seems to offer a hedge against changing the sum to prove the answer: good reasoning starts with rules and ends with decisions that conform to them; bad reasoning goes the other way, from decisions made first to laws fabricated to justify them. But moral laws are formulae that represent the shape of moral reality, not the reality itself; their relation to the reality can be probed and clarified, and must be, if we are to learn more about morality. That is why laws are capable of exceptions; as formulated constructs, they apply, as Saint Thomas says, "for the majority of cases."[30] The

---

29. Paul Ramsey's exposition of the logic a generation ago remains unparalleled. See "The Case of the Curious Exception," in *Norm and Context,* pp. 67-135.

30. *ST* 2-1.96.1 ad 3.

moral order lying behind them in reality is not capable of exceptions, only of further inquiry and more careful understanding. Claims to have advanced in prudence must be tested against this wider understanding. For example: the claim has recently become popular that the rule confining marriage to persons of the opposite sex is open to certain kinds of exception, of which earlier generations of humankind had no inkling. Is this a genuine case of learning from experience, or is it a rationalization of desires? The only way of dealing with that question is to expose it to the full philosophical range of the understanding of marriage that revelation and nature have given to us. A more peremptory answer may seem to offer immediate gratification, but it will in the end fail of conviction.

Circumstances and Consequences

Action is conceived in the mind and executed in the world. To understand a particular action is to understand it in context, not only as it has formed itself in the agent's mind. Which is to say that an act is not merely an operation to be classified in isolation. Its significance extends out from the core operation to the surrounds, its "circumstances," as moral philosophy has traditionally labeled them. Two instances of the same operation may represent different kinds of act *in mente,* acts conceived, as we say, with different "ends" in view. A surgical incision performed in clinical conditions is not the same act as an assassination by stabbing, even if the assassin were infinitely careful as to how and where he inserted his knife. But what shall we say of two surgical incisions both performed in clinical conditions and with similar ends in view, differentiated by the fact that in one case the patient has given understanding consent, while in the other it is contrary to the patient's will? As Saint Thomas noted acutely, there is a difference between the way theoretical and practical reason understand the relation of species to circumstances.[31] The unusual circumstances of a beached whale do not affect in any way my recognition of it as a whale. But with a debatable action I cannot recognize the species until I have considered the circumstances. In the case we have

31. *ST* 2-1.18.10: *"In rebus naturalibus id quod est accidens alicui rei non potest accipi ut differentia constituens speciem. Sed processus rationis non est determinatus ad aliquid unum, sed . . . quod in actu uno accipitur ut circumstantia superaddita objecto quod determinat speciem actus, potest iterum accipi a ratione ordinante ut principalis conditio objecti determinantis speciem actus. . . . Per hunc modum . . . oportet quod circumstantia dat speciem actui morali."*

given the two acts are very different kinds of animal, the one an act of medical care, the other an assault.

Suppose that someone's eccentric behavior suggests to my mind an amusing comment, a comparison, perhaps, with Don Quixote's adventure tilting against windmills. In making my comment I have it in mind simply to amuse, and perhaps to relieve some tension the behavior has generated. Will it constitute a "sneer"? Before I can decide that, I shall have to assess various factors: how much do the hearers know about Don Quixote? Will it actually relieve the tension? If it is reported to the person it describes, will it seem like kindly teasing or a mortal insult? These factors, though circumstantial, are material to the moral character of my remark. I cannot defend it by saying that it was a perfectly harmless joke that just *happened* to give offense. It is a harmless joke only if I correctly judge that it will not give offense.

And as it is with circumstances, so, too, with "consequences." What is it that is asked of us when we are told to consider the consequences of what we propose to do? Certainly, to make use of the mind's capacity to anticipate. To that extent we must judge Saint Thomas (and Cicero) justified: there is a kind of foresight involved in prudence. But we are not told to give anticipation free rein, but to focus it upon the interface of act and context in the situation that we shall act in. The "consequences" we are to weigh are not any future *sequelae* that may possibly transpire later on, and subsequently be traced back to the act. They are anticipations that are prompted immediately by aspects and circumstances of this particular act in this particular setting. There may, indeed, be other events that will follow later, and some of them may be anticipated. It is not these that I am bound to consider when exercising prudence, but the contribution my projected act can be expected to make to its present context. Much nonsense has been spoken and written about acts having consequences that run on forever into the future — a false-historical point of view which treats the future as a joined-up history. The consequences of an act are finite, tied to the act itself, which, belonging to a passing moment in time, will soon be overwhelmed by other acts performed by other people. Suppose I deliberate an offer of reconciliation to someone who has been an enemy. I may anticipate that it could evoke a new outburst of hostility, but that is not a reason not to offer reconciliation. What I have to weigh is the tendency of the act itself to turn events in one way or another. The more remotely consequences follow, the less informative they are about the act that lay behind them. Which is why the words "I told you so!" are so utterly unhelpful to moral reflection, even if it happens that they are true. *Anything* may have been foretold in advance if our imaginations were busy enough, but only *some* anticipations were material to the deliberation.

Deliberation may, of course, take an interest in unpredictability itself as something that a given act may be *expected* to produce. It may find an overwhelming reason not to do something in the consideration that the consequences are too difficult to anticipate, so that the tendency of the act is to open a Pandora's box of uncertainties. An important example of this reasoning arises from time to time over the effects of a determined and combative gesture on the stage of international politics, such as massing troops along a border. There could be good prudential reasons for discouraging such an action even if the rhetorical certainties in which the public likes to take refuge were unprovable. "It will start a war!" they cry, though actually we do not know that it will. Yet even not knowing that, we can form the responsible view that the action would be very dangerous, and without some very great countervailing reason that should be enough to dissuade us. In the arguments against a nuclear first strike the dissuasive effect of unpredictability is sufficient to ground a decisive prohibition: the consequences lie so far beyond anyone's anticipation that such an act could never satisfy the conditions of political rationality.[32]

The important formal point to make about this and other such judgments of consequences is that when they are made, before ever the act is performed, they are *as true or false as they will ever be*. If you said, "It will start a war!" and it doesn't, you were wrong. If you said, "It is very dangerous!" and it doesn't start a war, you may still have been right. It was not a *prediction* of what would happen, to be verified or falsified by events. It was a warning, founded on the inherent tendency of the act in its context. We can misjudge such tendencies, nervously exaggerating or confidently underestimating dangers, and that is a failure of prudence. Warnings are not well-founded merely because events cannot prove them ill-founded. But it is not a failure of prudence to note possible dangers (or, indeed, benefits) which do not materialize in the event. A provocative act that does not start a war can be every bit as reckless as one that does. Everything turns on how well we have weighed the tendencies of the action. Prudence is not a pudding whose proof lies in the eating, but an illumination shining into dark corners and distinguishing solid shapes from shadows.

32. For this argument see my *Peace and Certainty* (Oxford: Oxford University Press; Grand Rapids: Eerdmans, 1989).

Ideals and Compromises

We look for an action obedient to moral laws, but the moral laws are mediated to us historically. We acknowledge them through experiences we have had, through understanding we have previously gained, and also, not unimportantly, by decisions we have previously taken. One of the criteria that prudent deliberation brings to bear is consistency with its own past determinations. It cannot be a final criterion. We can be consistent in vice as well as in virtue, and the question of whether a past decision should be stood by or repented of can never be simply ruled irrelevant. However, in that the course of wisdom is a course of learning, there is at least a heuristic presumption in favor of building on insights we have been given. There is also a moral presumption, in that we find ourselves committed in some degree by longer-term purposes we have formed in the past. There may be formal promises given to others, or reasonable expectations created, but even if not, the sight of an agent reinventing himself and going back to work out everything afresh is distressing. We are not occasional agents, but called to live in continuity with ourselves. Repentance is a serious duty when we find ourselves in error, but by the same token it must not be lightly engaged in for no cause.

This is not, of course, to cast ourselves back on dull repetition. Our self-binding is not absolute; we do not deprive ourselves of the freedom to adjust our purposes. A purpose once resolved on is decisive for *immediate* action, but all long-term purposes are to a greater or lesser extent hostage to events, so that prudence is required to find new implementations of past purposes. A scholar who has always resolved to write a book may be caught up in the tumult of academic administration willy-nilly, and may need to think of other ways of fulfilling the scholarly mission — a series of articles, perhaps, which can be polished off one a year in the course of the summer.

We speak in this connection of "ideals," by which we mean the longer-term policies we form, with greater or lesser self-awareness, for ourselves (and not for others) to guide action in the future. And we speak of "compromises" as the prudential adjustments we make to them. *What* we compromise in such a case, it must be clear, is our own policy, the ideal. To compromise the moral order itself, or the moral laws grounded on it, would be quite another matter. The adjustments we have in view here are not to moral norms but to imaginative projections. There are good ideals and bad ideals, good compromises and bad compromises. Some ideals were never rightly formed, and the best thing to do with them is repent of them outright. But good ideals can be served by good compromises. Not every compromise is good; not every difficulty in executing a policy should make us retreat. Courage and daring, too, are needed in great enterprises, not only prudence. Yet a good ideal must be a possible ideal, and a good compromise focuses the attention sharply on its possibility. Moral consistency is not a matter of holding stubbornly to first-conceived ideas, or refusing to accept that circumstances change. Prudence must manage disappointments, find new courses of action in the wake of failure or frustration. Its compromises may be occasions of renewal, recovering disappointed ideals and finding new paths to realize them in new conditions. Compromise in the wake of persistent moral failure can prove especially controversial, as was illustrated by a discussion of great importance held among Roman Catholic moral theologians thirty to forty years ago about what they called "the law of graduality," the proposal that a struggle to over-come besetting sin might involve interim steps, decisions *towards* holiness rather than immediately *for* it.[33]

The context of the discussion, the bruising disagreement about artifi-cial contraception, was a misfortune. A thought-experiment ought to work with an instance on which there can be no substantive moral doubt. So let us imagine someone wrestling with obsessive and murderous desires for vengeance. Let us suppose him or her a serious Christian, who knows that nothing less than forgiving charity is demanded, who, indeed, in moments of self-possession wants nothing less. Prudence may suggest a strategy: to write down an account of the supposed injury, pouring into words the an-ger which might otherwise take up weapons. Such an account, it must be obvious, is likely to be very hostile. Yet it may serve to objectify, and to an extent correct, views formed in anger. The possibilities of self-deception are obvious. But in any compromise there may be self-deception. The proposal of graduality at least draws attention to the difference between justified and fraudulent appeals to what we claim that we "can't" do. It points to some tasks of moral self-direction which cannot be accomplished in one leap, but may be amenable to strategies of self-reflection, to inch-by-inch acquisition of new disciplines of mind. The "law of graduality" is not a first-order moral law as such, but it is a second-order one. In this it closely resembles the tra-

---

33. The concept was given official currency in John Paul II's 1981 encyclical, *Familiaris Consortio*, p. 9, which speaks of "a continuous, permanent conversion which, while requiring . . . adherence to good in its fullness, is brought about concretely in steps . . . advances gradu-ally with the progressive integration of the gifts of God and the demands of his definitive and absolute love." See generally Alain You, *La Loi de Gradualité: une nouveauté en morale* (Paris: Le Sycomore, 1991).

ditional "rules of conscience," "tutiorism," "probabilism," etc., which offered perplexed consciences criteria for decision *other than* the simple right and wrong of the action proposed for times when they could not know where that right and wrong lay. "Graduality" differs from these only in supposing that the right and wrong is clear enough, but the possibilities of obedience are in doubt. It is concerned with finding *subjective* means, reaching proximate outcomes in the habits of the mind, which will then be more amenable to the moral law.

How can we distinguish good compromise from the consequentialist strategy of doing wrong to achieve good? The latter is concerned with *objective means* to *extrinsic ends.* If we take the example of deliberately targeting civilian populations in pursuit of a war with a just cause, it seeks a proximate state of affairs *in the world,* tactically ordered to the achievement of a further good, disregarding the moral quality of the act that is to bring it about. In the illustration of the obsessively vengeful person who seeks to deflect wrath from madness, the proximate state of affairs is sought not in the world but in the mind — like someone working out frustrations on a punching bag, which does no wrong to the bag, however regrettable an impulse punching may be. We might contrast this tactic with another: if the plan were to assuage obsessive thoughts by *publishing* the hostile account and persuading the world to support our hostile point of view, that would be a consequentialist tactic, unjustly blackening another's name with the purpose (remote, alas!) of avoiding worse outcomes.

In this case, as in others, the only anticipation we allow is that of a possible course of action which bears witness to the order of goods. Here we give due place to Augustine's proposal that the relation of prudence to the future is *intentio.* Maintaining it depends on the hope of personal and cosmic fulfillment, but the "anchor within the veil" is not an object of clear sight. Neither, for the most part, are the various possible futures that occupy the middle ground of anticipation. It is by attributing false definiteness to remote or ultimate futures that prudence is corrupted to the devising of practical means to a goal of history that is taken as somehow given.

CHAPTER 9

Discernment

Indeterminacy

Deliberation searches for something it is right to do, assembling all the objective determinations that may point to one or another course. These may settle it. Informed of a guest's allergy to dairy foods, I stop wondering whether to serve crème caramel or fruit, even though the fruit is not at its best. But I may still be left with alternatives. These may be "indifferent" — should it be apples or pears? — which is simply to say that there are no further considerations to resolve them. But some undetermined alternatives are far from indifferent. Weighty decisions that do not fall under any moral law — what work should I pursue? should I marry? where should I make a home? — may be pregnant with the greatest good or harm to myself and others. It is not that such matters *cannot* have objective determinations — if I cannot stand heights, work as a roofer is closed to me — but they *may* not. Reasons that would point in one direction or another are not accessible, usually because they depend on future consequences beyond reasonable anticipation.

In such cases we do not quickly resort to tossing a coin. We face a deficit of moral normativity, and our sense of rational freedom demands that the deficit be made good. We persist in looking for determinations for as long as there is hope of finding them, and we are generally expected to spend time and trouble looking for them. It is striking to what lengths people will go to *invent* reasons that allow them to escape from arbitrary choice in major matters. We need determinations, and when moral laws or circumstantial constraints are insufficient, we look for some source of direction particular to the moment in which we find ourselves.

When we ask how and why the deficit arises, we see that they follow quite necessarily from our position as agents in time. Indeterminacy is a moment in an ongoing task of moral determination, a phenomenon perpetually presenting itself, perpetually to be overcome, as much part of our exercise of freedom as determinacy is. It is the condition of our present moment, this need to get a purchase on the future horizon as an opening for reasonable action. "As *at all times* you have obeyed . . . , so *now* . . ." (Phil. 2:12). "So now" posits the analogy of the future-present with the past, the law-governed rationality of the action we seek. But the "now" also posits the *difference* between all past exemplifications and what is to be given, the "absence" of formerly experienced determinations, the need to seek and find the analogies of law afresh, responding to the newness of the moment. Let us say that deliberation must conclude in an act of *discerning the time.*

The history of Western moral thought is full of only partially successful attempts to describe this step of deliberation into the uncharted. The earliest, perhaps, and not by any means the worst, was the Stoic distinction between "middle" or "imperfect duties" imposed by the law and the "perfect duty" *(katorthōma),* which concluded all questions and allowed of no further deliberation. The moral theologians of the last century tried to frame the distinction in terms of law and conscience — conscience being the individual's *particular* sense of what must be done, law the *universal* norm universally applied — a conception with the disadvantage of confining the individual's view to the particular, while generic thinking was the prerogative of legislative bodies such as states, churches, and societies.[1] An approach favored by Barth found in the moral law only negative approximations, drawing the line to exclude what generically must not be done, leaving divine command to determine concretely what must be done.[2] But moral law can certainly tell us what is to be done: it can tell us to educate our children, to contribute to the welfare of those in need, to love our neighbor as ourself. If it could not, we could form no idea of a sin of omission.

What is it, then, that the moral law cannot tell us? It cannot tell us what is to be done *next.* It gives generic forms by which we can understand the moment in which we find ourselves placed, but it does not tell us what time it is. It casts no light on the immediate horizon. And so it cannot formulate an *agenda* in which things that demand to be done can be ordered

---

1. See, e.g., K. E. Kirk, *Conscience and Its Problems* (London: Longmans, Green, 1927), pp. 3-105.
2. See p. 189 above.

by their timeliness. Where law prohibits, of course, all we need to do is to understand it. Once I recognize that my creative accounting is theft, there is only the smallest step from "this should not be done" to "stop doing this now!" But where the law is positive, a further discernment is needed. We may fully understand that we are morally bound to send our child to school, but whether that comes first before, say, giving the child something to eat, depends on what o'clock it is: when does school open? when did she or he last eat?, etc.

Deliberation terminates in forming a purpose, which is deciding to do something *now*. The "now" does not mean that the whole performance follows pell-mell. Not every decision can be given effect in the very next moments. That would mean that decision consisted entirely of a moment-by-moment *triage* of pressing duties, settling which email of the hundred in the inbox to answer first, and so on. Longer-term policies, too, have immediate effect, even though the initial moves may be some time away. We have decided to send the child to *this* school; the necessary steps will follow at the appropriate moments: writing to the head teacher soon after the fourth birthday, acquiring school equipment and clothing, and so on. Yet the decision *has* taken effect; we no longer spending whole evenings sorting through prospectuses and saying, "We must find out more about the other one." A decision, once made, determines how we arrange our practical tasks. It determines *us* — whoever "we" may be, for deliberation is by no means confined to individual actors; collectivities, too, achieve their discernment of the time, and fit the laws they obey to the possibilities and constraints that confront them.

The Path

In this context we characteristically look for, and may very well pray for, a sequential ordering or direction in the complex of circumstances, objective and subjective, which comprise our narrative situation. Action is not a mere eruption; it is the realization of agency in history, and implies an order and direction. Using a common metaphor, we say that we look to find a "way" or a "path." How does this metaphor illuminate the object of our search?

It happens quite frequently as we cross a bare hillside or open countryside that we ask about the surface formation of the ground we are walking on: is this a path? What is it that we are asking? The terrain has certain occasional features: worn patches where the vegetation is stunted or beaten down, bare earth or stone breaking through where nothing grows, and in places these features — let us call them "traces" — join up to form a "track," no more than a yard or so wide but indefinite in length, running roughly straight and maintaining a roughly consistent gradient. If this track persists beyond our view, we may ask whether it is a path. (We do not ask whether the ensemble of traces is a track; we can take that in at a glance.) In search of an answer we may look for secondary traces which suggest a practical intelligence: circumvention of natural obstacles, prolongation in a straight line over a distance, evidence of construction (a row of stones forming an edge or paving, steps cut in a steep slope, rubble filling in holes), even evidence of usage like the imprint of a boot in soft ground. If we see these, we are ready to infer that the track we have found is a path. Is that, then, what the question meant? Whether the track was made by an intelligence? No, we have no interest in what produced these traces on the ground; we are not archeologists but travelers. If we speculate about the track's origins — "I expect this is where the shepherds bring the flocks down to the village" — that is no more than a secondary hypothesis, for logic infers the shepherds from the path, not the path from the shepherds. The fact of a path licenses speculation on the purposes that formed it, but we can assume nothing about purposes till we have established that there is a path.

Are we asking, then, about the usefulness of the track to our own purposes? Do we want to know whether its direction brings us forward on our journey? We may well do. But until we know that it is a path, again, we cannot ask whether it will be serviceable. There is no direction at all in a set of scrapings in the mud. We must first know whether it is the *kind* of track that might lead us to a journey's end. Its convenience is the next question; the first is simply whether it is a path leading anywhere at all. What do we mean, then, by asking whether it is a path? Simply whether it has *a direction*. Not simply an orientation and a length — running east to west for thirty yards, let us say — but *somewhere it is going*. Most tracks go nowhere; they peter out or stop at the edge of a precipice. If this one leads from here to somewhere else ("somewhere" in the sense of a place with a cultural meaning), we deem it a path. We need not know where it leads nor why those who made it wanted to get there — not even whether they were human (for some animals make paths they follow, not only tracks they leave behind). We do not need to know whether it can be followed to its destination, for paths may be washed away or overgrown, or lead to a riverbank where a ferry or bridge has disappeared. We know only that there is somewhere the path leads. It has a direction discernible on inspection. But its direction is not a *further* empirical trace, different from the crushed vegetation, worn ground, stepped inclines, narrow width, elongation, moderate gradients, circumvention of obstacles, etc. It is a teleological form, which the traces display when they are seen together as a whole.

A ruined building has a teleological form, too. By studying what remains of it we can build up a picture of how it once looked, and infer the generic purpose for which it was built — a castle, a bakery, or whatever. The teleological form of the path is different. The ruined building has a generic end, which may be inferred from its form alone, but the end of the path is a particular place, a somewhere which is not some other place, and what that place is we cannot infer from the form. Its end is not revealed by generic function, but can only be wondered about, or, if we have the spirit of exploration, followed until we get there. That is why this metaphor is so potent in talk of practical attention to the future. In acting, we set off into the future with a purpose and a degree of anticipation, but though we may, and must, form anticipations and purposes, we know that these are projections only and that we have no clear sight of the actual future where our action will fetch up a *fait accompli*. The path, its direction abstracted from its goal, mirrors the purposiveness and uncertainty of action. In following it we do not use it as an instrument, turning it to serve purposes of our own; we commit ourselves to its direction, trusting that where it leads is where we want to go. We rely upon the direction it presents to us, and hope to be led somewhere consistent with our overall purpose.

The article on דֶּרֶךְ (*derek,* a "path" or "way") contributed to the ongoing *Semantics of Ancient Hebrew* by J. K. Aitken in 1998[3] identifies 706 occurrences of the noun in the Masoretic text of the Scriptures. Building on the explorations of D. A. Dorsey, it assigns these to three broad sense-groups: (i) a road, (ii) a journey, (iii) a course of travel or route, treating all metaphorical applications of the word to the living of life under the third sense-group. It would be better to say that each of the three senses has a metaphorical application: (i) A *derek* may be a be a road chosen in preference to others at a division, and so, as a moral metaphor, be a *decision.* (ii) It may be a journey followed from starting-point to destination, and so, as a moral metaphor, a

3. *Semantics of Ancient Hebrew,* ed. T. Muraoka, Abr Nahrain Supplement, vol. 6 (Louvain: Peeters, 1998), pp. 11-37. I must express great gratitude for drawing my attention to this article, and for assistance in philological matters of which I am inexpert, to my Edinburgh colleague Dr. David Reimer.

consistent course of life or conduct. (iii) It may be a prescribed route to travel by, and metaphorically a prescribed pattern of conduct, or *law.* When Moses reproves Israel for departing from "the *derek* which YHWH your God commanded you" (Deut. 9:16), the third sense is in play. But in Psalm 37:5, "Commit your *derek* unto YHWH," the righteous individual, portrayed as a dispossessed landowner outwitted by scheming and avaricious rivals, is assured of God's care for his future in the second metaphorical sense. It is the same at Psalm 5:8, "Lead me, YHWH, in your righteousness because of my enemies. Make your *derek* plain before my face!" And if we consider the phrase "the *derek* of righteousness," recommended in Proverbs 16:31 as a recipe for grey hair (and the opposite of "the *derek* of falsehood," which the poet of the Long Psalm says he shuns [Ps. 119:29]), it is a "way" in the first metaphorical sense, a fundamental decision for moral obedience and responsibility.

The three senses of the metaphor are in practice interwoven, so that a prayer for a path in an emergency can lead to a prayer for instruction in the path of God's commands. This interweaving is evident in the Long Psalm (Ps. 119, which, for all its textbook classification as a "law Psalm," has a strongly existential character: "O that *my* paths may be safe!" as the poet cries in verse 5). A whole stanza of that poem is devoted to the metaphor of the path:[4]

> *Cleaves* my soul to the dust! Revive me according to thy word!
> *My paths* I have recounted, and thou hast answered me; teach me thy statutes!
> *The path* of thy precepts make me to understand, and I will meditate on thy
>   wondrous works.
> *Melts* my soul for very sorrow; strengthen me according to thy word!
> *The path* of falsehood put far from me; and graciously teach me thy law!
> *The path* of faithfulness I have chosen, I set thine ordinances before me.
> *I cleave* to thy testimonies, YHWH; let me not be put to shame!
> *The path* of thy commandments I shall run as thou dost enlarge my mind!

4. The fourth stanza (vv. 25-32), which, following the alphabetic structure of the Psalm, begins each of its eight lines with the fourth letter of the alphabet, *daleth.* The poet often gives a special character to a stanza by repeating a word in initial position, indicated here by italicization. In this stanza five lines begin with forms of the noun *derek*; there is no other root-word in initial position so frequently anywhere in the Psalm. (This generalization excludes the use of verbal prefixes in stanzas 5, 10, and 22, and the prefix *w-*, "and" or "but," in stanza 6.) The striking emphasis on the one word is reinforced by using it as a bridge to the fifth stanza, where it occurs in the first line: "Teach me, LORD, the path of thy statutes." As one of the eight synonyms for divine revelation recurring throughout the Psalm, *derek* is standardly in the plural with a possessive prefix, "thy paths," but in this stanza the only occurrence in the plural is in the second line, referring to the poet's past life. The paths in this stanza are all the poet's own.

The stanza describes a drama of moral transformation, framed by the contrast between two uses of the verb "to cleave," *daqab,* in initial position in the first and seventh lines. Impotently sprawling on the ground at first, the poet ends up running off down the path he has been shown. In between these framing moments comes a varied encounter with paths. In the fifth and sixth lines he faces the radical decision between two broadly defined paths open before him. In the third and the eighth he combines *derek* in the singular with another expression for law, pointing not simply to the pattern YHWH has prescribed, but to *his* life formed according to that prescription. So the metaphor stands guard over the congruence of vocation and world-order, the agent's particular prospects for action bearing the hallmark of God's purposes.

Deliberation is not an inferential train of reasoning, its conclusion contained in its premises and only waiting to be laid bare; it is a focusing of vision upon ourselves and our circumstances, so as to effect an act of discernment. It looks for the appearance of a path of life and action, a direction that will emerge within the complex of circumstances. When the search is successful, we light on something not already present in our thought (except, perhaps, as anticipation), an immediate opening for action. We find it when certain features fall into line: the constraints in which we are placed, the moral obligations and expectations that weigh upon us, the particular mission we are embarked upon, all coming together within our field of vision to afford a precise opening. They present the appearance of a direction, leading towards the fulfillment of the promise of God. Sometimes, aware of the constraints, we think of our path as an obligation imposed on us; sometimes, aware of the opening, we think of it as a happy opportunity. Either way, constraint and opening must coincide.

How do we make the discernment? Not, certainly, by a kind of feeling. Feelings of excitement or calm may or may not accompany it, but feelings may be aroused, and aroused relevantly, by features in the situation, not only by the discernment itself. If we have some bad news which we wonder whether to impart to somebody, we will feel distaste for the task and anxiety about the reaction, but that is because the news is bad. It is not a sign that we are wrong to think that we must impart it. Nor, for that matter, do we reach the discernment by deductive inference. There is no deduction that can lead to the conclusion that this, and not something else, is presently to be done. It is a matter of observing correlations. In searching for a path, we search for a congruence of normativities, where the ordered demand of the creation, the agential powers which we are conscious of possessing, and the moment of opportunity into which we are thrust all flow together. We have no a priori assurance that we shall in fact discern such a confluence; we are always aware of the risk of being proved impotent to act. When we do discern it, however, it suggests to us the operation of a purpose.

Whose purpose? and for whom? That we cannot immediately know. The assertion that we are being led by God is not implied by the way things look. We may ask whether the devil or our own subconscious has suggested a direction that will lead to disaster — a possibility raised even in the narratives of the temptations of Jesus. Yet this is a question we can sensibly ask. If no combination of circumstances could invite such a construction, it would be meaningless to wonder whether we were misled in this or that instance. The question would be vacuous, and a good deal of commonplace moral experience would have to be written off as superstition. Believers, at any rate, are taught to wait and pray for such indications, ready to recognize in them the leading of God. So in the well-known narrative in the Acts of the Apostles where Saint Luke recounts how a series of frustrations prepared Paul for the dream in which a "man of Macedonia" cried out, "Come over to Macedonia and help us!" Luke comments, "we set about getting a passage to Macedonia, concluding that God had called us to take the good news there" (Acts 16:6-10). The verb "concluding" is all-important; the call was not the dream as such, but what the dream, taken with all the other circumstances, permitted them to recognize.[5]

Waiting and discerning is not an experience peculiar to the religiously attentive. It is part of the ordinary discourse of decision-making that we "see our way" to doing something, or "follow the obvious course." What these common phrases have to tell the theologian is that self-consciously religious experiences of being led by God are no departure from ordinary patterns of moral thinking, but a heightening of certain features of them. What it has to tell the general theorist of norm and decision is that a theory of moral discernment must not be squeezed beyond recognition simply to gratify a prejudice against loose ends. Moral thinking is closer to religious thinking than it has been fashionable in recent times to acknowledge.

But faith becomes explicitly involved when the waiting and discerning is turned into prayer: "Lead me, YHWH, in thy righteousness because of mine enemies. Make thy path plain before my face!" (Ps. 5:8). To pray for a

5. The sense of συμβιβάζοντες is "converging on a common judgment." The English translators' "convinced" seems to have no lexicographical support.

path is to pray for God to be our guide, which is to say that we pray for the Holy Spirit, given to lead us into all truth (John 16:13). We pray so because we need a path if we are to act. It is to be *our* path, the possibility for *our* acting in the moment *we* presently occupy. Yet it does not follow from the fact that a path opens up that it is the right path. We face danger as well as an opportunity: at the very moment of reaching out to live and act, we may destroy ourselves as agents and assume the impotence of an object with no possibility left to us but self-pity. So the path for which we pray must also be God's path, defined and determined by his commands, given by him to us here and now for the moment of dangerous opportunity.

Vocation

The discernment is a particular one. We look for *our* path, not for a generic rule. There is a fitting time and occasion for a young man to consider what makes a good wife, generically. But the weak Trollopian hero, torn between two rival objects of affection, is beyond the help of such considerations. It is not *a good* wife that he needs to find at that point, but *his* wife.

Here, for the third time, we encounter ourselves. We met the self first as an agent responding in faith to the summons of God, and then again as a human participant in the created world — one among many. Now we encounter the self in the future, not yet realized, offered in the moment available for action, unique to us and different from all others. Others confront their moment, too, of course, but that is something we can say only as observers and by analogy. To know what such an opening for action *means,* we must discover the one and only moment that lies open before ourself. Of some situation and of some opportunity we must find ourself asked: "Who knows whether you have not come to the kingdom for such a time as this?" (Esther 4:14).

How, then, is the self offered when we face the future? Is it simply a poetical reflection of the forward reach that belongs essentially to agency? Is it that in seeking a purpose of doing this thing or that (say, taking a journey or writing a song), we seek ourselves as the doer of that thing, and consequently hope to find ourselves more completely than we find ourselves now, as a traveler or a composer? It is certainly true that we do seek our future selves. Every end-of-action we entertain is, as we shall seek to explore at a later stage, a communication; every communication has two poles, that of initiator and that of recipient. There is no end we can seek that does not include ourselves as initiating a communication, and this self-anticipation stimulates our sense of agency. That, as we have seen, is the implication of eros. We may, perhaps, exaggerate the significance of the communication and of our role in it; it is a matter of moral maturity to deflate pretentious visions of ourselves, as traveler, composer, or whatever, with well-aimed self-mockery. Yet even so the seeking of ourselves in action, the expectation of a future self realized in agency, however carefully kept in its place, is essential to the dynamic of action.

Yet not every such anticipation of ourselves is satisfying. Our future self beckons through each next act that we purpose, but like a ghost cannot tell us whether it portends weal or woe. Together with the gratifying prospect of ourself as composer goes the mortifying prospect of ourself as a failed composer ignored by competent critics. Together with the prospect of traveling goes the prospect of missing the plane and being mugged in a foreign city. As every purpose may fail of success, so every end-of-action has its shadow side. We glimpse the possibility of ourselves as failures in life and action. No security is possible in anticipation. "I saw that there was a way to Hell, even from the Gates of Heaven," as the dreamer said.[6] A completed and secure self must be found, if at all, in the promise of God.

The promise of God, essentially and fundamentally the promise of his own unhindered rule over all that he is made, includes, as an aspect of it and not as a separate or secondary promise, the promise of the security and completeness of the believer. Nowhere is this more strikingly illustrated than in the Apocalypse, where visions wholly focused upon the course and climax of world history under the judgment of God are prefaced by a series of seven short letters to particular communities, each with a promise to the faithful individual within it, "the conqueror." In this sharp way John stresses the provisional nature of the empirical church; what ties it to the triumphant community of saints is this single someone, to be found in any of the churches "alive" or "dead," who remains faithful in action (2:26), who has heard the voice of the Lord coming in judgment, and has welcomed his return (3:20). The seven promises draw their imagery from the substance of the visions yet to come, thus tying the single believer into the triumph of Christ in world history. Life and death are the theme of the first two (2:7, 11); others deploy images of triumph and civility, throne, temple, government, banqueting and white garments, etc. There is also a persistent reworking of the metaphor of naming. The name to be conferred upon the conqueror will

---

6. Bunyan, *The Pilgrim's Progress* (Oxford: Oxford University Press, 1900), p. 148.

be a "new name," replacing that which he has borne, and a name of agency, interpreting the unique living and acting that the one agent has done, which is why "no one knows" the name "but the one who receives it" (2:17). As the old name summoned the agent to self-aware responsibility, so the new name crowns agency with achievement.[7] As the achievement is concretely unique in the case of each, so the name eludes repetition by those whose achievement it is not. Yet it is not secret, but acknowledged "before my father and his angels" (3:5), receiving the ultimate public reality through the judgment of God. With this new name we find, as in the first naming, a reciprocal gift of being able to name God: the name the agent bears is "the name of my God, the name of the city of my God, the new Jerusalem" (3:12), an identity established wholly in relation to the rule and community of God.

Let us speak of *vocation* as the way in which the self is offered to us this third time, though not without a degree of caution over three ambiguities this word carries with it. In the first place, it can refer both to the event of calling and to its object, the concrete form of service to which we are called. It is the latter rather than the former that is in view in this discussion, the promise of a realized self that is to take shape in history. Our vocation is the course of our life that *will come to be* our unique historical reality, but is not yet so, for our history does not extend into the future. In the second place, it has often been diverted, especially in German-speaking Protestantism, to refer to the forms of work in which our service is socially recognized as a useful contribution to the common good, the "vocation" as trade or profession. This restriction loses sight of the self within the function. Vocation, properly speaking, is not a single function, but an ensemble of worldly relations and functions through which we are given, *in particular,* to serve God and realize our agency. Sometimes, perhaps, vocation may be shaped by the recognized social role, though there is nothing to say that it must be, and even when it is, it is not exhausted by the role, but consists precisely in the concrete opportunities that arise, within and beyond the role, to do works that can never be exhaustively categorized according to their types, but can only be narrated as unique interpretations of the role.

A third misunderstanding, more refined but still a misunderstanding, speaks of vocation as a consistent, wholly preoccupying undertaking to which we subordinate all other practical concerns and accord a special devotion. In this sense only a few people have a vocation: doctors, nurses,

---

7. Rather than the changes of names we find in the patriarchal narratives, which speak of a new start in the light of vocation, the echo here is of texts such as Isa. 62:2 and 65:15.

teachers, writers, film directors, and actors, perhaps, but not clerks, house-wives, and general dogsbodies. That will not do from any theological angle. All are called to a service that can stand the test of fire at the last before God. Happy, perhaps, is the person whose service has one great unifying theme! Happy the theologian, the musician, the poet, whose gifts are focused upon one great and persistent undertaking! But their happiness lies in having a favored, absorbing occupation where they can find themselves; it arises wholly within the penultimate terms of this world's existence. It is not free of moral danger, especially idolatry. Our vocation is not just one strand in our practical life, not even the most important one; it is always woven of many strands. Those who have many different things to do, who must of-ten lay aside one task and acquire new skills for another, may bear witness more effectively to the resourcefulness of God's calling, may be more flexible in the face of difficulty, more immediate in their response to the needs of their neighbors. The life of the poet or theologian may be a poor thing to recount at the last, shrunk in upon its preoccupations while relationships are poisoned and opportunities missed, while the life of the odd-job-man may contain a thousand dramas that display the grace of God to perfection.

The temptation with the promise of vocation is the same as that with the promise of the Kingdom itself: to forget that it is a *promise,* the full content of which eludes us, and so to propose a view of our future self which claims the simple factuality of past history, shuffling off the task of discernment. If we are sure we know what our vocation is, and are no longer ready to see in circumstances a new challenge or opportunity, we have abandoned the task of discerning it. The poet who locks his door and gets on with the poem while war rages in the street outside, may discern the guidance of God, for we must all at some point ignore the merely harassing — but it cannot be simply assumed. The moment may have come to put the poem by and serve the neighbor's more urgent need. Vocation is to be accomplished, never done with, always mutating into new forms, ever and again to be attended to and discerned. Nor can it be detached from an exercise of prudence which looks backwards as well as forwards.

We take these questions a step or two further with the help of observations advanced half a century ago by Karl Rahner, the fruit of his meditation on the *Spiritual Exercises* of Ignatius Loyola.[8] His starting-point was one

8. See especially "Prinzipien und Imperative" (1957) and "Die Logik der existentiellen Erkenntnis bei Ignatius v. Loyola" (1956) in *Das Dynamische in der Kirche* (Freiburg: Herder, 1958) [= *The Dynamic Element in the Church,* trans. W. J. O'Hara (London: Burns & Oates,

that demands appreciation: "There is a real guidance by the Holy Spirit. . . . A man has to reckon, as a practical possibility of experience, that God may communicate his will to him."[9] As Rahner reads Ignatius, there is guidance that operates through rational considerations (Ignatius's "third time of election"), guidance that consists in direct revelation of God's will (the "first time"), and an intermediate "second time," where one is granted "enough light and knowledge" to discern something one must do in particular. It is here that Rahner lodges his claim for a special cognition (not mere "feeling") by which we discern obligation "comprised . . . in the facts themselves, not consisting in an ordinance of God transcending them and freely disposing of them: . . . something individual in the matter itself which, as something positive . . . can in the concrete be an object of the divine will just as much as the universal can."[10] This he calls "the imperative"; it is an "existentiell-individual" obligation (for which the coinage "idiomorphic" may serve as a more manageable synonym in English.)[11] To reach that object one cannot simply take a general principle and apply it to the case as an "instance." A man, by his spiritual nature, is not an "instance" of the human species. "His activity is always more than the mere application of a general law. . . . It has a content which, in what makes it imperative, can no longer be totally expressed in propositions . . . composed of general concepts."[12]

Rahner's argument responds to a moral philosophical tradition which excludes idiomorphic obligation on the basis that moral norms are generic. An obligation must be describable in impersonal terms, the criteria applicable in principle to any particular situation that instantiated them. In that view all action is rule-governed. A situation lying outside all rules would lie outside all categories of description, allowing no way to recognize the features that made it exceptional. Exceptions to rules are themselves rules.[13] And if a situation falls under two rules pointing in different directions, we

---

1964)]. Christian Ethics at the time was preoccupied by the question of "situation ethics," and if Rahner's argument was noticed at all in English-speaking Ethics, it was mistaken for a contribution to that discussion.

9. Rahner, *Das Dynamische in der Kirche,* p. 83 (Eng., p. 94).

10. Rahner, *Das Dynamische in der Kirche,* p. 95 (Eng., p. 108).

11. Rahner, *Das Dynamische in der Kirche,* p. 17 (Eng., p. 17). The distinction current in German (and French) phenomenology between *"existential"* and *"existentiell"* does not acclimatize well in English. Rahner's translator has done not badly with "individual," but has strayed in choosing "prescription" for *"Imperativ."*

12. Rahner, *Das Dynamische in der Kirche,* p. 99 (Eng., pp. 113-14).

13. On this Paul Ramsey's discussion is decisive: "The Case of the Curious Exception," in *Norm and Context in Christian Ethics,* ed. Paul Ramsey and Gene Outka (London: SCM, 1969).

naturally ask which paradigm it approximates more closely to. Even our dilemmas are uncertainties about how rules apply. To take the textbook case, where we hide the refugee from the secret police and wonder whether we can say he left the country last Wednesday, what we ask ourselves is whether this act, on the face of it both a lie and a rescue, is *more truly* a lie or a rescue. Such a question may be difficult to answer in a given case, but in principle it is answerable and important to answer rightly.

So a mother who imperils her life to save her child replies to those who would restrain her, "Any mother would do the same!" The homeomorphic appeal to "any mother" is what makes her response a moral one. An idiomorphic claim, "I must do what I must do!" might express the *pathos* of the situation very well, but would offer no moral intelligibility. "Universality" is the name which philosophy has assigned to the doctrine that what applies in one case applies in another, i.e., that morality has objective validity, not merely subjective — an unfortunate name, for what it indicates is not an obligation that applies to everyone all the time, but to generic structure of the moral demand, deriving from the order of worldly goods. An idiomorphic claim, then, cannot justify action, since it does not regulate *thinking about* action. It is infinitely available for self-excuse, creating a vicious circle of appeal that justifies what I do by the fact that it is I who am doing it.

Rahner by no means rejects this traditional position root and branch. He accepts the homeomorphic structure of almost all our moral thinking. But he denies the refusal of idiomorphic obligation which seems to follow from it. There is, he thinks, a moment of excess, in which the generic rule passes into the particular, and the particular may, in its very particularity, carry the force of moral obligation. Within the sphere of what is generically permitted, my decision may not be morally indifferent. Obligation may go further than generic rules, however elaborately formulated. When Paul obeyed the dream summoning him to Macedonia, his course of action was not only not dictated by a rule, but was one that Jesus at one point had forbidden his disciples (Matt. 10:5). So we may have obligations which do not replicate those of any other person. A doctor who feels morally bound to work in a remote hospital in the African bush cannot entertain the belief that everyone — not even every doctor — is bound to do the same.

The question that confronts us here is not whether particular obligations arise, but whether they arise (for they certainly do) in such a way as to qualify the claims of generic moral law. There is an argument that they do not, on which, in an earlier attempt to explore this question, I reposed my confidence: to heed a calling of God is in itself a generic rule; it is what everyone ought to do in the circumstances, even though the *content* of the calling is particular to the agent.[14] The category of "vocation" thus serves to frame the particular, non-replicable obligation within a replicable principle. To be called to do something is an event in life to which one may refer. When someone says he or she has a calling, I understand the kind of event referred to, though I cannot verify it. It is certainly no cypher for the purely inexplicable "I must do what I must do!" A calling is open to question and testing, at least by the one who seeks to discern it, though those in sufficient sympathy may usually help. They may even have grounds to suspect that the supposed calling is a mistake, which certainly means that they understand what is claimed. It is not very different from hearing a profession of love. Though I cannot imagine what she sees in him, I have no trouble understanding what she is *supposed* to see in him.

The reply may be made, however, that in such a matter the phrase "anyone in the circumstances" can have no meaning, since the circumstances are unique and nobody else *could* be in them. Rahner puts it charmingly: God can create many angels, but not a second Gabriel. There is only one "instance" of the requirement laid on Gabriel; there is no one in Gabriel's circumstances.[15] The vocation is coextensive with the person — not a "situation," but an identity conferred on Gabriel by God's calling him to his task. One admission that Rahner hopes to elicit here is that moral experience spills over the sides of a syllogistic model of deliberation, in which cases are subsumed under principles and "the minor premise follows easily."[16] We need have no difficulty granting this. As we have said, the "practical syllogism" (if we entertain such a conception at all) is marked out from the theoretical syllogism by the fact that the minor premise *never* follows easily, but is always the focus of whatever moral disagreement there may be. Deliberation is not a deductive train of thought, and moral thinking requires reading the situation and its circumstances.

But Rahner wants to take us a step further than this. Concrete obligation is "comprised in the facts themselves . . . something individual in the matter itself." Such obligations Rahner ascribes not only to personal agents but to "historical individualities of a collective sort" — nations, that is, and political communities of every kind — which have "their precise moment, their unique *kairos*, their historical task."[17] Political prudence, indeed, is very

---

14. Cf. my *Resurrection and Moral Order* (Grand Rapids: Eerdmans, 1992²), pp. 43-44, 220.
15. Rahner, *Das Dynamische in der Kirche*, p. 17 (Eng., p. 17).
16. Rahner, *Das Dynamische in der Kirche*, p. 97 (Eng., p. 111).
17. Rahner, *Das Dynamische in der Kirche*, p. 22 (Eng., p. 22).

much to the fore of Rahner's train of thought, burdened as he is with a sense that the church, in repeating generic principles, has often seemed to miss the political boat. He values prudence with "the capacity clearly to perceive the added extra, the singular feature," to reach "true decisions, obligations that accomplish for their time a historically unique individual reality," and to make a choice that is "the right one, the historically successful one."[18] Possible examples we might suggest could be assassinating a tyrant, giving the first performance of a new and difficult musical composition, breaking a world record in some sport, composing *Paradise Lost,* even (for which Rahner himself endured public controversy) opposing a war or denouncing inhuman threats in biotechnical innovation. All involve doing or saying something that could be done or said only in the light of the moment.

And here we should refuse to follow. We need not, of course, seize upon the word "success," by which he certainly does not mean "making history come out right" in the sense that Hauerwas has decried it. Rahner is the last to deny the martyr a role in history. Yet the point he stands to is that "right" decision (for martyrdom, Catholic Action, or for anything else) is sufficiently determined by the moment. What he hopes to reach with Ignatius of Loyola's aid is an immediate perspicuity of a unique moment in time, securing obligation with the fore-anchor of anticipated "success" and needing no anchor aft in the universal moral order. That cannot be. There is no way of grasping a "historical" moment in relation only to the future. History is not a seamless whole, extending from past to future; it is open to account only after, not before, it has happened. The particular contribution to history that each actor makes, the unique role that he or she has to play, and, above all, what will count as the "success" of the action at the end of the day, is, at the moment of decision and commitment, an object of hope, not open to historical verification before the event.

The actor cannot confront the future as though it were the past extended forward, like a historian with eyes in the back of his head. The only way to confront the future is in freedom, prepared to determine the indeterminate. But that means confronting it in ignorance of what "success" will amount to. In order to comprehend the action, then, the actor must submit to the generic forms the world offers, consenting to be "a" physician, "a" parent, "a" friend, or shuddering to become "a" cheat, "a" fool, "a" bully. It is these forms, combining and commingling, that shed intelligence on any calling we may think we are given. John Milton's unique vocation had to start by his being

---

18. Rahner, *Das Dynamische in der Kirche,* pp. 23-25 (Eng., pp. 24-26).

"a" poet composing "a" poem. He could not know that it was *Paradise Lost* he had to write — "our" *Paradise Lost,* that is, the one we pull off our shelves and read. His projected poem only became "our" *Paradise Lost* in the providence of God, as the poet fulfilled his famous service of standing and waiting. Or, to return to Rahner's own example, when Gabriel was sent to a maiden in Galilee, he did not share God's foreknowledge, but knew only what he was commanded to announce. (Or alternatively, Gabriel is no fit example for us.)

We must return, then, to the point we made in the past, that vocation frames the unique historical role within a generally intelligible category. For an obligation to be generic, it does not have to be replicable in history as an experiment is replicable in the laboratory; it is enough that it can be replicated in the imagination of those who understand it. But replicable to *that* extent it must be, if it is to be an obligation at all, for only so can it be recognized as an exercise of prudence. If that much is granted, we need find no further difficulty with the idea of an idiomorphic obligation based on "something individual in the matter itself." For what is individual will then not be cut loose from principled interpretation.

Historicism

Our fourth and last sounding in the sin against time explores the penetration of our reflection on time by anxiety, a theorizing of temporal experience in which we retreat from discerning God's call in the immediate horizon of the future-present, and turn instead to a reading of present experience which we hope may deliver the future up to clear and masterful anticipation. We look for "the way things are going," the direction that can be read off the present. This hope, of course, is the other side of the ambition to narrate the future as joined-up history. Let us call this *historicism,* with a reasonable confidence that our use is close enough to the center of gravity of a rather wide usage given to that term. Time, rather than essence, is taken to be the primary dimension of reality, the source of all meaning that there is, a meaning which can be displayed as "history." The orderliness of nature is taken to be rooted in history, which is narrated as a quasi-natural unfolding of events, whether a simple cause-and-effect sequence or a more complex organic development, that can be projected onto the inscrutability of future history, too.

An attraction of historicism is that it seems to offer the possibility of dispensing with moral concepts. All we seem to need for the direction of our action is that the next step will be known in the same way as the last step, i.e., by narrating the story that led up to it. What we shall do will follow seamlessly from what we have been, and the need for a decision will be avoided. What this leaves us with is action without a purpose, which is not an action at all. To purpose action, we must frame it in our minds, while it has no presence in the world, as a *non-necessary* event. We cannot purpose the whole of the future, to be sure, nor even much of it; a tiny fragment, comprising how we are to deploy our own freedom, is laid upon us as something we must take conscious responsibility for. To frame it in our minds as a non-necessary event, we must conceive it as an act of a certain kind which can have, in a given context, a certain practical rationality — even if the kind to which the act belongs is rare, the context exceptional, the rationality prophetic. We need to know "what we are doing." And for that we need moral concepts. The most that narrative logic could tell us is what we were *experiencing*. "We are on a perilous margin when we begin to look passively at our future selves," as one of the great nineteenth-century novelists observed.[19]

One form of historicism, which sprang from a Reformed cultural consciousness and came to be referred to by the imperishable Scottish term "whiggery," acquired a strong philosophical resonance in the nineteenth century. It was a teleological account of history, which read the past as a self-elaborating progressive narrative. The burden of making predictions which this narrative seemed to impose was evaded by Hegel's strategy of announcing the arrival of an "end" of history — a notion inseparable from the viewpoint of the "whig historian" (an English adaptation of the term), for whom the narrative of the past aims to display the compromises of the present as the best conceivable outcome. Whig history was no mere cultural aberration; it belonged intrinsically to a culture for which all study, including study of the past, must be broadly useful. The most useful thing to be drawn from history was a positive approach to citizenship in the present, appreciating the upheavals that gave birth to the present age as a painful discipline that allowed the collective acquisition of wisdom, never to be gone back on. The logic by which this optimistic civilizational historicism turned to nihilism at the end of the nineteenth century has been traced many times.[20] And

19. George Eliot, *Middlemarch*, book 8, chapter 79. The continuation is also instructive: "and see our own figures led with dull consent into insipid misdoing and shabby achievement." *Both* "misdoing" *and* "achievement" lose their moral character when we conceive them as a script we have been given, since they have been drained of the element that makes them personal, the resolution of practical reasoning.

20. Among the most telling, relating them both to the positivist turn in Thomism, Jean-

of nihilism we need only say that its re-assertion of freedom against nature could only recommend itself by floating on moral planks, such as "courage" and "honesty," which strewed the waves after the vessel they had been part of had been sunk. To take nihilism strictly on its own terms is to agree that there is nothing to be said for it.

George Grant, an underrated figure in the criticism of modernity, whose work might have given guidance to advocates of later "green" concerns, had Nietzsche in his sights when he declared that "the conception of time as history is . . . not a conception we are fitted for."[21] "Time as history" Grant understood as "the mastery of human and non-human nature in experimental science and technique, the primacy of the will, man as the creator of his own values, the finality of becoming, the assertion that potentiality is higher than actuality, that motion is nobler than rest, that dynamism rather than peace is the height." Grant's refusal of those programmatic themes left open the question whether he was right to accept the pretensions of nihilism to expound the concept of history more clearly than had been done before. Is history really a totalitarian concept, substituting for nature and de-naturing the world? The Christian theologian is likely to have doubts about that, and to suggest, on the contrary, that historicism never, in any of its forms, succeeded in understanding history correctly. It could not take the tension between natural order and time with sufficient seriousness. The idea of history turns on the *reconciliation* of good and time: the progress of time does not reduce the goods of nature to meaninglessness and vanity, but allows of a succession with its own meaning, congruent to nature but not identical with it. It is possible to underestimate the theoretical demands of such a reconciliation, which is what a variety of historicisms, spinning the logic of history out of nature or thrusting a logic of history over the top of nature, have done. Every such purely historical meaning turns out to be unmeaningful. It cannot yield the "love of one's own" to which Grant gave such great weight. But if a reconciliation cannot be accomplished by immanent dialectic or nihilist decree, it may be disclosed to us by God, as promise. The difference between "my people" and "other people" depends on a special and particular gift, a narrative identity; and a narrative identity is a temporal meaning that is only to be received as a gift, not discovered as a truth of nature or imposed as a *fiat* of will.

Yves Lacoste, "Le Désir et l'inexigible: pour lire Henri de Lubac," in *Le monde et l'absence d'oeuvre* (Paris: Presses Universitaires de France, 2001), pp. 23-54.

21. *Time as History* (Toronto: CBC, 1969), p. 45.

But again it is not historicism as a theory, but the habits of mind encouraged by theory that demand our attention. The theory quite easily diverts our practical attention from what it should most attend to. Announcing the transparent advent of the future, historicism actually shuts and bolts the door against the future *as a horizon of action,* by substituting a narratable present, i.e., the past horizon of the present. The key to our conduct of ourselves is then *what has (just) come to be,* the "where we have got to" from which an illusory sense of direction can be projected into an imaginary "where things are going." And that is precisely why it cannot find a place for the deep past, either. The past is focused on the immediate, the just-having-come-to-be of the present, and cannot look back to take in the full range of memory and record available to us, which might educate us about the intelligibility of events. Historicism does not, in fact, value the science of history very highly. Since narrative, to serve the turn we have in mind for it, has to reach an end *right here and now,* it has to be very selective narration, screening out whatever might find no authentication in "where we have got to."

The roots of this theoretical false step in the sin of anxiety are clear from the way it reinforces a movement of regression, shrinking back from the danger of action in conformity to the patterns of behavior that prevail around us. "Where things are going" becomes a way of representing what other people are doing, and invests with a spurious dignity a rush for cover in the crowd. We regress into the pre-reflective "we" of the collective moral subject, ensuring ourselves not only against the burden of taking thought and making decisions, but also against the risk of damaging conflict with the common opinions of our society.

We have been here before. It is apparent that the most reflective types of the three forms of "possible sin" — doubt, folly, and anxiety — converge upon one reflective sin, of which each is an aspect, the substitution of gnosis for action, a gnosis which is, at the same time, the falsely constructed identity of an imaginary "we," a supposed collective viewpoint representing no concrete community. The detachment of doubt, the dogmatism of folly, the historicist relativism of anxiety coincide in a posture of gnostic knowingness, a claim to have insight into the hidden mysteries of what is going on. The historicist strand in the mix, presenting this insight specifically as a view of "what the times require," is the version most typical of our age, with its delusive sense of being cut off from all other ages and experiences of mankind. *Circumstances* may require specific and novel forms of action of us, but circumstances can be interrogated, analyzed, explained, and reflected on. "The times" do not require anything in particular; they are simply given to us to live in, to make something of eternal value out of. That is why present times are hard to read, and those who pretend to read them can always pose as magi. The character of the times is yet to be determined, and that will happen precisely as a result of decisions we have now to take. To rely on the times to guide the decisions is to commit ourselves to a circle of self-justifying sophistry.

We find a concrete illustration in the role of the news media — i.e., the "old media" of newspaper publishing and broadcasting. The new media of instant electronic communications have fascinated philosophers and interpreters far more than the old, but it is the old media that tell us about the civilization we actually inhabit rather than that which may possibly succeed it. Most political discussion focuses on the way journalists perform their role, it being assumed that the role is perfectly self-evident. What concerns us here is not so much what they do, as what we expect them to do and why we expect it. There is some truth in the claim that it is we who make the media, not vice versa.

The very name "media" conceals, and not innocently, the distinctive feature of *this* mediation, as opposed to the multitude of reflective mediations of art, history, philosophy, poetry, etc., which is its special concern with the *immediate*. It is immediacy that they mediate to us, keeping us in touch with what is unfolding — with the "new," the just-having-come-to-be, the past horizon of the present, not the past in its narrative depth, as tradition. The new has no predetermined logic, so that focusing attention on it requires conceptual pre-patterning to register and control surprise and to integrate it into a narrative sequence. The unheard-of must somehow be heard of. And this is where late-modern media have established their line of supply. Devoting their full attention to the breaking wave, they echo its roar to us; we call upon them to show us the world new every morning, as though there never was a yesterday.

Why are our first impressions of events so important to us, though even the ancient Greeks knew that second thoughts are wiser? It is because we feel our identities to be at stake. History and tradition, from which we derive identity, have to be brought up to the moment, made continuous with the present, and every culture concerns itself with news-bringing in one form or another. Proverbially, news was thought to be refreshing (Prov. 25:13, 25); it widened the narrow horizon and stale air of local culture to admit broader communications. What is striking about the speedy and wide-ranging communications of modern news is how on edge we are about them, as though we were constantly afraid that the world would mutate behind our backs if we were not *au courant* with a thousand dissociated new pieces of information. This is a measure of our metaphysical insecurity, which is the engine of our modern urge for mastery.

It is a feature of some importance that the media of news are *mass* media. They cater to a society "democratic" in its self-idealization, conceiving that every member, not only a small minority appointed to the task, will share responsibility for what is done in the collective name, and therefore has a right to know. For this reason we expect the media not only to *assure* access to the new, but also to *regulate* it — by exercising judgment as to what is true and false, what is important and what is not. There is good sense in this. If a critical mass of observers in a society will think and act solely on first impressions, those impressions must be filtered. Who, after all, would not rather be instructed by professional news bulletins than by rumor? But the good sense is political, not pedagogical. It does not make us more judicious or reflective, but directs our reactions into predictable channels. What we expect of the media, then, is to typify our reactions, to impose familiar appearances upon the unheard-of, to ensure a process of routinization of news.

This is why actual news coverage is so small a proportion of the media product. The blurring of the boundaries between news, entertainment, and commercial promotions, theoretically distinct and supposedly insulated offerings, serves the function of the social embedding of news. The celebrity is the handhold, the advertisement the bridge that connects the world we are shown with our personal interests. For filtering, categorizing, bringing the unheard-of within the bounds of the heard-of, the cartoonist or the satirist who represents a dangerous tyrant as a stage clown with his trousers around his ankles serves the purpose quite as well as a reporter in a war zone. Frightening new horrors are written of in a consciously bland and traditional way full of mythic recognition-factors. Interpretative techniques call on a small range of typical phenomena. You and I, if we emerge for a brief moment from our customary obscurity into the public eye, will quickly be classified as devious politicians, predatory capitalists, irrelevant academics, or cutting-edge boffins, heartbroken mothers, etc. The stereotype, the predetermined classification, this is the technique that "digests" what is happening, and digests it "safely," i.e., without our having to question our view of the world.

The media, then, are a democratic institution. Their own account is that they protect democracy by securing a bulwark of free comment against the tyrannous pretensions of government and money. What we have most to fear, they warn us, is the erosion of their editorial freedoms — by "barons," government, big business, or whatever — leaving the body politic prey to the machinations of the powerful. It would be ungrateful to overlook the element of truth in this. The media have plucked a feather or two from the proud turkey cocks. Yet the intense, and intensely trivial, news-and-entertainment saturation which forms ninety-nine percent of the media's stock-in-trade, the vast swaths of newsprint and hours of broadcasting devoted to sport, horoscopes, emotional intrigues of actors and models and much else, has little to do with the logic of *quis custodiet custodes?* It touches the deep politics of identity. This is what interprets us to ourselves, makes us feel at home with ourselves, represents the deeds and words we read as those of friends or enemies, molds us into a common identity, teaches us to see ourselves as part of a shared struggle, all quite independently of what we are, what we do, what we suffer, who we share our lives with. The constructed political identity competes not only with other reflective identities, such as that we may have as Christian believers, but with the immediate identity we derive from our social setting. This is democracy understood as *popular* government, not as *republican* government. The media shore up our faith in the stability and reliability of that essential element of democratic theory, the people, the "all-encompassing something that is nothing," as Kierkegaard described it, "the public."[22] They exist to assuage the lurking fear that democracy is an unstable mix of iron and clay, and that the grandeur of the world to which our existence is entrusted may be brought down by a well-aimed stone (cf. Dan. 2:42-45). Inevitably, then, they are parties in the struggle for popular power, soaking up whatever surplus of authority they can squeeze out of government, church, and (in Britain) the monarchy by carefully directing suspicions in long-habituated directions.

The news media can themselves be embarrassed by too much news. This is reflected in the ambiguous position of their most interesting and admirable creation, the front line reporter, that traveling adventurer who seeks out and describes things as they happen, and "gets the story right." Justly celebrated in legend and still, today, the one to whom we are likely to owe our gratitude for such moments of imaginative expansion as we may be given or for new sympathetic insights into how others live their lives, the reporter has long been kept within strict limits, and was regarded in some quarters as a threatened species even before electronic communications began to take over. As far back as 1919, in philosophy's most generous tribute to the "responsibility" of journalism, Max Weber ignored the reporter's role

22. Søren Kierkegaard, *A Literary Review,* trans. Alastair Hannay (London: Penguin, 2001), p. 80.

entirely; for him it was the political journalist, the promoter of causes, who deserved our admiration and was so ungratefully rewarded.[23] If getting the story right is the reporter's aim, the editorial staff have their own priorities; the "comment" column or staged interview is better suited to the purposes of routinizing, while even the headlines, those sacred pillars of "shock," may be confected of press releases and PR handouts, plans, reports, draft speeches circulated in advance, notices of engagements, statistical projections, contested scientific claims, the insipid flavor of the whole drowned out with the pungent spices of speculation. What we look to the media for is the construction of the world of the moment, and reporting on realities may have only tangential relevance to that.

If "new every morning" is the tempo of divine grace and the tempo of our personal responsibilities, it is because the morning is a time when one can look back intelligently and look forward hopefully. It is the tempo of practical reason. The media's "new every morning" (quickly becoming "new every moment") is, one may dare to say, in flat contradiction to that daily offer of grace. It serves rather to fix our perception upon the momentary now, preventing retrospection, discouraging deliberation, holding us spellbound in a suppositious world of the present which, like hell itself, has lost its future and its past.

23. *Geistige Arbeit als Beruf: II. Politik als Beruf* (München & Lepizig: Dunder and Humblot, 1919), pp. 26-27. [= *Political Writings,* trans. P. Lassman and R. Speirs (Cambridge: Cambridge University Press, 1994), pp. 331-34.]

Prospective Postscript

We have reached the limit of a theory of moral reason. Following the logic of agency from the first awareness of the self as agent through its admiring immersion in the world of goods, we have accompanied it in its deliberations to the forming of a purpose. There is no further a reflective discipline can go in this direction, for actual decision and action belong to the agent. The reflections of Ethics terminate in seeking, not in finding. Yet if Ethics ended at that point its concerns would be confined to the purely formal — understandable, perhaps, for a moral philosophy, but stopping too far short for a reflection informed theologically by God's deeds and words. What further lines of observation, then, are open to Ethics as Theology — safeguarding its character as a reflective accompaniment to moral thought and not as a surrogate for it? Let us pick up three loose ends, one from each of the threads that have run through the cloth we have been weaving.

(a) There is a question that has emerged, first of all, about the agent-subject: is it plural or singular, a We or an I? Though the focus on moral thinking seems to prejudice the answer in favor of the consciousness of a singular subject, we have made a point in this volume of keeping the question open with an occasional reminder that it may be either of them. In *Self, World, and Time* we said rather more, suggesting that the I of conscious deliberation emerges out of a pre-reflective We, which lurks behind it, and looks ahead to an ideal We implied in the discipline of universalization, on the moral horizon.[1] We can hardly be satisfied to let it go at that. There remains to be explored what we may loosely call the ecumenical task of moral

---

1. *Self, World, and Time*, pp. 43-66.

thinking, the ordering of the I towards the We, the responsibility that goes with thinking as a responsible and self-evidentiary I to uncover and give reality to the ideal We of moral agreement.

(b) There is then the question about the world. If love must grasp the universe of goods in its due order, and if that order is not only ontological but temporal, destined to fulfillment in the reign of God, ordered love of the world must follow the world's direction towards that destiny, and so be shaped eschatologically, in the light of the world's end. A doctrine of ordered love, then, must assume a temporal dimension, as it does in Augustine, and extend into a doctrine of love's "stages" in the epochs of world history, before the law, under the law, under grace, and in full sight.[2] Exploring this historical direction of love is a proper task for Ethics, which in this context takes a special interest in the "household of faith" as a focus of love, so that an ecclesiological reflection, as well as an eschatological one, is indicated.

(c) Third, there is the question known classically as the *ends* of action — the ways in which our purposes conceive not simply of an action we find it appropriate to perform, but of a hope lying behind the action, a future, however indistinctly envisaged, that the action seems to promise. The act we purpose, the "what" of what we think we are doing, contains in itself, and inseparably, a "why," a temporal, future-regarding final cause. Almost all that we have had to say so far about envisioning the future has been restrictive, reining in proliferation of imagined future states in order to focus on the immediate future of action. But a purpose rightly formed is the bearer of a promise, which, though its absolute content may be hardly imaginable, generates the conditions of further deliberation, action, and life.

The projected third volume of *Ethics as Theology*, then, will seek to draw these loose ends together and say more, though always in general terms, about what is given to us to purpose and to hope for. The end of action embraces a community of agency and directs our love of the created world towards the Kingdom of Heaven. Here Ethics is shaped by an eschatology that it cannot take direct responsibility for. It is only in listening to what it is told of things beyond our human practical ends that Ethics can speak convincingly of love as sovereign. The affective knowledge that rests in its object will always lead back into the further dynamic of faith and hope unless faith and hope can look to a decisive completion.

And that is why, though the author may owe an apology to his readers for the temporal and material conditions of thinking and writing which

---

2. Augustine, *Enchiridion* 118.

impose the deferral of the final stage into a future volume, it is not entirely unsuitable to stop at the point we have reached and draw breath. There is a logical fitness to the separation, too. When Ethics reaches the end of the sequence of faith, love, and hope, it must stand back further if it is to advance further. The completion of the trajectory demands a new turn of reflection. The crock of gold, they say, lies at the end of the rainbow. The thinker-agent who has followed the calling of God to the last step of practical thought and stood on the brink of action must hear once more the distinctive counsel of Ethics, "Find, and you shall seek!" Simply to know what he or she is doing, the agent must look further than what he or she is doing. Of its own resources Ethics can say nothing of an end of history, nothing of a final finding that will put an end to seeking. Yet it can know of a moral teaching that has presumed to unite its instruction on the path of life with a decisive and ultimate promise, "Seek, and you shall find!" An Ethics that reflects on where *that* moral teaching has left mankind, and so takes up its calling to be Theology, can accompany the further seeking still demanded of us, not in order to deflate our hope of finding, but to give it self-knowledge and confidence.

Index of Subjects and Persons

Act, Action, 2-3, 4, 20, 25-27, 43, 66, 77, 85-86, 88, 115, 124, 140-41, 144, 147, 150, 158, 163, 167-68, 170, 172, 173, 179, 182, 185-86, 187, 191, 194, 197, 202-4, 208, 211, 216, 226-31. *See also* Agency; Circumstances; Consequences; Deliberation; End-of-action; Faith; Life; Virtue
Adams, R. M., 29-30, 70-71, 89
Adaptability, 45-46
Agency, ix, 11-14, 22-23, 26, 33-34, 36-38, 41, 69, 90, 100, 132, 140-41, 147, 149, 156, 179, 201, 211, 222-24; I and We, 40-41, 59-61, 216, 238; responsibility, 4, 10, 17, 21, 30-32, 44, 51, 63-64, 89, 174, 219, 231, 239
Aitken, J. K., 218-19
Ambrose of Milan, 39, 49, 204
Anscombe, G. E. M., 202
Anselm of Canterbury, 47, 170
Anticipation, 27, 146, 150-64, 166, 170, 173-74, 186-87, 192-93, 201-5, 209-10, 213, 218, 220, 223, 230
Anxiety, 12, 22, 152, 173-78, 201, 220, 230, 233. *See also* Consequences: consequentialism; Greed; History/Historicism; Impatience
Arendt, Hannah, 75
Aristotle, 52, 93, 181, 193, 201

Arnold, Matthew, 32
Athanasius of Alexandria, 111
Augustine of Hippo, 13, 14, 18, 21, 22, 25, 49-50, 51-52, 53, 54, 75, 77-78, 107, 112-13, 120, 124, 137, 193, 194, 202, 213, 239
Authority, 8, 9, 13, 15, 29, 31, 59, 83-84, 88, 128, 133, 135, 138, 189, 195, 200-201, 236
Axiology, 113

Bach, J. S., 129, 170
Balthasar, H. U. von, 47, 68, 125-26, 173
Baptism, 37, 41, 128-29, 137, 155, 161, 182
Barth, Karl, 98, 137, 184, 188-90, 192, 215
Bayer, Oswald, 146
Beauty, 71, 85, 89, 106-7, 125-26, 162
Biggar, Nigel, 189
Blake, William, 34-35
Book of Common Prayer, 23, 36, 135
Boredom, 86
Bunyan, John, 23, 148, 223
Butler, Joseph, 51-52

Carroll, Lewis, 206
Cary, Philip, 49
Chaplin, Jonathan, 113
Chesterton, G. K., 46
Choice, 16, 181, 183-86, 214
Chrysostom, John, 15
Cicero, 124, 193-94, 203-4, 209

Index of Scripture Quotations